Dancing with the Dead

Dancing with the Dead

A JOURNEY TO
ZANZIBAR AND MADAGASCAR

HELENA DRYSDALE

HAMISH HAMILTON · LONDON

HAMISH HAMILTON LTD

Published by the Penguin Group
27 Wrights Lane, London W8 5TZ, England

Viking Penguin, a division of Penguin Books USA Inc.,
375 Hudson Street, New York, New York 10014, USA
Penguin Books Australia Ltd, Ringwood, Victoria, Australia
Penguin Books Canada Ltd, 2801 John Street, Markham, Ontario, Canada L3R 1B4
Penguin Books (NZ) Ltd, 182-190 Wairau Road, Auckland 10, New Zealand
Penguin Books Ltd, Registered Offices: Harmondsworth, Middlesex, England

First published 1991
1 3 5 7 9 10 8 6 4 2

Phototypeset in Linotronic 300 Baskerville
by Wyvern Typesetting Ltd,
Bristol

Printed in Great Britain by
Butler & Tanner Ltd, Frome and London

A CIP catalogue record for this book is available from the British Library

ISBN 0–241–12954–0

ACKNOWLEDGEMENTS

Like all journeys, this one depended for its success on the kindness of people who live far away and will probably never see this book. I thank them none the less.

Of course there was also much help and encouragement given closer to home. Listing everybody would make this book far too long, but I must mention Sir Mervyn Brown, Laura Drysdale, Ben Gaskell, Alan Hickling, Stephen Hobbs, Kate Jones, Dr John Mack, Lady Ann Newman, Sir Geoffrey Newman, Imogen Parker, Simon Peers, Richard Speir, Shane Watson and Jane Wellesley.

Above all I thank my husband, Richard Pomeroy, without whom I might never have set off, let alone got back. This book is dedicated to him.

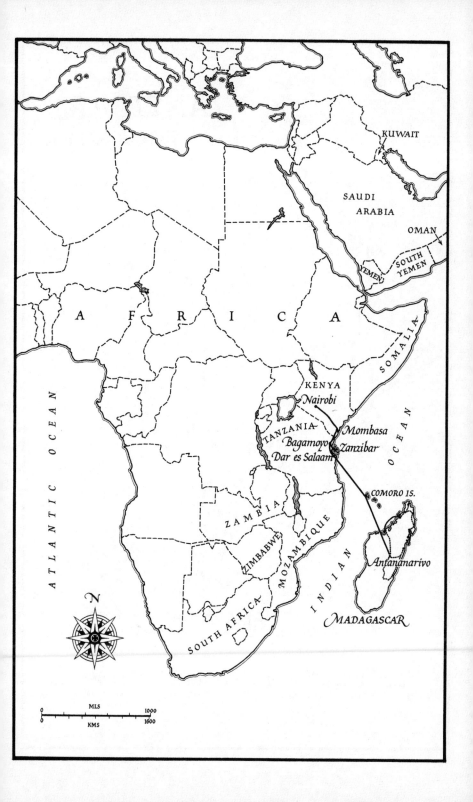

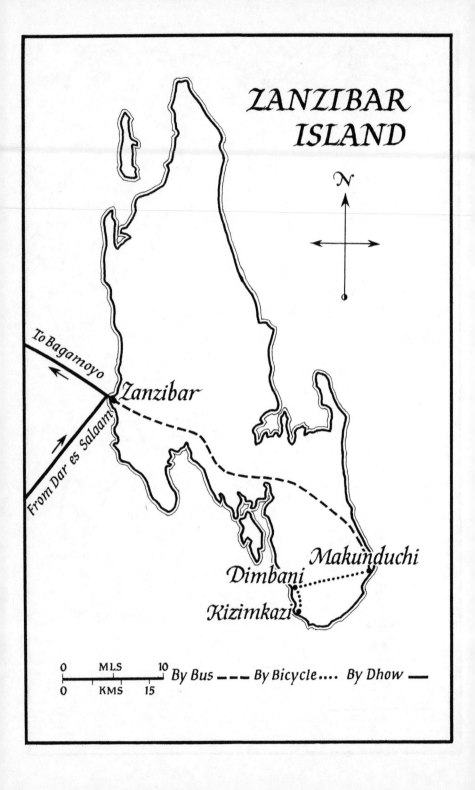

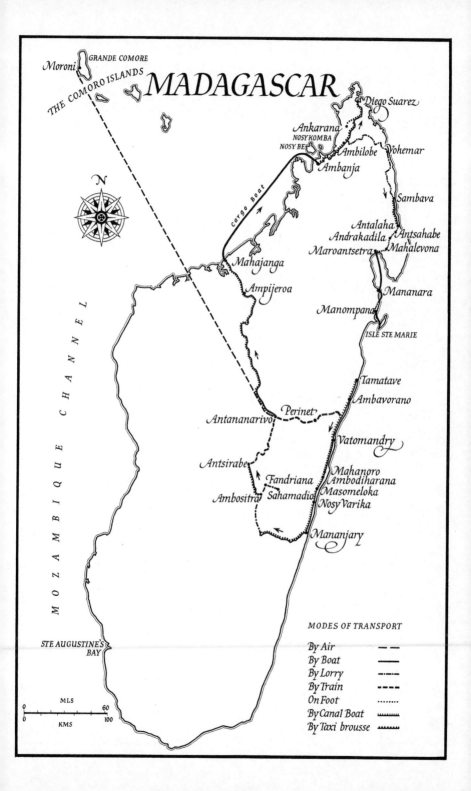

CHAPTER ONE

CHASING SHADOWS

In these rootless days we have to choose where we belong. I am drawn to islands, especially to the edges of islands, so I choose Dartmouth, on the southern edge of the British Isles. Though my family are only holiday visitors, this is our place: along the coast live cousins and aunts, uncles and grandparents. I fell in love here too, and married.

To belong somewhere is to have something to escape from, and a childhood spent in boats has given me a taste for travel. Or perhaps it's in my blood, for it is not just the living who root me here. In the fat hills and steep woods, down in the caves where the tide sucks and booms, lurk shadows of my ancestors, generations of buccaneers who set off from this smugglers' coast to ride the winds and currents around the seas of the world.

One day in 1987 my sister Laura received an unexpected phone call. 'This is the Honorary Consul for Madagascar,' an English voice announced. Madagascar? Laura had scarcely heard of the place. She had a tall friend who spent weeks in Malagasy caves in search of unidentified species of bat, and who imported Malagasy crystals, but other than that –

The Honorary Consul is blond and brokes for Lloyd's; he drives an Isuzu Piazza in which passengers lie rather than sit, and Madagascar is his passion. There is a palace, he said. It stands at the top of a precipice and was built for the murderous Queen Ranavalona, a queen crueller than Messalina and more lecherous. This Ranavalona had a bizarre taste in clothes and now headless dummies in dusty panelled rooms sport Victorian crinolines, Napoleonic coats, Arab djelabas, even Tudor bloomers. Would Laura, as a textile conservator, go to Madagascar to prevent these precious clothes from deteriorating further? Laura was intrigued.

She needed photographs, articles. My husband Richard could take time off from his contemporary art gallery and I was free . . . Gradually – inevitably it seems now – we were drawn in too. What did we know of Madagascar? It was home, people said, to the giant Rukh, a bird ten feet high; to the bat-eared aye-aye that is not a bat but a lemur; to winged foxes that are not foxes but bats; to upside-down trees that wave their roots in the air; and to tribes who dance with their dead. We didn't believe a word of it.

We spun the globe and found the island, as big as France, Belgium and Holland put together, as long as the distance from London to Naples, the fourth largest island on earth. Millions of years ago when the continents fell apart, Madagascar, like a great ark, sailed away from Gondwanaland with a cargo of weird fauna and flora which died out elsewhere and lived on here. Now it is besieged by flights of arrows fired by the South Equatorial current, as if they are trying to force it back into the dent in Mozambique where it belongs.

Months passed and Richard's Aunt Rosamund called. Did he remember the curious hat he used to try on as a child? I have it beside me as I write: a bowler on which something like a giant worm cast has landed. It is carved from one single piece of light wood, coconut perhaps, and in relief on the crown a crocodile freckled with woodworm grasps a fish between its jaws. Two green and yellow serpents stretch their eyes and coil around the sides, one reaching for the crocodile's leg, the other for its tail. Strangest of all is a tattered wine label; I can make out a few words only – *Vins Fins Fran-, Muscat de Fro- Maison Fron-.* But I turn it over to read, in curling sepia, '*Coiffure de la Reine Ranavalo, Madagascar. Authentique. Unique.*'

Perhaps it belonged to the Honorary Consul's murderous tyrant – its brutal imagery was surely her style. Will Your Majesty wear the crocodile bowler with the Tudor bloomers today? Or with the Victorian crinoline? It was bought as a curiosity in the 1930s by Richard's grandmother while on holiday in the South of France, but no one knew what the crocodile signified or how something so precious left Madagascar for Provence. The British Museum was excited but puzzled, and the Madagascar department sent it to the Peruvian department. In each the experts shook their heads.

Laura searched for funds for her project while Richard and I bothered magazines. Then Laura rang. She had just heard from a cousin that our ancestors used to trade with Madagascar.

'What?'

'The Newmans, traded with Madagascar, during the last century. The Atlantic was their main run, but apparently they also went round the Cape of Good Hope and up to Madagascar.'

'What were they trading?'

'Cloves I think – and probably slaves. At least so they say. They used to call it Black Ivory. And there was some sort of awful rum too called Screech. Apparently that's what it made you do.'

'I can imagine.'

'They were pirates really you know. Well, privateers. Letters of marque and all that. I've been sent a photocopy of this book written by Uncle Ralph.'

'I've never heard of any book.'

'Well it's here. *A History of the Firm* by Sir Ralph Newman (bart), 1932. Do you want it? I just can't think about it now. I'm too busy finishing this Hertfordshire museums report thing and getting the British Council to cough up the Madagascar money. I'll send it on.'

Uncle Ralph's book was never meant to be published but was typed and bound for the family, and a bundle of large-format sheets arrived. I scanned the Madagascar chapter greedily, wanting all the story at once, just a few phrases here and there catching hold. 'In the early 1800s . . . tempting bait to the Potentates and Natives . . . lairs of pirates . . . Your Majesty . . . wipe every man out . . .' There were Sim Sim, Dragon's Blood, Seahorse Teeth: what could they be? And Ramiaramona, Colonel Hunt, Seyd Aboubeker ben Shea Mossie Alhamidie, the Imam of Muscat – who were they?

I forced myself to concentrate, and began from the beginning. The Firm. It sounded like a band of south London gangsters. Done over by the Firm. The Intercity Firm. In fact they were Dartmouth merchant venturers who traded alone, together and then alone again over five hundred years – Newmans, Hunts, Holdsworths, Roopes and Christophers – inter-marrying, arguing, rivalling, with 'Houses' in ports around the world. Even Francis Drake was involved for in 1569 a Mary Newman married him. Believing him to be drowned off the Straits of Magellan on his voyage around the world, she betrothed herself to another.

But she was a practical woman and when he returned to Plymouth in glory on the Golden Hind, Mary forgot her new lover and rowed out to meet him, and without ado bundled her long-lost husband's booty under her skirts and smuggled it ashore. Or so the story goes.

In the early days the Newmans' Atlantic trade was supplemented if not by smuggling and piracy, then certainly by privateering. A 'letter of marque' (from the Provençal *marca* or *marcar* – to seize as a pledge) was issued by the crown, enabling a captain to attack an enemy ship and as a reward to seize its cargo. These captains acted as a sort of private and unorganized navy. The Newmans were involved in battles off Portugal and in the Chesapeake Bay, capturing hostile ships and being captured themselves. All this was legal but as Nelson remarked so sniffily, 'The conduct of all privateers is, as far as I can see, so near to piracy that I wonder any civilized nation can allow them.'

By the early 1800s the Newmans' trade with Portugal extended round the Cape and up the coast of East Africa to Aden and beyond. There were constant hazards and adventures, wrote Uncle Ralph, especially in the unknown and dangerous kingdom of Madagascar. He had never been to Madagascar, but he described it with gusto:

This huge island, with its war-like tribes, amazing lemurs, brilliant plumed birds, curious insects, fishes of bizarre appearance, bones of enormous extinct terrestrial lizards, and flora consisting of exotic Palms, Orchids, and Arums of immense size, coral-reefed rocky littoral (the former lairs of Pirates who attacked the treasure ships of the Great Mogul), must in the early 1800s have been the most astonishing place. ... In 1836 the Firm was trading direct with the Queen of Madagascar (Queen Ranavalona I), and we have a letter from her dated 21st November 1836.

This had to be the same Queen Ranavalona, cruel as Messalina, who sported Tudor bloomers and crocodile hats.

Uncle Ralph quotes from letters and ships' logs, and also from a nineteenth-century merchant named Trader Horn who claimed to have known this queen. With great excitement I sent the book to Sir Mervyn Brown, a historian and an ex-Ambassador to Madagascar, and it was then that my first doubts arose for Trader Horn was, it seemed 'quite valueless as a source on the history or indeed anything else about Madagascar'. Moreover, in his unorthodox way Uncle Ralph had jumbled up quotes from different sections of Trader Horn's book. There were other odd inconsistencies: the chapter headed Madagascar appeared to be more about the spice island of Zanzibar and its plump Sultans; and where Ralph meant Zanzibar he often wrote Madagascar. He ended the chapter with a Walter de la Mare poem which he entitled 'Madagascar'; it began:

> Far are the shades of Arabia,
> Where the Princes ride at noon.

and ended:

> He is crazed with the spell of far Arabia,
> They have stolen his wits away.

It was 'rather as if a poem entitled "Scotland" might expatiate on the delights of Cyprus', commented Mervyn Brown. Undermining my excitement came mealy-mouthed suspicion. Perhaps Ralph was crazed with the spell of far Madagascar; maybe he muddled up Zanzibar and Madagascar; or maybe he invented the whole thing.

I barely knew my Great Uncle Ralph. I remember a darkened room, flickering lights of a television and an aquarium, a figure in a wheel chair. He had had a stroke, and I wondered how something so pleasant could condemn someone to a wheel chair beside an aquarium. But I knew him to have been a brilliant man, and beautiful too. I picked up snippets: he created the sub-tropical garden with its waterfalls and tree ferns that the Pool House, where my grandmother and then my mother grew up, is banked against; he was a botanist and a zoologist and discovered something special inside the frog; he so loved the Gents at the Savoy Hotel that he installed an exact imitation at the Pool, stand-ups and all. Family photographs show a languid figure stretching long limbs on the beach below the house, eyelids drooping; some called him a Bohemian; my grandmother called him 'Old Bung'.

But Ralph was persuaded by his businessman father to give up his botany and become a partner in the family shipping firm of Newman Hunt Roope & Co.

He loathed it. I can see him, eyes glazed in front of bills of lading and whatever else occupied a shipping company in the 1920s and '30s. Those prosaic days of steam could hardly compare with the old buccaneering adventures, and as Ralph grew disillusioned with the present, so he escaped into the past.

Archivists were employed and he wrote his *History of the Firm*. Years were spent mapping out routes along which the family traded, as intricate as the routes along which they married and spread. The 'Pedigree' evolved into a great scroll encased in a metal tube, and to which new spouses and their family history were added in different coloured inks. Richard's ancestors, land-lubbers from up river, came into the story somewhere.

The archivists gave credibility to Uncle Ralph's book, but only the original documents could provide the proof. I rang my cousin.

'I don't have anything myself,' he said. 'In fact there's an awful story about that. When the Firm was moving offices they put out two piles of papers, one the precious old log books, the other just rubbish. The clerk threw out the wrong pile.'

'The wrong pile.' I could only repeat this stupidly. 'Everything lost?'

'Yes, as far as I'm aware. But you never know,' he added, 'there may still be something.'

Richard and I pushed against east winds to the headland at the mouth of the Dart where the castle stands guard. Here, in St Petrox church between the haven of the harbour and the open sea, the Newmans lie buried. We peeled the carpet from the aisle. Embedded in slate were familiar Newman names used century after century – Robert, Richard, Thomas, all merchants on my mother's side. In their midst lay another slab carved with a Jolly Roger. A pirate! So this was the company they kept.

Close by in the Pool House lived my Aunt Ann, Ralph's widow. Madagascar and Zanzibar were as much of a surprise to her as they had been to us. 'Those old documents – he was obsessed, you know. Hours and hours, weeks and weeks. I used to lose him. Lose him. He simply wasn't there.'

'Buried in his past?'

'Buried. Buried in his past. Quite honestly, I don't know what he saw in that old stuff, I really don't. He couldn't think about anything else.' She was resigned, amused, but I could imagine her loneliness as a young wife forsaken for piles of faded ink, for her husband's long-dead ancestors. 'He built an archive room here you know. Of course, I wanted it as a playroom for the children, but no, he was having none of that. It had to be an archive room.'

She sighed, tolerant as ever. Yet I had to admit that this was what I hoped for. If anything remained, it would surely be here. On the mantelpiece stood models of the Firm's ships rigged by my grandmother, some cunningly squeezed into bottles, and from the walls gazed unflinching Newmans who travelled the world in the full-sized versions. Did they visit the Indian Ocean? And in those frail-looking vessels? In their black jackets and periwigs they gave nothing away.

'Do you know if any of the original documents are upstairs?' I asked tentatively. I didn't want to intrude.

'I think it's just things about the Pool, but I don't really know. I haven't been up there for years – it's full of junk, freezing cold. The Firm's documents. I don't know. You see, the offices were bombed so it's unlikely anything was left.'

'Bombed?'

'Yes, during the last war. Completely flattened.'

Aunt Ann produced a photograph: two side walls – barely even a shell – remained. With the rest of the office, the desks and chairs and presumably the last of the documents, vanished my hopes.

'They found a few old port bottles afterwards that were flattened like biscuits in the heat. It was that intense. I think we've got one somewhere.'

There seemed no point in carrying on. Richard, however, was determined to persevere.

'You're welcome to look,' Aunt Ann said kindly, though her heart sank. Things were best left alone. She had enough to think about. 'If there is anything left, that's where it'll be, because nothing ever leaves this house.'

The archive room lurked at the end of a corridor which got steadily colder as we approached our destination.

'It was built right into the cliff. That's why it's so damp. See what I mean?'

The door was pushed open on the flotsam and jetsam of generations.

'I'll leave you to it. Bye. Good luck.' Aunt Ann fled, and I could see why.

No one would want to deal with this. In the greenish light of a window buried in leaves I saw that one wall was hung from ceiling to floor with Uncle Ralph's hats. There were embroidered Muslim *koffia*, floppy straws, Chinese hats, knitted hats, pointy witches' hats. No crocodile hats. We clambered past them and over more recent relics – Twister, Scalextric – through an obstacle course of broken clocks and chairs to forty years of *Punch*, old prints, Victorian scrap books ('For my own sweet darling'), leg irons, bugs and butterflies pinned to boards but eaten by living bugs and, behind them, a hundred and twenty Eastlight box files and a hundred and thirty-seven envelope files. It was a daunting sight. But at least there were files, and they were all meticulously labelled. One box entitled Newman Hunt Roope & Co looked promising. I wavered in anticipation, unclipped it, and out showered grey confetti: the documents had been shredded by mice. Mould dripped on a file beside it. Disappointment returned. The task was pointless; if the papers had survived the clerk and a bomb, they would have disintegrated here.

Again Richard insisted on continuing: it had become a sort of quest. We began each end of the shelf of envelope files and worked steadily towards each other, ignoring the title of the file in case something had mistakenly been slipped inside. Hours later, our hands immobile with cold, we knew more about Uncle Ralph's interests – fuchsias, succulents, flying saucers – but nothing about Zanzibar or Madagascar.

Laura came to look, and it was she who discovered the *lambas*. Tucked under a chair were two lengths of fabric. One was made up of two six foot long stripes of woven rusts, greys and yellows, their subtlety undiminished by moth and stains. What was unusual was the cloth; it was neither silk nor cotton, but some sort of plant fibre. Laura was convinced that it was raffia, a palm indigenous to Madagascar, and that it was a *lamba*, the shawl traditionally worn like a toga by the Malagasy, worn perhaps by the Queen herself with her crocodile bowler. The other was silk, the colours deep purple and black interwoven with metal beads in a style unique to Madagascar, and it stretched almost the length of the corridor. It was funereal and, Laura suspected, not a *lamba* for the living but for the dead, a burial shroud, a *lambamena*.

Were the *lambas* brought back from some trading mission? Were they gifts from Queen Ranavalona? Again, only the documents could tell. Day after day Richard and I searched and, far from diminishing, my desire to find them grew. It seemed such a chance that the Malagasy should call their island *Tanindrazana*, Island of the Ancestors, and that it should be the island not only

of their ancestors but also – in a small way – of my own.
Now it was Richard who retreated to the warm kitchen.

'She's got the bug,' warned Aunt Ann. Richard, thinking distractedly of a painting he had started and wanted to finish, went
home. But I couldn't leave. I was enclosed in the crepuscular
world of this attic room. Way below car doors slammed, affec-
tionate hellos and then goodbyes: cousins came and went with
children in tow. I could barely see. I tried to convince myself that
the letters did not matter. Even with documents and *proof*, the
past does not exist. It is elusive as a shadow. When I turn to
grasp it, the shadow will slip away to leave me with a handful of
air.

Then one afternoon Richard announced, cautiously: 'I think I
may have found something.' He had manoeuvred around a saw-
toothed man trap (anti-poaching?) to a metal cabinet. Smells of
must fluttered out like a bat. Here were more files and inside the
files were letters in florid hands. Some were still in broken-seal
envelopes, others brittle as leaves and more fragile. I held their
frayed edges lightly, as if in long-forgotten contact with flesh they
might turn to dust. Some were dotted and dashed with the morse
code of Arabic – Zanzibar! – and others were in a language
unknown to me, multi-syllabic and unpronounceable. It was
Malagasy.

— CHAPTER TWO —

MOMBASA

Night clamped down without warning on the old Uganda Railway.

'Open the window,' said Richard.

We breathed gusts of warm dung as we rocked in grandeur out of Nairobi and into a vast emptiness. Our lights flashed briefly over spreading horizontal trees and a cluster of round huts. Africa! I murmured it again and again as the train hooted mournfully at nothing. For hundreds of miles there were no other lights but the Milky Way spattered over a dome of black, and the odd mysterious fire. Africa. Africa.

By morning the gingery savannah had thickened to hills that rose abruptly from lagoons, as if in cheeky imitation of a nineteenth-century sketch that might have decorated the walls of the Firm's office. 'Scenes from Africa' – a silhouetted feathery palm, sun glittering on water, a solitary native paddling a canoe. Already we were leaving the dark continent for its east coast and the island port of Mombasa.

Our adventures beginning, every sense alive, we stepped lightly from the station into town. Richard had got fed up with trying to run his art gallery with no money and had left it for something even more precarious, a Karrimor rucksack and a few photographic commissions. This would be our first big trip together, and perhaps that would be the greatest challenge; both of us were more used to travelling alone.

It was now June 1989. Laura was finalizing plans, buying acid-free paper, a light meter and a humidity-testing 'whirling hygrometer', and hoped to meet us in Madagascar. Although Madagascar was also Newman Hunt & Christopher's main goal, their base was Zanzibar; this then was where we were heading now. We would continue south to the Comoro Islands and then cross the Mozambique channel to Madagascar. This was the outline of our journey, but we had no tickets booked, no return flights and little money; we aimed to travel as much as possible by boat. As the outline of the journey got coloured in, the same might happen to the story. Already I had been able to pick up where Uncle Ralph left off; the letters and cargo lists in the Pool contained stories not even hinted at in Uncle Ralph's book, and though in the carpeted hush of the Public Record Office in London I had found much more, there were gaps to fill. But mainly I wanted to see what people in my past had seen out of simple curiosity.

We found a room in a low dive close to the old dhow dock. It overlooked a yard – muddy now at the end of the rains – where at eight o'clock on a Sunday morning women pushed their black *buibui* scarves to the back of their heads (token *purdah*) and sat with legs apart swigging beer. 'Read Quran' exhorted signs hung between oversized elephant tusks across the main Haile Selasi Avenue. These women took no notice and the ground was littered with bottle tops. An African with heavy-lidded eyes slopped towards us in flip-flops, belly swaying over shorts, and kicked open a door.

'Choo,' he muttered. It was the predictably stinking hole in the ground. 'No water,' he added, without apology.

We had no time to waste. Narrow passages led us through the Arab quarter. Children played hopscotch in puddles and a man in a long white *kanzu* cleaned his teeth beside a well; carved balconies festooned in washing and propped on fragile struts teetered dangerously overhead. At the dock a corrugated iron shed was piled with sacks of strong-smelling tea, and two stevedores with rags round their heads sat on the sacks playing cards. In exchange for Kenyan tea, traders bring back scrap metal – wrecked planes and vehicles from civil war-torn Somalia – which, stripped of its power, was piled as artfully as a Tony Cragg sculpture.

And down below was what carried it here and what we had come for: dhows. Just six or seven, but dhows nonetheless, rocking together at the end of two jetties. No one knows the origin of the word, but 'dhow' is not used by the Arabs. They call these boats by their names – Booms, Dhangis, Sambuks, Ghanjahs, Zarooks – depending on the cut of prow or stern. They were a variety of shapes and sizes, but all were brown – brown wooden hulls, brown coir matting, brown rigging and dirty old brown sails.

We both thought at once of the dhows in Kerala with sails of patchwork fertilizer bags lumbering sedately up the backwaters. Here the sails were furled, and many had engines, but originally they would have been built on India's Malabar coast using teak brought down from the Nilgiri hills. New boats would have travelled north to the Persian Gulf and then on around the Indian Ocean, down the Somali coast to Mombasa. From here it was south to Zanzibar, east across the stepping stones of the Comoro Islands to graze the northern tip of Madagascar, and then up to India again. Cyclical, ever-turning, this is the ancient gyre of the trade routes. It depends on wind. For half the year the winds blow, without wavering, from the southwest, and then one night they turn and for the next six months blow steadily from the north-east. Fixed, intransigent, it has dispersed Arabs and Indians in a bladder shape all around its route.

In the fifteenth century the Portuguese punctured this bladder, and nothing would ever be the same. The dhows caught a ride on the wind and the Portuguese followed, catching up with the great maritime tradition of the Arabs. They even adopted the same triangular lateen sails. Until the raiding sea-farers of Oman reclaimed the trade for the Arabs, the Portuguese established themselves on the off-shore islands – Mombasa, Zanzibar, the Comoros, parts of Madagascar – and the Newmans followed in their wake.

In 1580 Mary Newman's husband was the first Englishman to show his face in the Indian Ocean. His wife's family came two hundred and fifty years later.

What brought them here? In the early 1800s most British traders rounded the Cape of Good Hope and set their sights directly on Bombay, pausing only at Mauritius, for the coast of the dark continent was thick with hostile shipping, with Arab and European pirates and warring slavers. But in 1824 two Captains of the Royal Navy named Emery and Owen surveyed the coasts of Madagascar and East Africa and declared Mombasa a British Protectorate. Much to the fury of Owen, who saw the trading and political potential in retaining a foothold in East Africa, the garrison was withdrawn by the British government. But in 1833 Owen published an account of his stay in the *Journal of the Royal Geographical Society*. Was it this that inspired the Newmans? Just one year later Newman Hunt & Christopher were to become the first British company ever to embark on a serious trading venture here.

We sat on the jetty gazing longingly at the dhows. Beside us a fisherman, expressionless as a fat Muslim Buddha, waited for a bite. He wore a malachite ring and a white embroidered cap; down below the water looked murky.

'I get good fish,' he suddenly said. 'Sometimes so big – as long as two arms.'

A boy with a thin snaky body dipped himself in and out of the water in his underpants looking coy. He was a pretty boy, voice high-pitched, named Khaled. His father was Yemeni and came south on a dhow when the Russians moved in. He did not intend to come to Mombasa, Khaled said, but he had liked it and stayed. One brother went on to Zanzibar, others to Dar es Salaam, and now Khaled has cousins up and down this coast. His grandmother was Bantu, and he embodied the mixture with his curly hair and pale skin. Now his family had moved to Saudi Arabia. They fascinated me, these links around the Swahili coast that were far more ancient than national boundaries. They had nothing to do with Somalia or Kenya or Tanzania, were created not by arbitrary lines drawn on a colonial map but by sea and wind.

'Do you think there'll be a dhow to Zanzibar?' we asked. Maybe, maybe not. They had to wait for good cargoes, and the winds were too strong now to sail. Maybe next week, maybe the week after.

'That is going north to Somalia,' the fisherman said, pointing at the nearest dhow. It was a Boom, the biggest there. 'But they have problems. They have changed the customs officers and these new ones –' He stopped abruptly as a large African encased in a grey uniform (a slab of muscle) strode past and stumbled into a tin dinghy, the dhow's skinny *nakhoda* hurrying anxiously behind. With an angry flick the customs officer uncovered the cargo.

'Flour,' muttered the fisherman. The customs officer bent and tasted it – drugs? – and the *nakhoda* smiled encouragingly.

We were joined by a Somali, slight and pale with a hooked nose and intelligent eyes. He seemed to know what was happening in the dock so I explained our story – as I was to do countless times over the next four months.

'My ancestors were trading here, all around this coast but

above all with Zanzibar and Madagascar. They were the first British traders to come here.' I felt absurdly proud of this fact, as if it was something to do with me. 'In their letters they mention using dhows, so you see –'

'Yes, yes, I understand. It's interesting. Your ancestors were here in Mombasa you say?'

'Well . . . I'm not sure.'

'I think they were. Come with me.'

He led us into the dhow office.

'This is where your ancestors might have auctioned their cargoes,' Abdi said. The Newmans would have been here long before this building, but I didn't want to dampen his enthusiasm. 'They've stripped out all the beautiful old interior panelling which would have been here then and made these partitions for offices.' Empty but for a few armed guards, lounging.

The dhow Registrar was a courteous Omani whose old white-capped head was sunken in folds below his shoulders. His heavy-lidded eyes and movements of almost painful slowness added to the feeling of ancient dignity that made the Africans seem brutish beside him. He too wore a malachite ring.

'Maybe he remembers your ancestors,' suggested Abdi.

'I can't believe he is 150 years old.'

'Ask him.'

The Registrar shook his head. He did not know his age, and the name Newman meant nothing.

'Look at these,' urged Abdi excitedly, pointing to old photographs above the Registrar's head. 'I think your ancestors are there.'

British East African traders sturdy in shorts and knee socks stared firmly over their moustaches at the camera. 'These are your ancestors?'

'No, I'm afraid they were here even before photography.'

Abdi was losing interest and we were noisy intruders in the Registrar's frail world.

No, he confirmed as we left, he didn't know of *any* dhows to Zanzibar.

We crossed to the island's opposite shore, to the modern container port of Kilindini, the largest in East Africa. Overlooking it, draped in flowers, stood the Yacht Club. If anyone knew of ships to Zanzibar and Madagascar, surely they would be here.

Hesitating at the Members Only sign, we watched from the door. How easily life turns into cliché: the chintz, the buffers at the bar in khaki shorts (who mirrored their thirties predecessors), the lovable grizzled African barman of unswerving loyalty. It was *White Mischief, Out of Africa*, unchanged despite nearly thirty years of independence. Conversation was convivial, a little bored, and hovered around beer. Should one drink Tusker, or White Cap? Coastal people opted for one, up country for another. The Commodore, a sturdy woman in her forties, bought us a drink. They had less than a hundred members now, she said, so they couldn't afford repairs. 'People are getting older, and less of them sail. Some Indians sail, but let's face it, it's a white man's sport. They sail, but they're not naturals.'

A race was starting, a crew was needed, so on our first day in Africa we set off in a dinghy. Even if we never found a dhow, at least we had been on the water, I consoled myself. Richard coped manfully with the jib, and I was given a scrap of paper and told to be navigator. It was covered in letters and numbers: LW14–16 2.90 14.25 START S LIKP S REEF. Perhaps that was why we got disqualified. All this was taken very seriously.

Our captain was tough little Johnny Close from Watford. As we scrabbled to and fro, he said he had been here a few years repairing boats. After his wife left him, he was employed to deliver a motor yacht from Spain to South Africa. Off the Somalia coast he ran into fearsome storms. He radioed a passing ship and the British captain tried to reassure him.

'I've been here thirty-two years and I know it'll calm down in a few hours.'

They waited a few hours and nothing changed. Waves broke over the wheel house, the engines were failing, then they sprang a leak and the bilge pumps broke; the three-man crew bailed ceaselessly for six hours. Eventually he followed the other ship down the coast, sticking a few yards behind by day, a few more by night, trying to avoid the reefs, but the storm never abated. At last they reached Mombasa, but when he was piloted in through the channel between the reefs the force of the wind behind him nearly propelled him into the pilot. Even now on a calm June day we could see the power of the Indian Ocean beating against the reefs beyond the fishermen (who seemed, oddly, to be walking on water). The pilot radioed Johnny to slow down, but he already had his engines in neutral. 'Sorry, mate, can't do nothing about it,' he crackled over the air waves. A tanker coming in had its stern right up out of the water. 'Almost arse over tit,' said Johnny. The other captain admitted that in thirty-two years it was the worst he had seen.

How often in their small two-masted ketches, brigs and brigantines the Newmans must have rounded the Cape after some ninety days at sea only to run into storms such as these. They were well armed against their enemies – blunderbusses, cutlasses, powder and ball – but not against the weather. They had no engines to help. The ships would have pitched and rolled, below decks foul with vomit, while one or two brave passengers struggled up on deck for air, clinging to the bulwarks, salt spray in their eyes. Somebody would be sent for'ard to reef the sails. Add to that an unreliable captain, and all could so often have been lost. On 22 January 1841 Mr Henry Angelo, their agent in Zanzibar, wrote to Newman Hunt & Christopher to express his extreme regret that Captain Ireland had lost their ship the *Herrick* at Brava, a harbour on the Somalia coast north of Mombasa. As far as he could tell, Ireland had tried to leave Brava at night. As the channel was very difficult, 'people' – natives? Arabs? other European traders? – tried to persuade him to stay until daylight, but he refused. So instead they offered to pilot him out for a small sum, but this too he refused.

Ireland was a pig-headed man. Tempers snagged but in darkness and silence, only the creak of the rigging, he insisted on sailing out of the harbour with one light glimmering on the mast. The inevitable happened. With a crunch that jerked the crew backwards and slopped coconut oil from its barrels, the *Herrick* hit the rocks. The crew pushed with oars and spikes, scrabbling against the jagged coral, but the wind was still and nothing could move them. They stayed all night. The next morning the same 'people' offered to haul him off for £20, but John Ireland – out of battered pride? – refused to have anything to do with them. He shouted from the deck, arms waving, and they returned to shore leaving him to spend the next five days sitting on the rocks. Did he hope to be washed off? The tide rose and fell, birds wheeled overhead, fishermen paddled out to look, laughing. 'The people say the captain was to blame, and that he made no attempt to get the ship off,' wrote Angelo. And on the fifth night (as Johnny Close could have predicted) a storm blew up so hard that the ship was wrecked.

'These, Gents, are the reports at present here, but God alone knows if they are true,' moaned Henry Angelo.

Much of the cargo was lost and eight months later a letter arrived from Mr Ireland's mother, who was concerned that she had not heard from her son since last year. 'Is he still in that dreadful climate?' she wrote. 'I hope and trust that you will remove him from such an unhealthy place if he is still living.' In fact he had not died of disease or even with his wrecked ship. Stubborn to the end, John Ireland had been advised to stay at Brava until his cargo, including the tanks of coconut oil, had been rescued, but even this he would not do. He was indeed still living, the Newmans reassured Eliza Ireland, but by May he had – not surprisingly – removed himself. He had found another 'situation worth accepting' and was expected home on the New-man's brig the 'Rio Packet'.

'Look! They're arresting a smuggler.' Johnny pointed out a police boat approaching a canoe. 'Oh no, seems they let them go, the bastards.' Johnny had stories about the 'smugglers'. They robbed any ship that came into port, and escaped with the booty to their mainland villages, up above the red-tiled villas and spreading gardens of the rich *mazungas*. They were rarely caught.

'The customs men, they're corrupt as hell. But there's been a big crack-down lately, people fired all over the place.'

'And the police?'

'The police!' Johnny almost spat in disgust. 'One hundred per cent – well, ninety-nine per cent corrupt.'

'What sort of thing?'

'This sort of thing, I'll tell you. The other day this idiot smashed my car, so I wanted to be a witness for the prosecution, and you know what? It cost me 700 bob. No secrecy about it, nothing like that. First I produced two 100 bob notes and this geezer, the officer, picks them up and says, loudly mind you, "Is that all?" "Yes," I said. "That's all. Look, I'm not one of your big rich whites, your big *mazungas*. I'm local." So this other police bloke says, "He's all right, he's one of us." Then I try to get my car back. Remember, I've done nothing wrong. So up comes this other officer. "I understand you want your car back?" "Yes." "Soon?" "Yes." "How soon?" "This morning please." "Ah, this morning. You know you have bald tyres?" "Yes." "And you know your suspension's gone?" "Yes." So I offer to make a donation to a charity of his choice. All smiles. "Thank you, Sir. And if you ever have any trouble with the traffic police about those tyres, just mention my name and it'll be all right."'

'Bastards,' said Richard.

'Well, it can have its uses. I had one Chief Inspector on my pay roll. He did some useful jobs for me.'

We didn't ask what.

'But the Afs are terrible people really. Give 'em a uniform and they think they're gods. Even the bloke that cleans the street. He's friendly one day, then he gets a uniform and he thinks he's God. Not that there aren't some nice ones of course – shit, I'm married to one. It's just the ones in uniforms.'

On the mainland a swathe of coloured cotton, drumming and chanting, ran down hill, over a beach and into the water. 'Baptism,' said Johnny. 'Had one of them last month,' he chuckled, 'and the priest went and drowned hisself.'

The evening was pink-gin-soaked, a confusion of ex-wives and new lovers, and of which faction supported whom. Children were sent away to school in the UK. It was always 'The You Kay'.

'I'm the sort of person who needs to be kicked from one thing to another,' said Hamish, 'then that really gets me going. But I've been here fourteen years and I'm still waiting to be kicked on, and it never happens.' He was charming and debauched. He could sing all of *Aïda* and most of *Boris Godunov*.

'Why should you want to be kicked on?' I asked. Below the terrace lights flickered on tankers resting in the harbour.

'It's too lovely. I'm getting into a rut. And you have to go back some time.'

'Why?'

'I wouldn't want to die out here. No friends, no relatives. That'd be awful.'

'So that's still home? England? That's where you belong?'

'Scotland actually, but yes. I suppose so.'

'Don't you find things changed when you go back?'

'Oh yes, I'm completely out of my depth. I can't even use the telephones any more. And my accent, it's awful – no one seems to understand a word I say.' It was Eton and Cambridge and he gave a mocking smile. His elderly mother tottered from the bar grinning foolishly.

'My mother's drunk,' he announced, with slight distaste. For the rest of the evening he ignored her, while she flirted with a younger man. From time to time she slurred that she wanted to go home. 'I'll drrive jush gimme the keys.' But no one moved. While Richard and Hamish played bar games I resorted to shredding matchboxes; like the drunken mother I was longing to leave but we were trapped, waiting for a lift. One for the road? If you insist – the wife'll kill me, last round, positively the last.

'Look who's here,' someone muttered. 'That's what happens when you stay late at the club.'

The club bore pinioned the newcomer. 'I can get you a ship to anywhere you want,' he boasted.

'To Zanzibar and Madagascar?'

'Ah. Zanzibar no. Madagascar? A few months ago, yes. Now the one and only ship is in dry dock.'

Edward 'Roddy' Rodwell had been editor of the *Mombasa Times*. He lived in Mtwapa, a few miles north of the city, and he invited us to tea.

At the end of a dirt track a bungalow stood in a sprinkled lake of grass. We wanted to ring the doorbell, but there was no doorbell. In fact there was no door. The house was ringed by an open verandah, so we wandered in calling, 'Hello. Hello?' A desk at the far end spilled books and papers – this must be the right place – and a puppy hairy as a small bear romped round our feet.

'Sparky! Sparky, stop that!' A tall woman appeared, smiling. 'You must be . . . come on in . . . Sparky, I said stop.' She patted him affectionately, looking up at us. 'He's very young.' We followed her over a polished wooden floor to the terrace. She was in her seventies with short grey hair pinned back, relaxed in red trousers but a little shaky. 'Roddy . . . I'll just go and tell him you're here. Roddy!'

The green lawn and trees fell down to a vivid blue creek. The terrace was crowded with pot plants.

'Hello!' 'Roddy' Rodwell tottered out, his eyes sealed behind glasses as thick as crystal balls, through which for years he has been gazing into the history of this coast. He was freckled with age and heavy on his legs, but he was proud of being able to remember our names. He sat with a thud, panting a bit, and placed a tape-recorder on the table – the old journalist. A servant brought a tray of tea and biscuits.

'Sorry about this tin,' said Olivia. 'Everything goes stale in seconds here, or gets eaten by insects.'

It was a breezy sunny afternoon. 'Lovely, isn't it?' Roddy observed, and he was right. He and Olivia came here over fifty years ago. 'Of course it was quite different then. None of these hotels.' He waved a biscuit towards a building almost in their garden that was put up recently by an Italian hotelier. 'Not that it's too bad, and we go there for dinner sometimes but nobody needs planning permission or anything, and everyone's so corrupt. But things always change, don't they? When we came we had the place to ourselves. There were even leopards in that bit of forest there.'

'Not any more?'

'Haven't seen one for years.'

Their sons had built their houses in the garden, married, had families, and become Kenyan citizens. 'It's the only way of getting jobs now. Everyone wants to become Kenyan. We're lucky all right, aren't we, Ollie? We've had plenty of adventures. Oh yes. We had a whale down there on the beach once. None of us could think what the appalling stink was. Stank to high heaven. And then we found this whale, rotting away, but we just couldn't get rid of it. Every time we towed it off shore, the tide swept it back again. Dreadful.' He coughed. 'But that's all by the way. Ollie always says I go off on red herrings, don't you, Ollie dear?' She smiled indulgently. 'Now, something about British traders wasn't it?'

I explained.

'Mmm. Newmans . . . it is a familiar name, but 1834 – that's frightfully early. This is fascinating you know. I'm vastly interested because this British stuff has never come my way before. I do know a bit about the American trade, but not Britain. The Americans were here first of course – I think the first ship was in 1809. They were trading here you know, not slaving. It was ivory, gum copal.'

'Gum copal! The Newmans were trading that too. It is on all the cargo lists. What is it exactly?'

'It's resin,' Roddy explained. 'It falls out of trees. I used to find it in the mangroves. Used for varnish. The Americans loved it, covered their wood in it. And ivory too of course. Ivoryton was set up because of the East Coast trade, and Pratton and Whittle became the third biggest piano factory in the world. But let's not chatter here. Come over to the office.' He stood, and saluted his wife: 'Ollie. Thank you so much for my tea. See you again some time.'

Olivia took Richard to see some ruins in the forest, and I followed Roddy through the house, past a Kenyan boy doing the ironing whom Roddy addressed in Swahili as 'Toto' – much as all chauffeurs used to be James – and without the slightest attempt at an accent. Across the spiky grass was an outhouse with a stable door. Its walls were lined with books and documents and files, the remains of his collection that is now with the Kenya National Archives in Nairobi. Every book was wrapped in anti-termite plastic.

'Now let me see, what have we here?' Roddy peered at the shelves and I waited.

'Of course I can't see a thing you know. Nearly blind.' He pulled out an American Ph.D. of which the footnotes were longer than the text, and blew off insect-repellent powder. Outside, the breeze shifted papery bougainvillaea at the window, and a cock crowed. 'This is all American stuff. The Americans were frightfully powerful, had thirty-six consuls out here, all backed up by their government, till Suez that is. When was it? 1869? After that the British boats could get home quicker, and supply things quicker too. The Americans had to go on going round the Cape.'

'That wouldn't have affected the Newmans. The last letter I have is from 1842.'

'Yes, it's too early. Hmm. Involved in slavery, were they? Shouldn't be surprised. It wasn't ended until very late here. You know, I bought a slave once.' His eyes gleamed with humour behind his crystal balls.

'A slave? But surely . . .'

'Oh, I didn't *mean* to buy him. He sort of came with the job. I was setting up a newspaper and was buying a printing press from an Indian chap, back in 1939. The Indian fellow said, "Look here, old chap, if you take the machine, I'll throw in the man as well. He goes with the machine." So I did. Now you can imagine I didn't know what to do with him, so I just said, "Look here, you're free now. You can go off and find another job, earn a living, do what you like. But you must look after yourself, find your own place to live, find your own clothes and all that." Well, he liked his machine, so he decided to stay. I employed him, and he worked for me for years. His name was Foot. He had a club foot you see. Foot. Yes, awfully nice fellow.'

'And Zanzibar? Did you go there in the old days, before the revolution?'

'Oh yes, often. They were a pretty rum lot, those Sultans. One of the great occasions was a party Sultan Said – that was the last but one – gave for the British High Commissioner. It was a tremendous affair, music, fireworks, the lot. We went upstairs in the palace to the balcony where we could watch the firework display over the water. My little god-daughter was there, so excited, but she went off for a pee. While she was away the most frightful thing happened. A rocket misfired and hit the firework store, and the whole place exploded. Rockets were going everywhere, into the crowd, nose-diving into the sea – a thousand pounds-worth gone just like that. The Sultan thought it was all splendid, applauding away, "*Mzuri, mzuri*, super", and then it was finished. You can imagine the disappointment when my little god-daughter returned and said eagerly, "Roddy, when are the fireworks going to start?" '

We laughed. 'So they were tremendous characters, the Sultans?'

'Yes yes. Barghash, you know, the second Sultan. They used to say that when he blew his pipe everyone danced, from Zanzibar to the Lake. That's Lake Victoria of course. Marvellous stuff. Your ancestors would have enjoyed it all enormously.'

I hoped they enjoyed it as much as he did.

'Of course the last Sultan fled here in 1964, and then went on to Southend-on-Sea. I suppose he's still there. You knew that, didn't you?'

'No.'

'Ah well. You know I'm the only one left who remembers all these things,' said Roddy. 'The other day I was asked to write a history of the Mombasa Club, and I realized that there was almost nobody I could ask about the old days. Nobody left. It's sad really.'

'But at least no one can correct you. You could just make it all up.'

He put his head back and laughed. 'Well . . . And of course my memory's so frightfully bad these days. Forget everything. I'm eighty-two you know. Nearly dead.'

It was early evening when we left. Roddy turned to Richard and said, 'Now let me get this straight. You're called Pomeroy, and she's called Drysdale, is it? But you're married, are you? So what do I put on the envelope? Mrs Drysdale?'

'No no. Ms. M.S. *Ms.*'

He looked puzzled.

'Roddy,' Olivia explained, 'you can put *anything* on an envelope these days.'

He sighed. 'Well I hope to see you again some day.'

'I hope so too,' I replied, but I wondered. He was eighty-two – nearly dead – and we were only passing through.

'Was it wonderful in the forest?' I asked. 'Did you see the ruins?'

'No, nothing special,' said Richard, airily. But after a few days he could not resist telling me, and we went back. We squeezed into the *matatu* bus again and rattled over the creek, past coral rag quarries – now dry red lagoons – and new five-star hotels, to be left at the roadside. The high sun pounded on the track and on my hair until it was too hot to touch. We dodged from meagre shadow to shadow. What little breeze there was rattled in palms and hummed through telegraph wires. A family squatted beneath a tamarind tree to eat lunch and call out '*Jambo, jambo,*' but otherwise the track was still. A man rested in a maize field, his skin so black it was purple, and matt as the bloom on a purple grape.

Shade swallowed us. Darkness; sudden shafts of light shifting with insects; silence. A thin black snake clattered through dead leaves and vanished. Shield-like cobwebs encircling horned spiders as big as a fist barred the way and tangled in my hair. Through the bushes flashed glimpses of blue sea. We stumbled over ruins, walls of coral rag now green with slime, roots clawing the rubble and wrapping tendrils round arched doorways and tiny rooms, dragging a once humming town back into the forest. Men in robes and veiled women would have flitted through these streets, for this was an Arab settlement, part of their great trading network that flourished on and off for over a thousand years before the Newmans arrived; even the Queen of Sheba and King Solomon came this way in search of gold and silver, ivory, apes and peacocks. The graffiti of a dhow just visible on a mossy wall was a touching human presence. We slithered from mound to mound, jumping holes that had been wells. A troupe of apes – big as hairy old men – glinted at us and loped away. Huge winged shadows travelled over the ground; above, giant hornbills flapped into trees and shrieked. For hours we sat and watched, scratching insect bites, waiting for a leopard; and from not far away came the rhythmic beat of drums.

A lumpen office block squatted behind the Catholic cathedral. Mr Barkat Hashmani of Ampees Shipping emerged from his chairman's office, a slight Asian with a quiff of hair and a moist handshake. I explained why we were looking for a dhow.

'I know already. I was expecting you.' A kindly engineer from the Yacht Club had phoned in advance. 'Sit down please.' His office was cramped, the desk strewn with telexes and brochures advertising the *Virgin Butterfly*, a recently introduced hovercraft that travelled from Dar es Salaam in Tanzania to Zanzibar. 'Why must you go by dhow? Why not this *Virgin Butterfly*? We are its agents, very quick journey, very comfortable.'

'No no, that's not the sort of thing,' we chorused.

He wanted to help, but was a busy man. 'These dhows, you know they travel so loaded! Two or three hundred passengers crammed together, no food, no water, just like slave ships. Very dangerous.'

'We don't mind. Anything will do.'

'Also it is not the season.'

'What do you mean?'

'The dhow season. The sea is still too rough, and the wind is blowing north. If a dhow is going anywhere, it will be north not south. What about Lamu?'

The Lamu archipelago, on the border between Kenya and Somalia: it was a possibility. It is the earliest Islamic site on the East coast, and also one of the first places where the Newmans traded, in hides and tortoiseshell. But beneath the text of this journey lies the subtext of possible other journeys, routes that might have been taken, landscapes and towns we could have strolled in, people we did not meet. Making decisions was hard – we wanted it all – but Lamu was north, and we were heading south. We must have looked so downcast that Mr Hashmani added, 'I do have a ship coming up from Dar es Salaam. Let me see.' He ran a jewelled finger down a calendar. 'Yes, it should have been here yesterday, and I think we have just received a telex to say it will be in at the end of the week.' He shuffled through the papers on his desk. If not a dhow, we would settle for a cargo ship. The fan turned, but not a hair on Mr Hashmani's head quivered.

'And then the ship will go back?'

'Yes. You could easily get from Dar to Zanzibar.'

A possibility.

'What's the cargo?'

'I send down soda ash.'

'And what do you bring back from Tanzania?'

'Nothing.'

'You bring back an empty ship?'

He nodded slightly. 'Tanzania has nothing whatever to offer.'

David Hill was said to know ways of reaching Zanzibar by water, and he lived above the old dhow dock. An unpromising passage where cats crawled over mounds of rotting filth opened to the fresh air of the harbour, and to an old warehouse whose door was pinned with messages. 'Knock three times with the big brass handle.' 'Please remove shoes before entering.' We knocked three times, but there was no reply.

In the last of the evening light we sat to write a note to add to the others on a flight of stone steps, and realized that these were the Leven Steps, built by a British Lieutenant from the ship HMS *Leven* – Owen's ship – in 1824, and without doubt used by any Newman captain who landed over the next twenty years. They were the original harbour steps. Now only fishermen came here to cast their lines. As the sun set behind the minaret of the new Bohra mosque on the waterfront, and the muezzin pleaded with the faithful, the fishermen laid down their rods, turned towards Mecca – here to the north – and bowed. Tonight was a special night; the Bohra high priest had arrived from Bombay; boys were in shiny white kurtha pyjamas, women in hideous ice-cream coloured hooded cloaks; and as the blue lights flicked on in the mosque we watched the women file upstairs and bend in prayer.

Richard prodded a thick brown centipede nearly a foot long.

'We call them Tanzanian Trains.' A tall white man in his thirties peered down from behind a red beard. We got to our feet.

'Tanzanian Trains?'

'Yes. Because they move so slowly. Why don't you come in?'

The door was unbolted and we entered – barefoot – into a cave of treasures. Rich reds; endless depths of shadows; portraits of

Zanzibari dignitaries proud in turbans; a sedan swinging from knotted ropes; a courtyard; water splashing over rocks and ferns. David Hill watched our response. 'You like it,' he observed, pleased. He glanced past us to his small neat-featured girlfriend. She flung open a door and we were plunged into the heart of this building to be deafened by its beating. Ticking, wheezing, chiming, swinging, every space was thick with clocks. Pale round faces gleaming out of dark wood. David and Deborah glowed. It was a triumph.

'All from Zanzibar?'

'Yes. All from Zanzibar.' David watched protectively as Deborah toured the room pointing out details.

'This is Ansonia, and so is this.'

'No, that's not an Ansonia but a Japanese copy of an Ansonia,' he corrected her gently. Deborah was still learning. 'You can tell because only the Japanese inscribed their clocks with the name of the shipping agent.'

Ansonia was an American clock manufacturer who, years before the Japanese, dominated the mass-production market; these clocks would have been shipped to Zanzibar from Salem, Massachusetts, perhaps in Newman ships. The Firm's cargo lists often refer to 'Arab clocks'. The Omanis in Zanzibar had, it seemed, a passion for time, for Muslim time, for prayers five times a day, until, in 1964, time ran out. These clocks were some of the few rescued treasures.

'This one's Japanese too. See the manufacturer? It's Seikoshi. We all know what that became. But the best are by McCabe, an English clock maker,' David said. 'The delicacy of the chime, the craftsmanship – they're wonderful. My very best is called the Prince of Wales Clock and I think it's by McCabe, although Sotheby's and Christie's know nothing about it.'

'McCabe . . . that sounds familiar. I have a letter from the first Sultan, Seyyid Said, to my ancestors that mentions a clock by McCabe. He wanted them to get it repaired in London.'

David was excited by this, and produced a photograph of a rather ugly Victorian clock under a cupola. 'Might it be this?'

'I'm not sure. My notes are at the hotel.'

'Then we must go there at once and get them. I'll drive. We can pick up some cold beers on the way. Oh, by the way, what did you say was the name of this family you're tracing?'

'Newman.'

He gave a short laugh. 'I don't believe it.' We all stared. 'In that case we are related.'

I looked blank. How could I be related to him? I had no family in Kenya. The clocks seemed to pick up momentum.

'My ancestors first came out to Madagascar in the nineteenth century, and then went on to Zanzibar. They were Quaker missionaries, brought here in the family ships, which were the Newman ships.' I could not take it in. Ours was not a big or important family, just merchants, and yet here, in Mombasa, by chance ... 'I am related,' he went on, 'through the female line.'

'Me too. All my links with Zanzibar and Madagascar are through the female line, generation after generation.' But this was the first I had heard of Quakers in the family, let alone missionaries. What would Uncle Ralph have made of that?

Deborah broke the spell. 'Let's go out for a pizza.' She was American and practical. Yes, I said to myself, this meeting is so extraordinary that I can only think about it if we talk of something as banal as pizza.

'No,' said David, and in his cool straight-backed way he was in charge. This was his house, his collection, his country, and Zanzibar was his obsession. Deborah had moved in only three years ago. 'I don't want to eat out. I want to get those notes.'

They were not the same clocks. In his letter, dated 1845, Sultan Seyyid Said described it as being in the French style, very light and so easily out of order. David's clock did not fit; it was later, and heavier.

'And you? Have you got any details about the family?' I asked David.

'My grandmother had all the family papers, but when she came out here all her possessions were lost in transit.'

'Oh.'

'Yes. But she remembered a lot. I wish you could have met her.' We sat on the balcony and it rained, almost silently. 'She used to talk about the family all the time, the Newmans and the missionaries. Now she's dead. Pity.'

'So you've got nothing.'

'I did have a few papers in fact, including a description of arriving in Zanzibar for the first time on a Newman ship. But something terrible happened.' Deborah drew in her breath. She had heard this before. 'Like you, I also wanted to arrive in Zanzibar by ship and experience what my ancestors had experienced. I was lucky. I sailed in on a yacht. But when we reached Zanzibar, I was lying in my berth with the hatch open, and someone scaled the side of the boat, reached in and stole the lot.'

'What a waste.'

'Yes, when they found what it was they probably just chucked the whole lot away. Probably just threw it in the sea. Everything gone. Immediately I tried to write down everything I could remember, but to tell the truth I felt so sickened I could hardly bear to think about it. Anyway, that's enough of that. I do have one sheet of notes.' He produced a scrap of paper on which were scribbled details about graves. St Petrox, it said. Dartmouth. And there they were: Thomas Newman, Richard Newman, Robert Newman. Merchants.

We drank beer and listened to jazz late into the night. We talked of travels in Asia (hence the bare feet), of Zanzibar and Madagascar. Like Richard, he had set up an art gallery. 'I left before I lost all my friends,' he said.

'The artists?'

'Yes. They were impossible.'

'I used to tell him, why don't you just tell them to get out,' said Deborah in a peevish voice. 'I used to say: Come on David, it's your gallery. But he never did.'

David shrugged.

What was it that created the intimate mood – the candle-light on the old brocades, the jazz, the beer, the soft rain? All of these, and perhaps the bond – however loose – of our Newman ancestors.

Behind us on the balcony but shielded by a screen was their bedroom; it overlooked the water and was romantically veiled in a mosquito net. I couldn't help being aware of their relationship, David cool and fair and straight-backed, yet with a sensuous love for beautiful things; Deborah trapped (by choice) in his dark palace above the water, a foreigner unable even to work without a permit. She sat hunched on a *chaise-longue* coiling and uncoiling a rope of hair, a restless person, a traveller. Zanzibar – where they met – was what held them together, but I wondered privately how long she would stay.

'Ex-patriates go through phases of loathing it here,' she said.

'The elephants all poached, the rhino wiped out, the economy deteriorating. Suddenly, all at once, it's too much for everybody in Nairobi. They all say they are leaving, but in Mombasa no one can understand, we can't think what they're complaining about. Then there's a change-over, and the whole thing happens again the other way round. Everyone in Mombasa wants to leave, and no one in Nairobi can understand why. Again and again it seems to happen like that. Most people end up staying. But you know Juanita Carberry?'

'*White Mischief* and all that.'

'Yeah. She's a friend. Well, after all these years she suddenly left Kenya today. Just packed up and went. But for people like David, they've been here their whole lives. This is home.'

Is it? I wondered. David had only once and very briefly been to England, yet he spoke like an Englishman, looked like an Englishman, was brought up on his grandmother's stories. He seemed torn. Like me, he was fascinated by his own roots, had trailed his ancestors to Zanzibar and Madagascar, yet he seemed to resent England, an unknown and cold place that still laid a claim on him, kept him from belonging here. He did not dream of 'The You Kay', but it takes generations for a family to transplant itself completely, for roots to be severed.

It was midnight when we ran back through the empty streets, alarmed by talk of thieves. We kept to the centre of roads, away from the shadows. Guardians curled up under blankets in shuttered doorways of jewellery shops. As we rounded the final corner of our hotel, a veiled Muslim woman hoiked up her black skirts and tiptoed past.

'Is there a policeman round there?' she whispered.

'No.'

'Good.' She giggled and vanished.

David Hill knew of no dhow to Zanzibar, and we pestered Hashmani with dwindling response. He had no news of the ship from Tanzania. In the evenings we wandered forlornly to the dhow dock, drawn there like castaways, gazing out to sea. I was getting impatient to leave this little island; we had to accept that road was the only way, and took the bus south to Dar es Salaam.

The shortages in Tanzania could be read from the luggage: polystyrene sheets, Imperial Leather soap, cow gum, and above all Omo. Everyone had their packets of Omo.

A man with glasses attached to his head with strips of yellow plastic stood in the aisle haranguing one pasenger after another, gesticulating, while they gazed back passive but entertained. He was yelling Bible stories to his captive congregation – a Muslim and Christian mix – and soon the shouting spread. A man in an orange blazer turned to his unknown neighbour to convince him of the Truth. He thumped the back of the seat, eyes glittering, voice high-pitched: 'YES! You must wait for God to jump out and surprise you. He will jump out and surprise you! Yes! You must ask God not for money but for peace.' He hit the seat again. 'Yes! With money you have guards on the windows and the doors, dogs and Securicare yes! But no peace. No peace!'

His neighbour nodded, and smiled, and stared at the neat rows of coconut palms and sugar cane of a still successful country. Oddly – perhaps it was a religious thing – one of the passengers had a cushion strapped to the top of his head.

The quality of the customs buildings epitomized the differences between these two hostile countries. On the Kenya side cleanliness and efficiency; over six miles of no man's land to Tanzania and we found ourselves in a tin shed in the middle of a field. Inside the shed stood a Mini van. It had been there for years, clothed in bird shit. The rafters were clotted with nests, both birds and spiders. 'They could be being cultivated for some exotic crop,' observed Richard.

Borders are always strange uneasy places, especially late at night. We shuffled from queue to queue dragging baggage behind us and slumped against it pale under neon lights until two in the morning. I sensed no warmth from our fellow-passengers, one of whom with a face like a gourd had made it her mission to keep me at the back of every queue. Every piece of luggage was unpacked and there was nervous talk of strip searches; we had none of the right visas, vaccinations, or onward tickets. 'They might not let us in.' I was panicking. The gun-toting guards were without charm.

'Oh good,' said Richard. 'You can worry about that now. Anything else?'

In the shadows I added 'cholera' to my Thomas Cook vaccination certificate and forged a typically illegible doctor's signature, and by the time we reached customs the guards were too tired to bother with it or our lack of other documents.

But it was the road that mattered. At the Kenyan frontier a

line drawn across the tarmac left us with twelve hours of bone-jarring hell. I have been on worse roads, but never before with such a cowboy of a driver. And we were at the back. We were smashed, jarred, shattered against potholes. For twelve hours we gripped the seat but often we were hurled with such force that we almost hit the roof, letting out involuntary cries.

'Slow down for God's sake!'

No one took any notice. Now the head cushion made sense. Soon we did not trust the seats themselves – they would come up with us – and could cling only to each other. For twelve hours my body was rigid, waiting for the next shock, and soon my neck was so stiff I could not turn my head which became an unbearable weight. Richard clutched his stomach – he had pulled a muscle. We took it in turns to lean on the polystyrene sheets, but they began to crumble under the battering of our skulls. Red dust invaded the ill-fitting windows, soon to be replaced by rain which streamed through rust holes on to the neighbouring seat.

CHAPTER THREE

DAR ES SALAAM

At last the industrial suburbs of Dar crashed in beside us. 'Shoddy' advertised his roofing and building materials: he was clearly responsible for most of Dar. We heaved on our packs and walked into town through vistas of featureless grey. Everything was smothered in filth – the roads, the vehicles, the drab East European flat blocks. We seemed to make a habit of arriving on a Sunday when the lifeless streets and shuttered shops drew attention to the imminent collapse of the buildings. No one cared about Dar. It was a place that had once been a city but was no longer, just a collection of structures decaying without charm. The only activity was around a secondhand bookstall which offered *Breast Feeding is a Wonderful Art, Class Struggles in Tanzania*, some well-thumbed Mills & Boon titles and a book of Swahili proverbs which fell open at the wise old saw: 'He who hides his private parts will never have a child.' Women eased vast bosoms and jutting shelf-like buttocks over broken pavings with babies strapped to backs, baskets on heads.

In the old botanical gardens a few scraggy roses clawed up from the grey dust. Once-smart colonial residences – German turn-of-the-century vernacular, all dark beams and high eaves – were now haunted by dogs. Creepers sprouted over shutters and cries of peacocks, lonely cries, added to the sense of desolation. In Mombasa this area would be filled with Yacht Club members, security gates and swimming pools; it was in a way reassuring that just a change of regime and this was what could become of all that glossy wealth. The next stage was the creeper-smothered ruins at Mtwapa, and then nature would reclaim it.

Change money, change money. The air of Dar es Salaam – 'Haven of Peace' – whispered the words. It came breathing out of litter-strewn doorways and from behind walls, change money, change money, taunting us. An official with a brief-case barked:

'These men are thieves! Stick to your programme!'

We made our way towards a well-known landmark, the clock tower, to find a stump in a roundabout with a broken digital clock on one side and a Coke advert on the other.

The Delux Inn was full. While Richard searched for an alternative I collapsed with the bags and fell asleep. I woke spasmodically as a succession of men peered down: I must have been an unusual sight, hair matted with red dust, feet and legs mud-spattered.

'You have roads like this in England, I think,' murmured someone in stone-washed denims and a tropical shirt.

'Yes.' I agreed. I was too tired to argue.

We ended up climbing four flights of stone stairs to a room once painted blue, now crumbling to reveal the rotted pink plaster beneath. The ceiling was tracked with twisting cracks and lianas of electric cable leading to a defunct speaker – again Eastern Europe came to mind. Buildings like these were provided by Communist countries sympathetic to Tanzania's post-colonial 'African Socialism'. Our room price included breakfast, which was served on the roof under a corrugated iron canopy. In the centre of a concrete expanse stood plastic tables and a sofa spewing foam. The black tea was so sweet my teeth ached, and the piece of dry bread spilled weevils. We shook them off and ate the bread: we had no Tanzanian shillings for anything else. We did have the luxury of a bathroom but the bath was plugged with a wad of newspaper and filled with cold water – the receptionist advised us to scoop up bucketfuls with which to wash and to flush the loo. We shared it with the next room, and Richard opened the door and banged it quickly shut again.

'There's an enormous and completely naked black man in there. I should wait a minute.'

The point of this room, however, was the bathroom window. It was a narrow slit, without glass, but from it we could see the docks.

Day after day we ventured along the harbour front, stepping over sewage pipes and coconut husks and rotting peel flung there by orange sellers, and unemployed men who sat gazing out to sea, dreaming of escape. A child on a concrete bench donated by the Lions Club swung her legs as we passed, but otherwise we were ignored. At the water's edge men dug shoulder-deep pits in the low-tide mud, bare hands feeling out worms in the slime. The carcase of a boat lay beached and waterlogged; a crow picked at its ribs and flapped off. A ferry for Mtwara was edging towards the harbour mouth, so laden with human cargo that it sank dangerously low in the water and listed to port. Like a slave ship, I thought, remembering Mr Hashmani – so many dispensable humans.

It may have been squalid, but here at least Dar es Salaam took on some form, some purpose. Cranes leant their heads sociably towards each other, like elegant giraffes. And below them were what we had come for: boats. Dozens of them, rusty tankers pumping bilges and hooting horns, pilot boats busying back and forth. But best of all there were dhows and not all were motorized. One glided past under its triangular sail, heavy with a cargo of coconuts, a sight unchanged except in detail for a thousand years. At the dhow dock the guard in his cubicle slept, head propped on rifle butt, so we tiptoed past and into the port. Here dhows jostled and bumped. Not just one dhow; not just seven, but more than we could count, all broad-hipped and brown as wenches, festooned with rigging and swinging wooden blocks and pulleys like medallions. We dangled our legs over the side of the jetty. Muscular seamen were already untying the sail and covering the coconut sacks in tarpaulin: they looked a tough bunch, black and scarred and grinning and dressed in rags. Yes, they said in passing, there might be a dhow to Zanzibar.

It was off-season, careening time, and a dhow was being rebuilt to take a motor. It was propped on logs on the grass, the old planks sawn away, new ones fitted in place. An adze aimed with deadly accuracy shaved the planks to fit. A boy in a pink T-shirt hauled out nine-inch nails with a crow-bar made from a steel reinforcing rod, and another chipped the old planks into pegs: nothing was wasted. The captain had paler skin and sharper features than his workers. He came from the north and wore a *koffia* and white *kanzu*, and he hurried about anxiously giving orders. We sat amongst wood chips on logs waiting to become planks, and watched. A head poked over the top of the boat.

'*Jambo!*'
'*Jambo.*'
'*Habari?*'
'*Mzuri.*'

'Karibu!'
'Asante.'
A chant of welcome.
'Speak Swahili?'
'No.'
'Small small.' He held up finger and thumb an inch apart.
'Very very small small.'
The head laughed and disappeared.

The tide sucked back from a sambuk lying just off shore, baring its underbelly. It listed on the mud, held upright only by ropes, and seemed oddly out of scale, a vast hull looming over tiny people like Gulliver pegged down in Liliput. We flapped on sandals over the slime to find a young Swahili kneeling below the hull among the scattering of white barnacles he had scraped off. Some had landed snow-like in his woolly hair and been trapped there. He was chipping out scum-filled cracks and filling them with rope, pressing it in, and painting over with fish oil. The elephantine hull swelled above us, way up to the gunwales, over which leaned a brown sharp-featured Arab face. They were from Yemen, explained Mohammed, a local who stood around watching with us, hoping for work. He pointed out the captain, an old man with fat ankles. His slim son squatted beside the African and pointed out cracks, working fast before the tide whooshed back in. It takes them nine days from Yemen, Mohammed said. Only nine days? An eight cylinder engine, 350 tonnes.

At the stern a rudder soared. I walked around it, taking care to avoid the thunderbox which was suspended overhead, a hole in a plank. Above it rose the poop cabin, transforming this boat from a humble dhow into a splendid galleon crowned with a carved rail and adorned with arcs of carved wooden roundels golden with varnish. And above it all two masts. This was the sort of dhow the Newmans would have used, surely. Even their own brigs would have been similar – two-masted, different only in form, not in feel. I longed to be invited aboard, but no one seemed willing and there was no ladder. Perhaps a dhow like this, I dreamed, will take us to Zanzibar.

At the port a young trainee pilot leant on the rails, crisp in white shirt and shorts, handshake firm. No no, he was not from Dar, he said. He came from the Malawi border.

'Do you like Dar?' Richard asked.

'I must say, no.'

'Noise?'

'Yes, too many cars. It must be as if you asked a Yorkshireman if he liked living in London.'

A Yorkshireman? An incongruous thought. I gazed down at a dug-out canoe half-submerged, an abandoned flip-flop floating at the bottom. The over-loaded ferry had paused in the harbour mouth. A woman aboard had been pushed by humans to the edge of a deck, had fallen, and cut off her leg; the crowd at the jetty was so thick that the stretcher-bearers had to fight to reach her. Spectators hurtled past a boy selling hard-boiled eggs, sending his day's profit bumping down the harbour steps. Birds of prey wheeled overhead: Yorkshire seemed a long way away.

'What are you doing here?' he asked.

'We're looking for a dhow to Zanzibar.' I anticipated the usual dismal shake of the head.

'A dhow? That's no problem. You can get one tomorrow, just buy a ticket in the morning.'

'Do you mean it? Tomorrow?'

'No problem.'

I liked this trainee pilot.

'Our harbour master's English. Would you like to meet him?'

'Very much, yes, thank you.'

He smiled. 'I'll call him on the radio.'

We heard a blast of crotchety English finishing: 'if they must.' The trainee pilot looked embarrassed. 'I'm sorry. The harbour master's English, but sometimes I find it very hard to understand what he says.' We changed the subject.

I couldn't wait to leave. We had been robbed, and narrowly escaped arrest for using the black market. But it was not just the city itself; it was also the wearying infinity of Africa that yawned behind us, the millions of villages and thousands of miles. I longed to get back off shore onto a self-contained island where I knew where clear boundaries lay. I longed to get to Zanzibar.

The trainee pilot hurried away to deal with the woman and her leg, and a slight boy named Mohammed Khamis Hamza leant on the rails beside us. He was the first Zanzibari we had met, our first link with the island, but he had left it to seek work on the mainland. It was hard. Sometimes he hung around in the port looking for day work but there was too much competition. He missed Zanzibar, I could tell by the way he said it – *Zanzibar*. He caressed it with its name.

'There many many beaches, so clean, not like this,' he said. 'Zanzibar peoples cool, high cool. Here people thieves. Many peoples drunkards and thieves.' He had been befriended by an English student and had memorized his address in Edgware. 'Mr Andy, he very good man, he smoke so much marijuana. At end of letters, he always write: "Take Care".'

'That's nice.'

'And Captain Harris, he going to find me a ship.'

'Where to?'

Mohammed Khamis Hamza shrugged. 'Anywhere. Europe countries, America, Australia, anywhere. Maybe I see you in London. Captain Harris, he very big man, ooh, so big, and he help me.' Everyone, it seemed, was trying to leave Dar es Salaam. 'You go Zanzibar by dhow?'

'Yes.'

He frowned. 'Very dangerous. So many people.'

I looked at the ferry still sitting in the harbour mouth. British newspapers often carry reports of Third World boats sinking under the weight of passengers. Crushed in a dhow we wouldn't stand a chance. 'And shark,' he added.

'Sharks?'

'Five day ago, dhow Zanzibar to Pemba turn over. Two people from eighteen found.'

'The rest were eaten by sharks?'

He nodded slowly. 'Nobody know. But Zanzibar Pemba very deep, many many sharks. Dar Zanzibar not so deep,' he added reassuringly.

To fill time we rang a friend of a friend who had lived in Dar for eight years and was said to know this coast well. He will help you in your researches, my friend had promised.

'My office is the most hideous building on the street. You can't miss it,' said Alan Rogers by way of directions. But all the buildings were hideous – it was impossible to choose – and by the time we found his he had gone out. His wife met us at the door. She stood tall and large-boned in a conventional belted cotton dress, a pale woman in her late thirties.

'Are you expecting him back?'

'Yes.' She tapped her fingers on a counter. 'What are you doing here?'

I explained and her pale eyes glittered.

'I suppose they were trading in ivory, were they?'

As I spoke I saw my mistake. On the walls posters advertised a Tanzanian wildlife preservation campaign.

'Ivory?' I looked to Richard for help, but he could do nothing. 'Maybe. I don't know,' I finished lamely.

Of course they were trading in ivory: it features on almost every cargo list. It was possibly the dream of ivory that drew them here in the first place, as it had drawn Arabs and then Portuguese for hundreds of years. What was it that tempted Kurtz into the Heart of Darkness and sent him mad? His passion for ivory. It was the search for ivory that led coastmen to penetrate into Africa's interior in the mid-nineteenth century, and it was ivory that was behind the slave trade. Slaves were used to carry the tusks to the coast and when slavery was finally banned, the trade in ivory increased as a substitute.

The Americans had been at it for years. By the 1830s their annual export of ivory from Zanzibar was worth £60,000 to £80,000. The Americans also imported ivory to Britain, and the Newmans were the first British company to attempt to short-circuit their control and bring it direct to Britain themselves. They fed an insatiable demand. By the mid 1830s some twenty-five tons of ivory were imported from East Africa to England, most of it by Newman Hunt & Christopher.

And now there was almost no ivory left. Sue and Alan Rogers had recently started their campaign to save it, and pictures of dying elephants accused me from the walls. I knew that I bore no responsibility for my ancestors' actions; though I talked of 'my' ancestors, they did not *belong* to me. How could something that no longer exists belong to me? I do not belong to my descendants. How could I belong to people not yet born, whom I may never know, never see? We were unconnected except through some very diluted blood lines marked out like a problem chart on a scroll. They lived their lives in a way that was acceptable enough at the time and then evaporated into nothingness, leaving no trace but a few chilly graves. And yet I was ashamed.

'And what has our project to save the African elephant got to do with your ancestors?' Sue Rogers' voice was hostile.

'Nothing . . . I was just interested. How long have you been out here?'

'Thirty years. My ancestors came out here too, but they weren't trading ivory.'

We did not ask what they were trading. She was busy. The phones rang and behind her two Tanzanians tapped at typewriters. Our interruption was more than she could stand, and she tried hard, but not hard enough, to hide her irritation. Her husband was more amiable.

'Sit down. Hasn't anyone offered you a cup of tea?'

'Er, no. We've just arrived,' I lied.

Alan resembled his wife, with the same taut features and dry skin. They embodied this drab city, their faces the colour of the ashen dust that heaped the roadside. Perhaps they were friends of the crotchety harbour-master; perhaps to be English and stay on in Dar meant you had to be as mean as the city.

We were interested in their work, tried to press further, but information was grudgingly given.

'How many elephants are left in Tanzania?' I asked.

'We never count heads,' snapped Sue. 'How can you possibly be accurate, and you waste enormous amounts of money and man hours doing it.'

I seemed to gall her every time I spoke.

'Can you at least give us some idea?' Richard persisted, bravely.

Alan was more forthcoming. 'It is thought that between 1979 and 1987 we lost more than 70 per cent of our elephants. About half a million. The poachers are mainly Somalis who slip over the border undetected and sell the ivory to people like the Poon brothers in Hong Kong through their operations in Dubai.'

'What do they use?'

'AK-47s, automatics, Land-Rovers. They are incredibly well-organized and well-funded. The Poons buy two to three hundred tons of ivory a year at $3 a kilo and sell it for $220, so they can well afford to cover themselves, pay the bribes and finance the whole thing. It's thought that there are now about 75,000 elephants left in Africa.'

'Alan, I meant to tell you,' Sue interrupted, her eyes suddenly bright.

'Moi burnt the ivory.'

'When did you hear?'

'Just now.'

'Good God.' A beam passed between them and I saw how charged was their mission. They resembled the Christian missionaries who fought slavery here a hundred and twenty years ago. Their fervour was as intense, and right now, in their hideous office, ivory seemed an even more emotive issue. This was man's inhumanity to animals at the point of near-extinction. It seemed worse. To try and destroy the market President Moi of Kenya had sacrificed thousands of pounds worth of government stocks of ivory recovered from poachers, and ceremoniously set it alight.

'He had the world's press there, TV cameras, the lot.'

'Good God,' Alan nodded slowly. 'But we don't need all that, do we? We can do it without.'

'Yes.'

We want not only to stop people trading in endangered species, the Rogers said, but to stop people wanting them. The Tanzanian government is very supportive, they said. Yet in the Government Tourist Corporation was a Game Trophy Shop where we could buy zebra handbags ('popular for executives and teenagers'), impala head and antlers, and zebra shoes. There was even a brochure pinned to the wall suggesting, 'At the end of your visit to Kilimanjaro, just pop in at the taxidermy factory. This is where you can pick up an elephant you can sit on (an elephant footstool) . . . you can even wear an elephant or python and walk away with it (shoes made from elephant or python skin). When in Hong Kong or San Francisco just lift a phone and place your order for ivory, or place an order for a huge lion (mount) – in a few weeks your ivory or lion will knock at your door.'

We asked an assistant about the lion.

'Yes,' he said blithely, 'you can easily buy a lion skin, no problem, beautifully cured.'

'How much?'

'A lion would cost $6,000. Very cheap.' He was tantalized by the prospect of a sale.

'Where do you get the lions?'

'From the game parks.' But now he began to suspect that we were not potential clients. 'The zebras are culled,' he insisted quickly. 'The lions and elephants are taken from poachers.'

'But you create a market, don't you see?' We were hectoring the man. It was not his fault.

At midnight we arrived at the dhow dock to find – confirming our worst fears – over 300 people waiting with us. Everyone had their eyes fixed on the far end of the jetty. I leant against a wall, cushioned by my rucksack. The harbour glittered, glamorous now masked by night. Lights from cargo ships stretched down into the black water in orange and white bar graphs. Dinghy lights bobbed. An oil refinery flamed on the distant shore; the Mtwara ferry, still sitting at the harbour mouth, shimmered like a cruise ship. Then, at last, an unassuming little boat worked its way towards us. Surreptitiously we all sidled forward, manoeuvring our bags with our feet. The *Ras Nungwi* tied up alongside. It was long and very low in the water, and covered with a canvas roof. I felt a moment's disappointment: if this was it, we would not sail.

But it was a dhow all the same, and we squeezed ourselves happily up wind of the engine. A hatch opened on sacks of flour: our packs were dropped on top. Passengers travelling lighter optimistically put their bags beside them, stretched out their legs, settled in for the night, but soon other passengers nudged between their knees. More and yet more people. One fat man stood amidst hummocks of seated bodies and swivelled his head in search of a space.

'Give me your bag,' I called, trying to be helpful. 'There's a space here.'

'It is not my bag I am thinking of. It is me, sitting down.'

His trousers hung well below his belly and Richard turned (with some difficulty) to say: 'Poor man, he's suffering from builder's bum, that legendary disease.'

No one resented him forcing his way in. However many people, however large, there was always room for more. Beside me a boy lay with his legs splayed around a barrel; he remained like this all night, never complaining, and rested his bare foot in the palm of my hand. They were different, these Zanzibaris, I could see it at once. They lacked the aggression that simmered on the mainland. They were smaller, paler, sharper-featured: their Arab blood showed.

Off in a dhow at last, off to Zanzibar! We lurched out of the harbour and coasted north, then east across the twenty miles of Zanzibar channel. The captain unscrewed the light bulb and we vanished into darkness; the only light was the orange dot of his cigarette which drew Arabic calligraphy as he bent to the wheel and peered over bodies to the bow and beyond. We leaned over the gunwales and watched phosphorescence dance in our wake.

But the swell got up and Richard began to shake his head. 'It's no good,' he kept saying. 'It's no good.' I felt his panic spread. 'We can't make it. Don't you see? If the sea gets up any more the waves will break over us. We're too low in the water.' He was shaking his head and sighing. 'The flour will get sodden, and we'll sink, just like that. We're overloaded. It's just no good.'

I also remembered now, after all my longing to go to sea, that I was often seasick.

But the hours passed and a flock of dhows setting out to fish intimated land. A bleak dawn broke on Zanzibar.

CHAPTER FOUR

ZANZIBAR

In 1837 Robert Newman Hunt was a gaunt man of delicate health. Though thirty-two years old he was unmarried, and lived still at his parents' home in the appropriately medicinal environment of Upper Harley Street. Oddly, although he was a partner in the Firm and one of the central characters in its story, he is barely mentioned by Uncle Ralph and does not feature on the Pedigree. But I know he was my great-great-great-uncle.

The damp London air was unsuitable and Devon proved no better; the doctors prescribed a cure. His father allowed him to fit out a yacht – with no expense spared – and with a skilful surgeon he proceeded on an aquatic excursion of more than two years' duration.

'An aquatic excursion' sounds a most dignified venture. Robert, wrapped in shawls, leans against the mast. His cheeks are hollow, his Byronic curls lift slightly in the breeze. I see his surgeon, an older man with whiskers, emerging from the cabin with a glass of brandy and laying a hand on his patient's arm, gently urging him inside. The sun is setting and the evening quickly chills. 'An aquatic excursion' gives no hint of the burning sun on the hot becalmed days or of the monsoon winds that destroyed the *Herrick*. But Robert Newman Hunt had the sea in his blood: both his parents were of old Dartmouth merchant stock, and he would have trusted his captain in the knowledge that if you can sail in the spasmodic gusts of the river Dart against a running tide, you can sail anywhere. Robert Newman Hunt smiles weakly and accepts the glass, but he barely notices his companion; he has other cares on his mind. The Sailor King is not yet dead, but the Victorian age is on the horizon, and he carries the burden not only of his own business ventures but also the responsibility of spreading the words of Profit and Civilization.

According to the letters at the Pool, in visiting various parts of the globe he was very flatteringly noticed at Zanzibar by His Highness the Imam of Muscat, and encouraged the Imam to look favourably on England.

It must have been an exciting time. The Imam, the great Sultan Seyyid Said, had moved here from Muscat with his court of Omanis and vast retinue of concubines only two years earlier and in 1840 made it his capital. Zanzibar and East Africa were part of his Sultanate, and as a merchant in his own right he saw what both island and mainland had to offer. All of Africa's resources would converge on Zanzibar, from where they could be shipped around the world, and on the island itself he decreed that for every three coconut palms a clove tree must be planted. They flourished, and so Zanzibar was born, on the brink of becoming one of the world's great entrepôts.

The Newmans had arrived at much the same time. But already the Firm was in trouble. It was not just diplomacy that brought Robert Newman Hunt here; nor can it have been the search for a cure. Zanzibar was always a haven for malaria and dysentery. No, the reason for his visit was to sort things out.

Trade had begun well. Within months of arriving in the Indian Ocean the Firm's vessels swarmed the coast. The *Sandwich, Vulture* and *Argus*, the *Kite, Kingfisher, Swallow* and *Rio Packet* – all these and more were dispatched from England laden with salted beef and needles, muskets and poison. These were sold for Maria Theresa Austrian dollars (half a dollar being simply one dollar cut in half) or were exchanged for aromatic gums and resins exuded by different East African trees and used for darkening paints and varnishes, with such tantalizing names as Arabic, Olibanum, Dragon's Blood, Myrrh, Colombo Root and Aloes and for coconut oil, hides, aloes, simsim (sesame) seed, sea-horse teeth (walrus tusks), cloves and ivory. (I loved reciting these names and handling the worn cargo lists that the Firm's captains had held, striding booted round the 'hard' at Zanzibar giving the crates and sacks a final check. How could they have envisaged that over a hundred and fifty years later I would be earnestly deciphering their scribbles in a freezing attic in Devon?)

The Firm's agent, Norsworthy, went into partnership with a Swahili slaver named Khamis bin Othman. He seemed ideal. He had accompanied Owen on his voyage in 1824, and was said to speak fourteen languages and have an intimate knowledge of the natives and their trade. In 1834 Norsworthy brought him to London on the *Kingfisher*. Robert Newman Hunt, delighted at the arrival of this exotic 'Ameer', wrote to Lord Palmerston that 'Armeia bin Hafman (they seemed to have trouble with his name) is desirous to . . . be presented to His Majesty at the next levee.'

The request caused the Foreign Office some consternation. Who was this 'personage'? East India House reported to Palmerston that 'The party does not appear to have any title to be presented as a diplomat', but warned that 'the Imam is, you know, a friend and ally of ours'. Eventually Lord Palmerston denied him access to the King but agreed to see him himself.

Despite his dubious qualifications, Newman Hunt & Christopher took up this Arab gentleman with enthusiasm and invited him on a grand tour of Great Britain. He was taken from Manchester to Liverpool by the newly opened railroad. 'We did the thirty-one miles in rather less than one hour and a half. We saw the docks on Sunday (after church of course). The Ameer says he wants a plan of Mamhead House and Park (the recently built family seat near Exeter) to take back to Zanzibar.'

But the triumphal start to business proved a hollow bubble. Khamis bin Othman's reports of the potential trade were wildly exaggerated and by 1837 the Firm was on the brink of losing its massive investment.

Each day I woke long before the light. The mosquito net breathed beneath the fan, lifting and falling, while I awaited the procession of morning. First the town crier, '*Allah, Akbaaaaar,*' and the slap slap of his bare feet receding and returning as he embroidered his way through the weave of alleys. '*Allah, Hamdulillaaaah.*' Heard but never seen. Only then did the cats begin their shrieking. On the roof with the water tank I forced myself to practice yoga as the sun rose; I was hidden, up above the rusted leaves of corrugated iron. From down below floated shouts of children at hopscotch already and the scent of wood smoke and frying coconut oil; crows squawked and a goat browsed, unconcerned by all that had come and gone in Zanzibar, under a swollen baobab.

We tried to get lost in the old Stone Town.

'Hey *mazungo*, where you go?' a boy asked, arm round a friend.

'Nowhere. Just looking. And you?'

He shrugged. 'Going roving,' he said, over his shoulder. Passages interlocked and doubled back between curtains of limewashed coral. They parted on foetid courtyards where fat ladies leaned on balconies. Men kicked off their sandals at mosque doors, and hooded women flitted past like blackbirds. Turning their backs on the wide sea that brought them here, each separate race squeezed together into the smallest possible space, and closed their heavily carved doors; fish carved on the doorframes evolved into flowers and pineapples. Above them the houses craned towards the light, like trees in a rainforest.

And then we'd be almost blinded by a brilliant vertical stripe of blue. Not for the first time, I thought of Venice. With relief we escaped on to the breezy seafront where boys splashed after a ball. Here customs offices and palaces and old godowns and consulates rose high and stained, crenellated and arched; map in hand and heads in the air we tried excitedly to identify them. Was it here that Robert Newman Hunt plied his trade?

The customs office was a flat-faced slab of a building which the British had tried to prettify with flimsy metal columns. One hundred and fifty years ago Newman Hunt climbed the steps and pushed open the massive carved doors with their Indian brass spikes to admit himself into the formidable presence of Jairam Singh, the 'farmer of Customs'. All imports went through him, and if he did not want them himself, he could choose the purchaser, and with the connivance of the Americans and the Sultan fix the price. It was a monopolists' ring which the Firm threatened by trying to circumvent it, and Jairam Singh determined to squeeze Newman Hunt and Christopher out. It was only after complaining that the Firm was at last given the protection of a British consul, to be not only the first in Zanzibar, but the first in all East Africa, so indirectly the Firm was responsible for the area becoming, in the end, a British Protectorate.

This, surely, overlooking the harbour in colonnaded splendour, was Seyyid Said's palace, Beit el Ajarb, the House of Wonders! Robert Newman Hunt would have paid his respects to the Sultan here (it was smaller then, and more delicate) and seen him enthroned with some of his one hundred and twenty children. Much changed, of course, and now taken over by the Communist Party, but there nonetheless.

We searched for Mtoni, Seyyid Said's other palace, where each day between nine and four he held court. Squeezing into a

Toyota pick-up which serves as the bus north to Bububu we were dropped beside a BP petrol depot. A large dilapidated building with a tin roof stood on the shore beside it.

'This can't be it!' I had hoped that it might resemble neo-Tudor Mamhead House in Devon, which had been built for the Newmans by Anthony Salvin and had so inspired Khamis bin Othman.

'No, I agree. But let's look anyway.'

We pushed through a rusted sheet of tin into a hall thick with weeds and ducked our heads as fruit bats streamed out in alarm. Fig roots squirmed over walls. If this was it, all that remained were squat pillars and arches, and the tantalizing roof of a Persian bath that we could see but not reach. It looked like a warehouse, something to do with the petrol depot, but what warehouse would bother with a Persian bath?

'It's such a hideous building. So heavy.'

'But it must be it,' said Richard. 'Where else could Mtoni be?'

I saw Robert Newman Hunt as the stars dripped onto Prison Island being ferried from his yacht to the little dock here, a turbaned slave guiding him into a hall of riches. His eyes take a moment to adjust but through a haze of incense he makes out walls clad in decorative plasterwork in the Persian style. That same year, he recalls, the Sultan had married the huntress Scheherazade, the ravishing granddaughter of the Shah of Persia, and the Sultan hoped to tempt her to join him in Zanzibar.

Champagne for the Englishman! (Newman Hunt recalls that along with the buttons, slates, snuff boxes, whitewash brushes and gunpowder in the Firm's store are half a dozen champagne glasses – he could pass them off on the Sultan! But he quickly dismisses such base thoughts.) The Sultan is more than hospitable – nothing is too much trouble – for he is somewhat taken with this pale but civilized gentleman. A pleasant change from the red-faced Norsworthy. Robert for his part is impressed by the courtesy with which the Sultan treats his own family and his slaves, and is convinced of his genuine goodness.

Ethiopian concubines, statuesque against the candle-light, serve sweet coffee and halva. The silk cushions on which Robert reclines, the heat, the wafts of scented skin and his great distance from home: does he feel a momentary freedom from his business worries and his ill health? Does he allow the sensuous languor to overwhelm him? Who knows.

*

We walked the five miles back under a perfect crescent moon. A Muslim crescent. Beneath it, and behind a high wall in the town centre, we found Sultan Seyyid Said's tomb. It was crumbling and littered with tins and bottles.

Everything was falling down, propped up, yet resonated with past glories. We found ourselves wondering, where *is* everybody? Zanzibar was that sort of place. In the sea-splashed houses with their glassed-in verandahs that rotted in the damp air I was suddenly reminded of the Pool. Of course! With its exotic garden – palm trees and giant ferns basking in the Gulf Stream, another ocean's gyre – it was not so far away. The same smells of mildew, the same salt-dusted windows, the same steaminess. No wonder Robert Newman Hunt felt at home.

What was seen as the golden age of Sultan Seyyid Said ended with his death in 1856. Thirty-six of his children were still living, and he was succeeded (in turn) by four of them. Although they continued to wield power over the island, in 1890 Zanzibar became part of the British Protectorate. Then in the early 1960s, when a mass of African countries gained their independence, Britain recognized the independence of the Sultanate of Zanzibar, in 1963. One year later the Africans in Zanzibar, many of whom were descended from slaves, rose up in armed revolution against the wealthy Arabs, their one-time masters. The alleyways filled with shooting and bloodshed, and the Arabs fled back to Oman. The new radical rulers of Zanzibar were quickly supplied with aid – including military aid – by the USSR, China and Eastern Europe. Within weeks monolithic concrete flats were built by East Germany on the edge of town; Zanzibaris complained to us of the British who sat off-shore and prevaricated, not wanting to get involved in their ex-protectorate, while the Communist Party established power. 'The Africans were used by everybody,' people told us. 'They couldn't do anything about it. In three weeks the island's fate was decided.'

The more moderate President Nyerere of Tanganyika, less than twenty miles away, doubtless feared the build-up of military aid and so brought Zanzibar under his control, creating in 1964 the United Republic of Tanzania.

People told us of post-Independence craziness, but it was hard to know how much to believe – the forced inter-marriages between Africans and Indians, Africans and Arabs; illiterate village boys made government ministers; spies everywhere.

Now Zanzibar's government square, once as spruce as the old Treasury gardens in Mombasa, was overgrown. A rusted car stripped of its wheels was propped in the centre of a patch of grass – abandoned here, or perhaps erected as a memorial to a capitalism long dead. Hills of rubble where houses had collapsed were foraged by chickens, goats and rats, and pawpaws grew tall. A man virtually dragged us into his house.

'Come with me, I am responsible, no sweat, follow me,' he urged. He had fourteen children and stank of alcohol; we expected to be mugged. But he led us up a stone staircase to see where the back of his house had simply disappeared. A carved door was suspended in mid-air. The owner, an Omani, had fled, and this man and his children were squatting here.

'Curios and fancy goods' were sold in a heavily arched building on the seafront where (surely) the Newmans would have stored their goods. I hoped, foolishly perhaps, to find some memento of them, or at least of Seyyid Said, amongst the Dutch export bowls and the inevitable clocks. (They were everywhere here, in mosques and government offices and *en masse* had become ugly, their round faces crude.)

'All the clocks are working,' said the Gujerati owner, not really hoping for a sale, 'but we don't wind them because it interferes with the telephone.' He called himself an Indian; his family had traded here for generations, since long before Partition. Other Gujeratis had come to East Africa as coolies to work on the Uganda Railway, and had stayed in Mombasa and Nairobi and got rich, but not in Zanzibar. The man shook his head mournfully. 'This is just junk,' he said, waving a dismissive hand at the brass pots, door knockers, tatty models of dhows. He was having brass studs added to the old Arab chests – the Omani tourists preferred them like that he said, despising them. 'So many troubles. Everything changed.' He had smooth pale skin and fixed his eyes on the middle distance and spoke wearily in a monotone with pursed lips. His children were at school in Bombay; there were no schools here. 'My son wanted to be an engineer but I told him, "No, we must stay in business, then we work for ourselves. We are our own boss and we can make a quick getaway if that is needed." ' The Indians: the Jews of the Indian Ocean. 'Zanzibar is finished. Had it,' he muttered. He

planned to leave for (of all places) Bromley. 'This place! It used
to be a piece of heaven. Now it's a piece of grave.'

Gazing up at yet more ruins under scaffolding, a thick-set man
paused to chat. He wore a sports jacket and his English was
good. 'It's terrible. I've been away for seven years in the merchant navy in Greece, and I come back and find the place has
collapsed.' There was shame, and disgust, in the way he spoke.
Rashid was forty-eight years old, a Comorian brought up in
Zanzibar. He had got embroiled in the fighting in 1964 and been
shot in the chest by revolutionaries, after which he thought it
wise to leave the island. Like a knight on a quest, for seven years
he had roamed the seven seas, but as he hung out in New York
bars and toured the brothels of Rio, cruised up the Panama
Canal and crossed the Pacific, as one year melted into another, so
his vision of Zanzibar did not dwindle but grew more vivid. To
the Greek sailors he was just another black, at the bottom of the
pile, but he saw the mosques crowded with bare-footed men and
the ginger tea near the port; he saw balmy evening strolls with
friends through the Jamituri gardens, pausing at lamp-lit stalls to
buy hot grilled squid. It became increasingly difficult to quell his
longing to return, yet for seven years he was tied to his ship. And
when at last he made his way home, everything had changed.

Now he wanted to change money on the black market. With a
blow, my sea-faring knight became a portly man with warts on
his neck and a stutter. I couldn't bear his humiliation. He looked
around distractedly; it wasn't just the money; fear lurked here in
Zanzibar, fear of the authorities, fear of thieves, just fear.

He strolled with us in search of Mr Ah Chu, a friend of a friend
in England. 'This is a Chinese house, we'll ask here.' A Chinese
youth with long hair emerged from a grey concrete house that
could have blotted any modern Chinese city. He spoke
courteously to Rashid in Swahili. For a moment I was surprised
by his fluency – I had forgotten that the Chinese have been here
for generations too. Richard said suddenly: 'We are travellers in
a travellers' world. Everyone has come, by dhow or cargo ship,
from somewhere else. Everyone shares ancestral stories, like a
collective dream, of leaving and arriving.'

It was low tide and boats leaned at angles on slate-coloured mud.
Through an open door we found Ah Chu's wife in printed cotton
pulling apart skeins of vermicelli.

'Ah Chu in Hong Kong,' she explained. 'Our three children in middle school there.'

She knotted the vermicelli ropes and placed them in rows on a wire mesh. She did it efficiently and her flat face shone with the effort and the heat. Behind her a wood-fired furnace steamed the vermicelli under a sodden cloth.

'Primitive huh?' grinned a Chinese youth, baring discoloured gums. 'No machines here but it works OK. Don't touch! Very hot.'

Her family had been here three generations, said Ah Chu's wife. 'Long time, but funny thing, we still eat our vermicelli savoury. Swahili people like it sweet.'

'Are there many of you Chinese families left now?'

'Now only six or seven.'

Rashid remembered Chinese friends from school. One had left for San Francisco, another for Hong Kong, a third for Dubai. Others were in Australia, more in London. The great whale of Zanzibar that sucked in so many people during the nineteenth century had, in 1964, spat them out again and sent them spinning across the globe.

'Will you stay here do you think?'

'I think so. I like it here. People nice, we have good business. I sell 500 kilos a day of vermicelli! We have this too.' She leant over a basket and produced what looked like an old rubber shoe. 'This sea cucumber. We have divers. We export for Chinese food to Hong Kong.'

Everybody knew Mr Mitu. He was not a prepossessing sight – a bandy-legged Sunni Muslim, an Indian-Omani in a shirt stained with fruit – yet as he clattered around the island in his decrepit taxi not only children but adults too ran to the road waving 'Mitu! Mitu!'

He was a happy man. In his youth he wanted to leave the island to travel and work abroad, but his father could not bear to see him go. And to keep his son there, he burnt his passport. So Mr Mitu, without bitterness, stayed, married, had children. Then one day his father regretted it. 'My son, I am sorry. I was wrong. You can go now.' But by then it was too late. The Communists were in power and he had no foreign currency. He shrugged. He did not mind. All he cared about was looking after his 'Mama' (we took her some medicine on the outskirts of town) and his family. But above all he wanted to finish his cottage. At Independence every man was given three acres of land to farm or build on as he chose. The government tried to tempt people in to the newly deserted palaces, but they were dangerous structures, and did not belong to them. What about the new East German flats? People did not want to live there either. So, on their three acres, they set about building their own 'cottages'. First the door was carved, then a stockade of mangrove poles were filled with coral rag, mud and cement, and then the roof was thatched or covered with tin.

'I want something to leave my children,' said Mr Mitu, simply.

He did not resent the police. Each time they stopped him in his taxi he willingly paid the bribes.

'They earn about 2,000 shillings a month. No one can live on that! If they wanted to buy only one loaf a day and nothing else they couldn't. How can they survive with families too? I earn so much more I am happy to share a little with them.' Everybody liked Mr Mitu.

We took a fishing boat to Grave Island. A swollen-bellied boy dealt with the ropes.

'He's so young!' I said.

'Trainee fisherman,' replied the captain.

We hiccuped on the outboard past arc-sailed dhows that hovered on the water like winged insects poised for flight. Behind a whitewashed wall on the beach marched rows of British graves. The captain pulled up weeds, and then lay by the boat to smoke a joint while he waited for us. There was one particular grave I hoped to find, that of a young seaman who died while in the Firm's employ, a boy barely older than our trainee fisherman, but we found nothing.

Evening turned Zanzibar cupric but weightless – like the dhows it too seemed to hover, floating free. Again I thought of Venice, and suddenly of Othello too. It was obvious! That was why he was at home in Venice; after all, the Swahili were the original Moors. He, like so many ancestors of these Zanzibaris, had been sold into slavery, and he too despite his love for Desdemona 'would not my unhoused free condition / Put into circumscription and confine / For the seas' worth.' But I was getting carried away. Apart from a few medieval mosques and villages, Zanzibar had barely existed until Seyyid Said arrived.

The red disc of the sun slid down a flat sky to be sucked into the sea. Night in the black streets threw up isolated images: men and women sprawled in front of houses on still-warm stone ledges; shuttered candle-light striping Richard's face; a labyrinth writhing away from us in all directions. I loved the anonymity of night – observing, unobserved ourselves. A woman in black crosses a single pool of light; mothers sit together cross-legged on bare stone floors; a baby screams; a man snores over his stall of grilled maize.

After being constantly together for the past few weeks it was difficult to part, but we each had our own projects. I left Richard to his photography and retreated to the National Archives. Sudden cool and professionalism: air conditioners whirred and the desks were wrapped in plastic. It could not have been more different from my freezing Devon attic. A languid Indian assistant flopped his hand towards mine, and looked me up and down with the beginnings of a sneer. I saw myself through his eyes: hot and grubby, in shorts and flip-flops. Not an impressive sight, though I felt better when I noticed that he was in his socks.

'What did you say the name was?' he drawled.

'Newman.'

'We have a photograph of a Newman.'

I could not believe my luck. He drifted next door and lifted a cloth from a glass table. Beneath was a photograph, but it was of Ahmed bin Nooman, Seyyid Said's ambassador to America. Sadly, no relation.

In their neat bindings (the British bureaucrat's passion for order!) the early British consular documents lacked the excitement the letters had held in Devon. They bore the same looping nineteenth-century script, the same dried-blood ink, but none of the sense of discovery. There were some intriguing marginalia: 'Relative to Sayyid SaOod and all his rascally conduct'; 'Relative to the plunder of a dhow under the British flag by the people of Fungani'; 'Relative to my complaint of that old scoundrel Seyyid Suleiman interfering in cases between British subjects; all false, this old Suleiman is a notorious old slave dealer.' But I found not one mention of the Newmans or even of Norsworthy. The Firm was here even before record keeping began.

But in a history of East Africa, laden with dull graphs, called

Slaves, Spices and Ivory by Professor Abdul Sharrif, I at last found mention of the Newmans; here they received their stamp of historical approval. They expanded too quickly, I read, alienated Jairam Singh, and by 1838 'wound up their East Africa trade'. What was this? 1838? But what of Captain Withycombe and Henry Angelo? What of the wreck of the *Herrick*? Their letters, filed in Devon, are dated 1840–42. Clearly the professor knew nothing about them. A historian proved wrong! I remembered my Cambridge tutorials with the great Professor Ullmann, and the many times I had tried to impress him by quoting from some obscure document only to be told that he had long ago declared that document a forgery. Now, at the risk of being proved wrong myself, I must admit that I couldn't resist a glow of triumph.

On landing in Zanzibar Robert Newman Hunt discovered (to his embarrassment) that not only had Khamis never been an ambassador of the Sultan, but had come to England 'obliged to fly his creditors', including the Sultan himself. To think that the Firm had tried to persuade the King to receive this charlatan! Particularly galling was the fact that in 1838 the *Kingfisher* brought to London another 'Ameer', but this time a genuine relative of the Sultan who was entertained not by the Newmans but by their rival, Robert Cogan, and was a tremendous success. He too was taken to Manchester and Birmingham – though at the public's expense – and was then extended the highest accolade of all: not only permission to see the Queen, but an invitation to stay at Windsor Castle (and to bring from amongst the Sultan's gifts the more *portable* items). The Newmans had backed the wrong man.

Norsworthy turned out little better. Found to be embezzling the Firm's funds, he was unceremoniously sacked and fled to Bombay. Two years later Norsworthy, back in Zanzibar again, wrote to the Firm that 'Armice Oton has made me his dupe' and had the nerve to ask for a present in return for his three years of service. This was not the last of him. In 1841 he must have been caught smuggling, for he wrote to the Firm to apologize for having sent a box of Dragon's Blood in the *Rio Packet*. 'And I am sorry to add that I have deceived Captain Withycombe with the contents of this box.' He begs the Gents to look over it, as it was to pay for his son's schooling.

Who was this Norsworthy? The headmaster of my prep school in Surrey was also called Norsworthy, and it transpired that he had an ancestor named Robert Brown Norsworthy who was christened at St Saviour's church in Dartmouth in 1802. How could anyone have envisaged that a hundred and thirty years later the rogue's descendant would be striding through a school, black academic robes flying, while Newman Hunt's descendant would be his awe-inspired pupil?

The trade did not wind up but continued under the efficient agency of Henry Angelo. His spiky handwriting reports regularly on the state of the market, the price of ivory, the wickedness of the Americans. So I was not prepared for the professor's rude assertion that Newman Hunt & Christopher failed in Zanzibar. I took this as a personal rebuke. But he was right. They were failures. And not only failures but mean too. A year later when the invaluable Henry Angelo at last receives his salary he finds it is less than the agreed amount. Surely the Firm could have treated this charming agent more handsomely? And what of the non-existent grave? Why did the Firm take two years to return the boy's meagre effects and outstanding wages to his distraught father? There in the Archives Robert Newman Hunt metamorphosed from a Byronic adventurer to a greedy, piggy little man with a protruding lower lip and a sac of fat beneath his chin that dangled like the dewlaps of a Red Devon cow; his extremities were veined with port. The Sultan was secretly revolted and far preferred Robert Cogan. No wonder he never married!

Having been so intrigued by my ancestors I was suddenly filled with disgust. I wanted nothing more to do with them.

Day after day we walked as if searching for something, and not finding it – perhaps some kind of heart. We were beginning to bicker. I was impatient and restless, wanting to move on, thinking of Madagascar, while Richard, like the buildings, turned in on himself. We paced the streets, me irritably pointing out this carved balcony and that lintel, while Richard's eyes glazed. The sea would be the only relief from the claustrophobic passages and the aimless wandering. But leaving Zanzibar town was difficult. We needed a permit to travel and could only have a permit if we had a place to stay. The only place to stay was a government bungalow; no camping was allowed.

Bus 10 was not a bus but a lorry built of wood, with hard wooden benches onto which passengers flung themselves in the now familiar scrum for seats. Veiled women hoiked up their skirts and battered to the front with baskets and rubber-limbed babies that seemed never to cry or urinate. We argued for the five hours to Makenduchi, not with each other, but with a toad-faced bureaucrat and his basket. He insisted that we, as rich tourists, should travel by taxi and not be allowed to use the already crowded buses, and in a way he was right, except that we were not rich. He had bribed the police to drag off two Swiss men (who did not have travel permits) and so made more room for himself. 'Do you operate some kind of apartheid on your buses?' we shouted. He was an official; fellow passengers were amused, but wary.

We passed from the lush centre to the scrubby south of bracken, leafless baobabs and stumpy bushes, and ended at Makunduchi. It was a village like any other with mud and coral houses and tiny wooden stalls selling bananas, but was given the status of New Town by two incongruous blocks of flats that sat here as if they had uprooted themselves from East Berlin and paused for a rest on their way somewhere else. The stained concrete was boarded up and squalid.

On the coast a square white house stood alone in a grove of *mviji* trees. These were rangy and feathery, and spiked the earth with small cones. We stayed several days in this lonely place. Ali, with red alcohol eyes, soft voice and buckled toes, cycled from the village each day to cook. 'Of those that remember life when British was here,' he used to say, 'one hundred per cent want them back.'

Each day we watched the dawn, huddled together on the beach out of the wind. The roar of the trees and of the breakers on the distant reef was the roar of the clouds welding and parting overhead, and of the great machine of the sun cranking up into the sky. Molten copper trickled round the edges of the clouds and lit up the slender Wahadimu women who strutted to the beach with baskets of coconut husks on their heads. Daily the ritual was the same: down went the heavy basket, the rolled cloth that acted as a head cushion was unravelled and pinned under a rock, then the *kanga* wrapping the cotton dress was knotted round the head, and the *kanga* beneath the stone was wrapped around the dress. In the roar of dawn they squatted to unearth buried coconut husks and slap them against rocks, making coir. Children vanished over the reef in search of whelks, and a boy cycled, singing, on cow-bitten grass between hovels that gaze, forlorn, out to sea. Men bailed double outrigger canoes that teetered on the beach with arms outstretched, unchanged after a thousand years. The Wahadimu are Zanzibar's oldest tribe.

It was an eerie place, the roar of the waves the roar of a planet being formed. The reef was alive with primitive creatures – sea slugs, weird opaque fish and snakes; it was ever-shifting blues and greens, and the incessant wind blew waves not on to the beach but across it in jerky ripples. Long-legged sea birds tried to make headway but were battered back. At low tide we walked to the far end of the beach where grassy cliffs turned into coral which jutted, dripping, over our heads like the bumpy roof of a mouth. In amongst the tonsils crabs scuttled, waving whiskers from behind slime-covered stones.

'The wind's coming more or less directly from Madagascar,' Richard said.

We passed time reading – in a junk shop we had bought a worm-bored copy of *The Chrysalids* labelled 'Zanzibar Book Club 1955', and two collections of new Tanzanian Stories, one called *Poisoned Love*, the other *Killer Drink*. We fed two starving kittens who poured with dysentery, and rats ate our soap. In the evenings we sat in the lamplight on the verandah, out of the wind.

'We must be two of the most immobile people I know,' said Richard.

At night Ali made us lock ourselves in. He was afraid of thieves and of the armed guard.

'Not give him seat if he ask. He just sleep all night,' warned Ali. But when we tiptoed out over the *mviji* nuts there was no sign of anyone, just the stars and the half moon and the lighthouse. On our last night, however, into the lamplight veered an old man with a twelve-bore shot gun. He saluted. 'My name is Alias.' It was a British Police Gun, and he pointed it at us. 'This gun shoot anything,' he growled proudly. 'Lions, elephants, people.'

Pushing it gently aside, Richard asked, 'And have you ever used it on a person?'

'*Many* times.'

We rented bikes from a friend of Ali's, and banged over potholes for all of one day.

'*Jambo, jambo!*' Shrieks of delight and amusement followed us, but we could whizz on past, waving breezily, until a tyre punctured. I left my bike in a village and joined Richard on his, him pedalling, me trailing my legs behind, past maize and paw-paw struggling to survive on the coral.

Dimbani was a perfect village. Square mud and coral houses lined a street of trodden earth, and plump women in headscarves sprawled with their babies on warm stone, or sat together stitching *koffia*. An old man let us into the mosque, pointing out the gourd with which we were to wash our feet. It was cool inside, painted dark yellow and green; the straw mats were scattered with rosaries and copies of the Koran. We wanted to see the clover-leaf *mihrab* and a twelfth-century inscription, proving that this is one of the oldest mosques in Zanzibar, a relic from the early trading days of the Shirazi Persians. The guardian lit a lamp, and held it to the inscription. A girl watched from the door. No, she couldn't come in, he said. She put her finger in her mouth.

At Kizimkazi eighteen-year-old Aboubakar took the bicycle chivalrously and strolled beside us. He was trendily dressed in a patterned shirt and shorts, and he was more muscular and had straighter, whiter teeth than most of the southern people. He seemed clever and a little nervous, but the flat back of his head gave him a brutish look. He was studying English, physics and chemistry at school. 'But there are no jobs,' he said. Down on the beach a catch was landed. All the men raced to haul up the boat, excited and laughing, and Richard joined them. The boy murmured, 'I would like to speak with you but in my English I make many mistakes. We go here now? I would like to escort you. Look, this is my teacher.'

A toothy man helping the fishermen paused to shake hands. In the bottom of the boat bundles of squid glistened, not much for a day's catch. I was introduced to Omar, whose teeth had been hurled at him from all directions, and whose skin was prematurely wrinkled. Omar was the teacher's younger brother, and in his long white *kanzu* and rotted white cap he resembled a sleepwalker who had strayed in here and woken suddenly. He did not seem to fit.

'We would like to take this opportunity to show you our village,' Omar announced.

'Yes, we would be pleased to see your village.'

We talked like characters from an Ionescu play, on the brink of getting the pages of our phrase book muddled. 'Omar, do you take American Express?' 'Yes, the weather is fine for the time of year.'

*

We were led past small shops where posters of a woman turning
a man from her door warned against AIDS, and paused for
oranges. Our new friends obligingly demonstrated the art of
peeling while the rest of the village watched from a distance and
then trouped along behind as we made our tour.

'Our café.' They pointed out a wooden shack where men sat on
logs playing board games.

'Our cave.' This was the well. Aboubakar let Omar do the
guiding while he looked about anxiously, and shifted from foot to
foot, hands behind his back. His chin was jutting and he smelled
of sweat.

'My brother's house.' The teacher invited us into his compound with its floor of beaten mud. 'This is my other brother's
house, and this is my other brother's house . . .' Omar was one
of twelve. 'And this is my house. This will be a bedroom and
this will be where we dispose of our body's waste products. I
began the construction four years ago but it still is not
complete.'

'Are you married?'

'No, because I have no house so I cannot marry.'

'Why don't you finish your house?'

'Because I have no job so I cannot buy materials because of
our economical situation. I have no job and I do not like to fish. I
would be very pleased if you could help me, because I can only
get enough money by cutting wood, just thirty shillings a
bundle.'

That was about twenty pence. I could not envisage him fishing, or even cutting wood; he looked and spoke like an intellectual, but his brother already had the village's only intellectual
job. It had been so tempting to see these villages as perfect rural
idylls – the women sewing, the men helping with the catch – but
just beneath the surface lay utter hopelessness. Families with
twelve children: how could any village support them all? Omar
was desperate, and that explained Aboubakar's nervousness: the
two of them had been through this routine before.

'We'd like to help you but I'm afraid we have very little money
on us.'

'Then I will come with you to Makunduchi.' We wanted to be
alone. 'At least we can escort you to our neighbour village.'

'No, you can't possibly come all that way with us.'

'We often come and go from that village.'

Was there no escape? At last we announced firmly, 'Thanks a lot for showing us your village, and here is all the money we have.' The rather small sum was taken grudgingly.

'So you will send me more from Zanzibar? It will take about two weeks? In two weeks I will get it?'

In fact Aboubakar followed us to Zanzibar and pestered us there.

We hitched a lift back to Zanzibar with a very different Ali. This Ali was a coarse fellow with a beard, large hands and a jovial laugh. He enjoyed life, loved his boss, loved his Land-Rover. He was a driver for a Norwegian aid project that was electrifying rural areas; work on these southern villages had for many months been diverted to the east coast, where the Aga Khan planned a hotel chain.

We passed an outdoor meeting of the Communist Party, but Ali was reluctant to discuss it.

'How many join the CCM?'

'About 60 per cent.'

'Why do people join?'

'Er, you can't be a manager or a leader without membership CCM.'

'Can anyone join?'

'You must study three months first.' He added non-committally: 'Some women join because they can get one set of free kangas.'

This was not a criticism of the women or the party, just a statement.

'I see. And are you a member?'

'Yes.'

He was much more forthcoming about marriage. This he liked to talk about. 'Many men – about 30 to 40 per cent [he also liked percentages] have two wives. Less than 1 per cent have four. Our Prophet say four is maximum. But you must be very rich and strong man for that,' he bellowed.

'And you?'

He shook his head. 'I have only one wife. I am not rich man. Nor strong enough man!'

'Children?'

'Five kids,' he said proudly.

'Five already! But you're so young.'

'I am twenty-five. You have kids?'

'No.'

He looked worried.

'Just married,' I explained quickly.

'Ah!' He rolled his eyes and grinned. 'Then they will come soon.'

'Yes,' I said, thinking: that's enough of that subject, though with Richard between us it seemed safe enough to touch on intimacies such as these. Richard was tired of talking and wanted to look at the view, but without him there I would never have had this conversation.

'Me,' Ali went on, 'I have five but I would like half a dozen.'

'Are marriages here arranged?'

'Some arranged, some not. For myself, I chose my first wife, very pretty, and I pay my deposit to her parents, but when I go to meet her I discover that she is already engaged!'

'That was bad luck. Did you lose the money?'

He nodded. He did not seem to mind. 'So then I say to my parents, "You choose for me."'

'And did they choose well?'

'Oh yes, I got this wife for just six hundred shillings.'

'Oh! Very cheap.'

'No, that was before our currency devaluation. Now that would be about three thousand shillings. The average wage per month is two to three thousand. A bicycle is thirteen thousand.'

'So at least a wife is cheaper than a bicycle.'

'Yes, but many wives can be very expensive. You may build separate houses, though if first wife is a kind lady then no need separate houses. Wives can live together and not be jealous.' (He pronounced this *jeeloose*.)

'And do the ladies ever go out to work?'

'Oh no!'

'Why not?'

'If women work, they might find a better man there. The husband would be *jeeloose*.'

I had a fleeting impression of a society that raged with barely restrained lust. He went on to explain the difference between our two cultures. In England women go shopping in the market, and the men just do their jobs. But in Zanzibar the men go to market and the women stay at home and cook and have children. They only go to market if they have no husband.

'And divorce? Is that possible?'

Divorce is easy, requiring a chief's permission. Men can re-marry at once, but women must wait at least three months.

'That seems a bit unfair.'

'No, it is good idea. Then if woman gets pregnant (*predgenant*) she can know whose kid it is.'

Throughout the day he shouted greetings to friends; everybody was making their way to a festival in Zanzibar town. Ali handed out cigarettes and welcomed them aboard. He was a popular man. At a roadside hut he chucked a shy boy under the chin and gave him fifty shillings. This was Ali's eldest child, who had been sent to live with his grandparents, to look after them and to make more space at home. Most families did this, Ali explained, but I pitied the small boy away from his friends with the old couple in the country. He did not come to the festival.

The Idd el Haji was in full swing when we reached the town at nightfall, celebrating the arrival at Mecca of Zanzibar's pilgrims. We plunged into a maze of stalls, the air thick with burning petrol lamps and kebabs; there were cones of peanuts, sugar canes squeezed of their sticky juice in mangles, rubbery samosas and castles of peanut brittle. After our days in the south it was like returning to some great metropolis. The beat thudded from a makeshift disco and stall-holders in jazzy shirts danced behind their wares, while children peered through holes in tents to watch theatrical performances, all deafeningly amplified.

Wolfgang Dourado's father, a Goan, had had a passion for Mozart. It was not hard to find Wolfgang's house: he had been Zanzibar's Attorney General and everybody knew him. A woman put her head out of an upstairs window.

'He's in London, I'm afraid. But why don't you come in?'

Although it was still early evening, Mrs Dourado was in her dressing-gown and slippers. She was rather squat, but the stiff short hair that sprouted upwards from her brow gave her a look of surprised intelligence. She asked us to sit down, but left the front door open. Perhaps it was the warm air, perhaps a pre-caution. The neighbours had seen us and she wanted to give them no cause for suspicion. Wolfgang Dourado had spent some time in prison for his vociferous anti-socialist views.

'My husband suffers so horribly from psoriasis and arthritis that I told him not to come back until he is cured.' She added: 'Our doctors here are not good.'

No schools, no doctors.

She was a third generation Goan; her Perera grandfather had, like most of the Goans, come over with the British as civil servants.

'He was very rich, had huge houses everywhere. And now we are left with only this,' she said, smiling sadly.

It did not look bad. The large room, unlike the more austere and tumble-down Swahili houses, was smothered in patterned fabrics and Catholic paraphernalia – a crucifix, a statuette of the Holy Virgin, a saintly picture of the Pope. There were books too – Kenneth Clark's *Civilization* and *Born Free*. It was a warm, lived-in room.

Two weeks had passed since I had been so disillusioned by my ancestors. I had had time to forgive them, which I had to do if this journey was to continue. Their failure, I convinced myself, was not their fault, simply their bad luck. I explained the story. 'The question is, who was Henry Angelo? I thought at first he might have been Portuguese, what with the Firm's connection with Portugal, but the Portuguese haven't been here for centuries, have they? Anyway, then I thought he might have been Goan.'

Mrs Dourado nodded. 'Almost certainly I would say yes. Though I've never heard that name myself. But it is a Goan name, yes.'

'And you see he also speaks excellent if rather flowery English.'

'Yes, that would be a Goan.'

'Do you know of any cemetery where I might find his grave?'

'There are Goan cemeteries, but you know, recently the government wanted to build on the land, so we had to dig up all the graves and take them away. Of course if you didn't have any descendants to take care of you . . . '

'You mean, there might have been a grave, but it would now be built on?'

'Possibly, yes.'

'And there are no Angelos left?'

'No. I've never heard of any.'

Richard asked, 'How many Goan families are there here now?'

'Only about twenty. To be quite honest, those that stayed only did so because they had not the means to get out. The famous families – the Perera, Alberquerque, Gomes – they've all gone.'

I wanted to ask why she and her husband had stayed, but was held back by a fear of intruding, and the open door.

'When they left Zanzibar, where did they all go? Back to Goa?'

'Some of them back to Goa, others to the USA, Australia, the UK – all over the place really.' Sucked in, spat out.

'But we've heard that people are coming back now.'

'Very slowly. Some of the Omani families. It's to do with the oil of course. Suddenly the government has seen what the Omanis can offer. Oil of course, and wealth. So some of the old houses are being repaired. Oh! You should have seen it – what – five or six years ago. It was terrible. Houses crumbling. No food in the shops. People were starving, literally. And they will have so many children! I don't know how they support them all – fourteen, fifteen.' She sounded weary. 'We've had twenty years of privation. Really hard living.' She spoke as if it was over, but even now a sense of desolation hung like a pall. Open-fronted shops that Captain Withycombe described as being 'gluted (sic) with goods' now – if they were open at all – displayed two aerogrammes clipped to string like washing, a cabinet of elderly biscuits, and unappealing bars of marbled soap over two feet long. In the market men sat over meagre displays of tomatoes; by afternoon it was deserted but for a cat crunching fish heads in the gutter.

'But,' Mrs Dourado said brightly, 'business is coming back. A few more tourists like you are coming.'

As we left she said, 'You should visit John de Silva. If anyone knows of this Henry Angelo it will be him. Also you should visit our Catholic cathedral. John de Silva lives just there. Look out for the twin towers, you can't miss it. The sung mass – it's magnificent. You'd enjoy that.'

We lurk on the balcony at the west end. A white-frocked Swahili priest emerges from the confessional and saunters, hands clasped behind his back, down the aisle beneath chandeliers and past marbled Corinthian columns and a gothic pulpit. A host of styles, imported from Marseilles. The women gather on the right, bright in blue and yellow *kangas* and shiny dresses, the men more sober on the left, grizzled heads bowed in prayer. A nun in a blue veil and functional shoes thuds past us to ring a bell. 'Get up, stand up, stand up for the fight,' sings Bob Marley from a house down the street.

The congregation rises for the green and gold Bishop and his acolytes, splashing holy water to right and left. The ladies bob, their hair channelled into squares and zig-zags, a geometric art of looped tendrils, pin-cushions, tea-cosies, interlocking mounds and zones. (Goans go to the earlier service.) The choir warms up with drums and tambourines and with a hard full-voiced twang the singing starts.

Later, there is Sunday School. Boys in shorts and girls in frills squash together into the smallest space behind a pillar in the emptiness of the cathedral, nudging each other, whispering and giggling, spying through the carved holes in the pews at us trying to be invisible at the back. A neat Goan girl in yellow lace clicks her white heels down the aisle to collect the hymn books, Miss Goody-Goody; when we tiptoe out every head cranes to watch and a broad nun smiles serenely at St Franciscus Xavierus up in his roundel.

Behind a carved doorway a flight of steps led up to a white-painted verandah. Mrs de Silva was in her forties, dressed casually in a denim skirt and white T-shirt. 'Won't y'all stay for a soft drink or a coffee or something?' We sat on cane chairs beneath trailing plants. Her husband would be home soon. 'Of course John will know of Henry Angelo. He has done so much research at the Archives. Weeks and weeks. He plans a book, but right now he is very busy trying to save the Stone Town, and be a painter.'

Richard's heart sank as she fetched a portfolio – he would have to be polite – but he lightened when she opened it. There were sheafs of ink drawings of Zanzibari doors and balconies, alive with energetic lines and swirls, and highly professional watercolours.

'He's self-taught, you know.' She was proud of his work, and we looked forward to meeting him. 'He wants to have a show in London.'

A slim teen-aged daughter with short hair and buck teeth asked from the door if she could go out.

'But you have school tomorrow.'

'I know, but not till ten or eleven.'

'School's at nine!'

'OK,' said the girl, rubbing one leg against the other, 'I promise I'll go at nine.'

Her mother turned to us. 'She's always trying to get out of it,' she said, laughing.

John de Silva was every inch the artist. A striped shirt was pulled tight over a spreading belly, face animated under wild hair.

'You know what his hair is exactly like?' Richard whispered as we left.

'No? What?'

'His drawings of the doors! All those swirls and loops. They're all drawings of his own hair!'

The curtains bulged in the breeze. Mosquitos were biting so John rushed about squirting a spray saying, 'Sorry, sorry about the smell.' But we didn't mind.

He confirmed Angelo's ancestry, though he had never come across an Angelo himself. Mrs de Silva smiled when I mentioned his elegant handwriting.

'Yes,' she said fondly, 'that would be typical Goan.' She had left Goa only when she married.

John was planning a history of Zanzibar illustrated with his own drawings.

'I've seen your name in the Archives visitor's book,' I said, and this released a flow of despair about only today seeing workers trying to restore the Marahubi baths, scraping off all the old plaster.

'I wish they'd leave it with all the mould and what not. It's better than scraping it off and whitewashing all over it. That way we'll just as quickly lose the original designs. So many layers of whitewash. They don't mind if I tell them off, they know me now. That Director of Archives, he's a good man I think, and he is beginning to learn. Only last year they were selling off one of those lovely old houses in the Stone Town, private sale, and I made him make a fuss. The new owner was planning to pull it down and rebuild, so I made him write a letter, and that's quite something when these people like their jobs – trips to the UK, Canada and what not.'

'Don't the old houses still belong to people?'

'Some belong to people and some are gazetted monuments, but even these are not safe. The other day I heard the Ministry of Agriculture – who don't even own it – sold Mtoni to a private person!'

'Sold Mtoni?'

'Yes! £1,000, plus £1,000 in bribes. This is illegal. It's a historical monument, you can't just sell them off – and if you can, I'd
like to know about it because I'll buy one.' He held out his cup
for his wife to pour him tea.

'Are there many other people like you who care about the
Stone Town?'

'None! But it's getting better. Even those new houses that are
going up – they're using all the wrong materials and are pretty
comical in style it must be said, but at least they're using carved
doors now, and the odd Arab arch around the windows, so that's
something.'

'You must feel lonely sometimes.'

'Oh, it's better now. Before I couldn't mention a word because
politics . . . ssshh . . . it was all politics. You couldn't mention a
word about the Omanis or even the British. Anything to do with
them was untouchable. Those were terrible times after 1964. For
ten years I tried to make a living from painting. I was selling a
lot, but then I gave up because I thought I was so bad.'

'How do you survive now?'

'I find more ways – photography, advertising. Dear, where are
my photographs?' His wife hurried off to find them. 'It's easy
enough to make money in a small way. Things are improving so
much since '84.'

'Most people seem to find it pretty hard still,' I said.

'Yes, it is hard. It's easier on the mainland. But it's easy for
me, let's say. And my wife earns a good living.'

She was a secretary in an FAO project encouraging rice pro-
duction. She smiled at him indulgently. He was the Artist, cre-
ative and entertaining, spoilt and egocentric, who needed
support. We admired his paintings and I mentioned David
Gentleman.

'But I know him!' John cried, delighted. 'He was here in
Zanzibar! I saw his work and he was very encouraging to me. I
hope to see him when I go to London next month and try to set
up this show. Have you seen his latest book? It's marvellous. I
wanted to buy it last time we were in London. I wonder why I
didn't? I remember! She didn't give me enough money.' His wife
seemed not to hear.

John's father had been a tailor for the Omani court. 'Those
were the days! The Arab ladies were gorgeous – silks and satins –
nothing spared.'

'But even now they still look pretty good, the women here, despite their poverty,' I said.

Mrs de Silva laughed. 'They'll pay *anything* for dresses – at least that's what I gather from the girls at the office. They won't spend anything on the house, it's all on the dresses. And then they wear their *buibui* on top.'

In Malindi district near the port we sat in a fly-ridden café while Richard ate a lump of goat with rice, and I drank Indian *chai*. An old man split his lips in a toothless grin. A rag knotted his head and trousers flapped useless round his knees, but he had a pocket and from the pocket he produced a clove, which with great dignity he gave me. I kept it for days; when we moved on I hated having to leave these useless treasures. He led us to his workplace where more half-naked Zanzibaris stitched up sacks of spices; a hill of cloves hovered like a shadow. The air was aromatic, medicinal. This sight and smell had barely changed, though in the 1830s they would have been slaves, transported in convoys, yoked together with forked sticks, from the lake regions of East Africa. Here were their descendants. A supervisor with a paunch sauntered over. Staring above our heads he muttered contemptuously: 'Please. Get out.'

A question I had been avoiding remained: were my ancestors involved in slavery? Did Newman Hunt (tall, debonair, wide-browed, fair-minded) try to convince the Sultan of the inhumanity of the trade that formed the basis of his success? Did he watch, eyes pitying, as men and women were dragged from their storage caves in the market to have their teeth examined and their limbs exposed and were made to run after sticks like dogs to show their paces? Did his booted legs stride forward, impulsively, to rescue a native woman with wild eyes from one excessive piece of cruelty? Did his hand rise in her defence? Did he beg the Sultan to ameliorate their condition? Or did he (portly, piggy-eyed) see the slave trade as essential for the economy, that they were much better off being clothed and fed by their masters than living in heathen ignorance in the jungle?

'There is a fear,' wrote Angelo in 1842, 'of the slave trade being prohibited, in which case Zanzibar will be *destroyed*.' Did Newman Hunt himself 'indulge'?

Uncle Ralph believed that Black Ivory was indeed one of the

Firm's cargoes. But he had no proof, or what there had been has disappeared. The only reference I found was a letter sent by the Firm to all their employees in the Indian Ocean.

July 29th, 1840

Gents.,
On no account whatever are you to mix yourselves up in any manner with the procuring, or engaging, or transporting of negros (sic), or any coloured people from any part of your neighbourhood to Mauritius or elsewhere, either for M. Giguel House or any other person And whether under the sanction of any British authority or not – And write to M. Giguel house to say that you have received our orders to that effect. This instruction is to stand good until rescinded by the signatures of all four of the partners of our house.

The ban is serious, but why was the letter necessary? In 1822 the Sultan had signed the Moresby treaty to suppress the slave trade with Europeans on the East African coast, but far from the liberal conscience of home, how easy it must have been to slip into local ways and to accept cruelty as a necessary part of life. How little relevance laws passed in England – 111 days away – must have had for the Zanzibar traders.

At the Pool I found a file of legal records, and a hand-written bill from Freshfields Solicitors fifteen pages long requesting Newman Hunt & Co to pay the (then) large sum of £211.10.10.

Respecting the charge of murder made against the Captain and Crew of the Ship *Caroline* belonging to the Imam of Muscat and the proceedings at the various police offices consequent thereon and the Writs of Habeas Corpus obtained by Sir George Stephen against the Captain requiring him to produce seventeen of the Crew alleged to be detained as slaves and the proceedings consequent thereon.

The Times of the winter of 1845/6 quickly dubbed it 'The Case of the *Caroline*.' and the Firm, acting on behalf of the Sultan, was at its centre. Oddly, Uncle Ralph does not mention it.

For the first time, the Sultan decided to bypass the European traders and send a cargo of his own to London in his favourite ship, the *Caroline*. Robert Newman Hunt was to act as agent and sell the cargo. But most important were the four full blood Arabian horses which the Sultan sent as a gift for Her Majesty. This was a high-profile visit.

The *Caroline* needed repairs, so Robert Newman Hunt rented a brig in the East London Dock and transferred the fifty-eight-man crew here. But in early December one of the crew jumped ship and made his way to Sir George Steven of the Anti-Slavery Society. Among the crew, the fugitive claimed, were twenty Africans held as slaves, unpaid, imprisoned on the ship, and mistreated as only slaves in the truest sense of the word could be. Legally all slaves on reaching British waters were automatically freed, but these were so hungry that they had been forced to pawn their clothes for food, and now – in mid-winter – were wrapped only in an old blanket and woollen cap. For the Firm, it could not have been more embarrassing.

Not only were the crew kept in a state of slavery, but two days sail from Ascension Island, one of those slaves had been murdered and his body thrown overboard.

It was not a happy ship. The captain and almost all the crew spoke no English, and the English sailing master and his mate spoke no Arabic, Persian, Swahili or any of the other African languages spoken by the crew. For four months they were trapped together in this micro-universe, this dark and wandering island of teak. Day after day the *Caroline* bucked over cliffs of angry water, the hull battered and the rigging lashed.

On the sixty-third day of the voyage Mahomed Bankah, an African slave belonging to (the now late) Robert Norsworthy, was coiling rope. The boatswain, a Persian, came up on deck and reproved him for negligence and threatened 'to give him the rope's end'. Mahomed Bankah answered insolently, and the boatswain punched him in the face. Mahomed Bankah, a huge African, hauled himself up and taunted him, threatening to return the blow. The boatswain fled to the captain's cabin. The captain immediately called three of his own men who grabbed Mahomed Bankah and forced him to the ground, one sitting on his neck while the other two were ordered to 'champoo' him. For ten minutes they whipped and kneaded him with their knees and elbows. When they finished, and dragged him down to his berth, he was vomiting blood. Within twenty-eight hours the man was dead. Soon after, shot was attached to his legs and he was thrown overboard.

According to Sir George Steven, this was the story of sailmaker and deserter Grant. But who was this Grant? Was he the hero Sir George portrayed in court, the only man brave enough to reveal the truth and to stand up for the mistreated Africans trapped in appalling conditions on the ship? Or was Grant a

pale-eyed liar and shirker as Freshfields and the Firm would
have us believe? Was he a whining scrounger who knew all about
his rights but nothing of courage or endurance? Was he, in fact,
the model for Conrad's Donkin, that pet of philanthropists and
self-seeking landlubbers? He was an Englishman who had
starved, who had been down to the pits of existence. In Jeddah,
for the meagre sum of $150, he had sold his religion to become a
Muslim. Circumcised, his name changed to Abraham, with the
muezzins whining and beggars plucking at his legs, he was
paraded through the streets on a white horse. Was he the worm
that turned in the belly of the ship?

Abraham Grant, on account of 'selling' his religion, was considered an unreliable witness, and the case was dismissed. The
crew did not appear to be slaves and Mahomed Bankah had
apparently deserted. However, Sir George Steven was not
satisfied and wrote to *The Times* re-stating his case. *The Times*
refused to print it as a letter, so he took out an advertisement,
whereupon Newman Hunt & Christopher, on behalf of the
Imam, sued him for Malicious Libel.

At the trial each crew member was asked (through an interpreter), 'Do you know the difference between a free man and a
slave?'

'No.'

'Are you a slave?'

'No.'

Perhaps they were afraid; perhaps they did not understand;
but although little was clear, they had, the Judge concluded,
been engaged for wages. They had pawned their clothes, but it
was to buy drink, not food; their food, supplied by the Firm, was
more than enough. The crew were sent back to their ship and
again the case was closed.

As for the murder, there was no proof either way. The
Establishment was firmly behind the Firm, and their name was
cleared. The British Government paid Freshfield's bill.

Forty years later the Firm moved offices, and found two vast
slabs of stone brought to England as ballast. They were rough-
hewn, smoothed with age, but cut into them were Hebraic
inscriptions. The British Museum was excited: they were
fourteenth-century memorial tablets to Madmiyah, daughter of
Sa'adyah, son of Abraham, and they seemed to suggest that there

was a Semitic colony in Zanzibar long before anyone had suspected. On being given them by my great-great-grandfather, the
Museum placed them opposite the doors of the main entrance.

'Perhaps they had nowhere else to put them,' observed the
present curator. They are now consigned ignominiously to the
basement and said to come from Aden.

No Newman ship would have needed such ballast – they
would have had cargo enough. But the *Caroline* had almost no
cargo and mainly ballast. The ship was then emptied for repair:
surely ballast of any interest would then have been moved to the
office. I became convinced that the *Caroline*, sailing from Muscat
past Aden to Zanzibar on the gyre of the winds, and then on to
London, brought these stones here.

'The case of the *Caroline*' is not mentioned in the Zanzibar
archives, but perhaps it was that which prompted the Imam in
1847 to appoint Robert Newman Hunt his first Consul General
in London. In his extravagant style the Imam addresses 'his
Excellency the truly dignified, the faithful and trusty friend,
Robert Newman Hunt Esq – may the Lord protect him and
render his times happy and in every way prosperous and may all
his wishes be accomplished, Amen . . . From a long time even
until now, whatever of our affairs we committed to your charge,
most truly and faithfully have you executed all.' The Imam
added as a postscript: 'Please accept these and excuse your
friends.' There was a jar of halva, a box of eight jars of preserves,
and a bottle of Otto of Roses. Not lavish, but charming.

One night I lay awake and heard a fellow traveller vomiting, and
was suddenly overwhelmed by the squalor of decay: it could drag
you down. Permits arranged with the tourist office and the
Police, we left the next day on a dhow – sailing at last – to
Bagamoyo.

The dock was a mess of boats and shouting. From it our dhow
disentangled itself and, like a great insect waving legs, was rowed
towards us with long spatula paddles.

'*Enzi ya Moja*? Nice boat,' people said. 'Not big but nice.'

We were helped aboard. Everything seemed massive, the sail
the height of the four trees that lashed together made the mast,
the blocks and tackles like shields, ropes thick as five fingers –
even the men were unusually stocky, with hairy chests and big
teeth. 'Where's the beef?' asked the captain's T-shirt. Yet we

moved with lightness, the captain barely touching the tiller as the wind rose with a round, full moon.

On board was a clown, a burly seaman with breasts and flat feet, brow creased by wind and sun, nose flat and chin hung with jowls. A grizzled St Bernard of a man. Throughout the six-hour sail he strutted about the deck while passengers slapped their thighs and wept, nudging each other and repeating his jokes. There should have been only the sounds of the wind in the sail and the churn of our wash, and the occasional order to pull on this rope and release that one, but instead the air shrieked with hilarity. We were a ship of fools on the great emptiness of sea.

Empty, but for flying fish and stray logs which bobbed past, signalling to each other on some secret mission of their own.

We peered beneath a thatched roof, and in a shaft of smoky light glimpsed blue-whites of eyes and teeth – slaves!

'Come in, join us!' they choroused. Of course not slaves but passengers. In stricter Moslem days a woman would have been shut in down here, meals delivered on a tray, but now I was free to lie with Richard on top of the thatch where we watched Zanzibar slide astern.

All the slaving dhows came this way with the British naval cutters in pursuit of the illegal traders.

Lights glimmered on the beach at Bagamoyo and in the old arched customs house, but there seemed to be no dock. We anchored several hundred yards off shore. A boat would be rowed out for us all, Richard and I told each other. The crew were jumping overboard: ah! they were going to pull us in. Then the young captain turned to us.

'Let's go,' he said gently, indicating the bows. There was no alternative, and so we climbed down into chest-high water, heaved our rucksacks on to our heads, and waded ashore.

But for the whirr of insects, the place was silent, just the customs officer and his candle alone on the beach. Though Tanganyika and Zanzibar have long been united, the rigmarole of customs checks is still observed. The captain was instructed to take us straight to the police. We walked down the empty street with a man close behind us, peering into the bushes. 'Seaman,' muttered the captain, as if that explained everything.

The police station was a decayed fortress with a tunnel (now blocked) down which illegal slaves were smuggled to the beach. We registered our arrival and the captain led us to the hotel. It was close to the police and fenced with barbed wire, on the site of the gibbet where Africans were hanged by the Germans for opposing their oppressive rule – Bagamoyo was the old German capital before they moved south to Dar es Salaam. A group of drunk Tanzanians chanted '*Mazunga mazunga*' and cackled. A boy with staring eyes unlocked a room with one single bed and a collapsed ceiling. I leant my pack against the barred window.

'Don't leave it there!'

'Why not?'

'Thieves.'

In the distance we heard drumming and chanting. As we were putting up our mosquito net a man banged on the door.

'Boss! No English. Boss, open door please.'

'Come back in the morning.'

The knocking continued for a while, and then footsteps went away.

It was when Seyyid Said turned his attentions from Muscat to his East African dominions, and the demand for ivory grew, that the slave trade took off. To transport ivory traders needed slaves.

> '*Wimbo huu uliumbwa*
> *na wapagazi was misafara*
> *ya biashara walipokaribia*
> *Bwagamoyo*'

they chanted. ('Be happy my soul, let go all worries, soon the place of your yearnings is reached, the town of palms, Bwagamoyo.')

But as demand for slaves grew with the clove and sugar cane plantations, so Bwaga-moyo – 'Throw off melancholy' – became Baga-moyo – 'Crush your heart'. The journey no longer ended here, but continued to the Zanzibar slave market until it was closed in 1873. Bagamoyo's last known ex-slave, Maria Ernestina, died in 1974.

Bagamoyo is haunted still by their misery. We were allowed to visit the Catholic mission established here for freed slaves only if accompanied by a plain-clothes policeman. With unease he fingered the revolver in his belt. Unemployed youths armed with knives have moved in from the country to infest this town, and no unguarded tourist on the beach, in the hotel, or at the mission, escapes. Walking up the mission's avenue we knew that unseen figures lurked behind the mango trees; we were not even allowed to visit a shrine amongst coconut plantations without our guard. He then escorted us, unharmed, to our room. That afternoon – as soon as we could – we caught a bus back to Dar; even Dar seemed preferable to this heartless place.

— CHAPTER FIVE —

COMORO ISLANDS

One of Robert Newman Hunt's main reasons for leaving his country was to visit the unknown kingdom of Madagascar. He sailed from Zanzibar and on his way south east he paused, as Arab traders had done for generations, at the Comoro Islands, part of Seyyid Said's dominions. After four days running before a northerly monsoon, Newman Hunt raised his spyglass and would have been astonished at what he saw.

Rising from the water is a landscape of the planets, a nest of hills with their tops scooped out, once boiling with lava but now clad in pale green fur. Looming over them, protective and angry, is the 'mother' hill, Mount Karthala, the largest active crater in the world. It disguised itself in a wreath of mist; unaware of its potential, a few stray huts dared to straggle up its flanks. Its black lava tumbled to a fringe of white coral which turned the sea a brilliant blue. Gleams of a lurid sun broke through the storm cloud and travelled over the green palm and banana leaves which glittered against the black rock to sweep the white coral and the blue sea; it was a place of vivid colours more familiar from dreams than from life.

It was not just what he saw that made Newman Hunt uneasy. He knew of the pirate canoes that annually used to set out from Madagascar, like the Norsemen who descended on Britain, to plunder the islands and any boat that lay in their path. Six months later, when the wind changed, slaves were shipped by the thousand back to Madagascar and the Mascarenes. Newman Hunt had heard tell of women who, rather than be taken as slaves, flung themselves from a volcano to the sea. It was at a village just south of Moroni on Grande Comore. He turned his spy glass slightly to the right, and shuddered. The Sultan had assured him that he had nothing to fear, that he had the Sultan's protection, but nevertheless as he moored in the small bay at

Moroni Newman Hunt must have felt dwarfed and, though he would never have admitted it, in need of a friend. Fortunately one of the Sultan's Amirs was resident here, an Omani, and he sent Newman Hunt the most delightful of letters.

May 25th, 1837

My best friend Robert Newman Hunt Esq,
How are you this morning, and I wish to know how you are every morning and every night. I beg to present you with a cow, and send one of your men to choose him out of four or five. This is not the proper thing to present to you, but it is the best I have got,
from your servant,

Seyd Aboubeker ben Shea Mossie Alhamidie

Newman Hunt accepted with pleasure.

Again we were thwarted in our efforts to travel by sea. During our brief return to Dar we searched for a ship to the Comoros, but the harbour master merely laughed. Any boat that might have traded this route was in dry dock. So we were forced to fly and with disorientating abruptness left what was once the British sphere of influence (with the legacy of drab clothes and fish and chips) for what was to become French. Suddenly baguettes, delicious coffee, a well-dressed bourgoisie, and French language. As early as 1847 Seyyid Said had complained to the Foreign Office of a growing French presence in the Comoros, so the British opened a consulate. But to no avail: in 1885 the four islands were absorbed into the French Protectorate of Madagascar. Three of them – Grande Comore, Anjouan and Moheli – achieved independence in 1975, but the fourth island, Mayotte, has chosen to remain a French colony.

The Frenchness was superficial. The evening we arrived a ceremony took place on the pretty, almost Mediterranean, sea-front beside the Friday Mosque. Sharp-featured men betrayed their ancestry – Bantu, Arab, Creole and, for the first time (we noticed with excitement) the high cheek-bones of the Malagasy. The men were swathed in silk robes and turbans: peacock blues, rich browns, pinks and greens, glittering with jewels. They sat in rows holding canes while prayers were chanted. Coffee and cans of Fanta and sticky orange cakes flavoured with rose-water were handed round on silver trays, and the women watched from above, hidden under patterned shawls with only slits for eyes. The local headmaster had reached a stage in life when he thought it would befit him to take a second younger and prettier wife. This, at vast expense, was the announcement of his *grand mariage*.

A warren of passages – narrower even than Zanzibar's – twisted away from the Friday Mosque, and we searched here for a place to stay. But as we searched, so clouds gathered and offloaded. Within seconds the streets became streams, swathes of water cascaded from gutters, and figures shrouded in plastic ran past candle-lit rooms and crouched in doorways behind water-falls. We sheltered in a tiny shop.

'You've found your man,' said the proprietor. We splashed after him over rutted lava, past the foundations of a new mosque that had been abandoned and already turned to ruins, to meet 'La maman de Dr Said Bakar'. She appeared to have no other name. A large pale Omani-Comorian wrapped in a green and red scarf from which hung green and gold earrings, she had a throaty voice and a world-weary air, shrewd kohl-rimmed eyes that had seen more than we could ever guess; she could have been a fairground fortune-teller, tawdry and mysterious.

The apartment was furnished with a blue plastic three-piece suite and its blue-washed walls were stained with damp. After some hard bargaining we agreed it was perfect. We were given soft drinks to celebrate, and three fat ladies sat in La Maman's front room to watch. They bulged in satin, faces heavy and impassive beneath make-up, feet wedged into narrow high heels, while we streamed on to the floor.

Early, the muezzin groaned into life, joined by another and then another as if the whole town was mourning in deep, disem-bodied voices. Gradually they died away, leaving one voice which came in waves, drowned from time to time by the rain pounding the tin roof. New sounds of getting up – the querulous voice of La Maman (perhaps she's older than she looks), cocks crowing, and a radio playing music lighter than African and more delicate: Malagasy.

Shouts from a café down below. I brought up cups of tea sweetened with condensed milk for Richard, who was wrapped in shawls with a cold.

'Why didn't you tell me?' demanded La Maman.

Her doctor son was home from Paris to prepare for the wedding of his daughter and, at the same time, his own *grand mariage*; he could have helped. (She was sure it was malaria.)

Toiliha Abdallah Charif had rented a windowless room opposite ours. He was a civil servant in the Ministry of Finance, recently transferred here from Anjouan where he had left his wife and most of his children. He had only half a moustache, and an eye blinded by diabetes which gave him a disconcerting lop-sided look, but he was a friendly neighbour. He sang the praises of the house – the view of the sea, the central location, the kindness of Maman. He had set up a camping stove on a box as his kitchen. 'If there's anything – *anything* – you need, please ask.'

'Thanks a lot.'

Toiliha had been educated in Madagascar. Only now was this country even mentioned. The Comoros were stepping stones not just physically but culturally; every perspective had shifted. I found this re-orientation one of the most exciting things about moving on.

One evening his two eldest sons arrived. Toiliha sprawled on the bed in his *kanga*, his sons around him. Stylish in French clothes, they invited us in with charming *politesse*. The eldest (Abdallah Charif Toiliha, his father's names re-arranged) had just returned from a year studying medicine in Algiers; before that he had been in France, but to his disgust the scholarship there had ended. You can't imagine how dreadful Algiers is after Paris, he said, yet he returned home as a glamorous emissary from the outside world, bags filled with treasures – new white trainers, T-shirts, French records. They were to celebrate at a disco tomorrow – would we join them? Toiliha urged us to come. He would reserve a big table and promised great music. But in the end Richard was too weak, and Toiliha himself lost his enthusiasm. He seemed deflated. It was OK for the young people he said, but he felt a bit out of things.

This island was full of mysteries. How come, in one of the world's poorest countries, there were discos full of expensively-dressed Comorians? How come in a country that produced almost nothing the roads were newly tarred and so many people driving Mercedes? How come the shelves were empty in the tiny shops but for a few tins of condensed milk and bars of soap, cigarettes sold singly, and yet their owners sat tuned to the World Service on their glistening stacks of Sony hi-fi equipment? How come when most people lived in tin shacks tomatoes cost the same as in Europe, and the boat between the islands the same (almost) as a cross-channel ferry?

The answer was foreign aid, corruption, family connections with the Middle East, and South Africa. Jumbo jets of South Africans were landing weekly, and they had just opened a vast hotel called the Galawa Sun. One day we tiptoed down its drive into a gleaming white campus, a world apart. After only a month, already the lavishness of the developed world seemed both grotesque and magical. The sprinklers on the lawns, the shops of sun tan lotions, the bar in the centre of the pool: we gazed open-mouthed and surreptitious, waiting to be found out. I noticed that my trousers were filthy. I would have liked a swim, but had nothing suitable; I was not even wearing any underwear. We were outsiders, yet deep down was the sickening knowledge that simply through having white skins we could get away with it.

We had a drink. It was early afternoon, hushed and sunsoaked. Moustached men with beer guts lazily smeared sun cream into their latex-clad women, from whose backsides thighs crinkled like warm butter. They were blonde and tough and bored. A grey-skinned honeymoon couple sucked on straws and stared at nothing. They waited for the next meal. I looked for signs of revulsion in the barmen, but saw none; they were the only people enjoying themselves.

As we left hilarity set in, and clutching our bellies we reeled back up the drive.

Each day Toiliha sat for hours on our plastic armchairs, pulling his feet up with him and wrapping his arms around his knees.

'It's all politics,' he whispered. 'Everything here – politics. The South Africans – President Abdallah just wants to make friends with everybody. Anyone who will give him money. And the French – they control everything.' He looked around him, alert for eavesdroppers, but the door was closed.

'Still? But you're been independent for what? Nearly fifteen years.'

'I know, but the French cling on. And you know this neocolonialism is worse than straightforward colonialism.'

'In what way?'

'We don't know where we are. We don't really know what's going on. And we could be less dependent, but they don't let us go. We could produce our own salt, but we don't, because the French want to sell their salt. Same with soap, tomatoes – you know we even import tomatoes? The people here with money are politicians and people in commerce – you know, "import-export".' He made the quotation marks with his fingers.

'Isn't it better now than it was, under Ali Soilih?'

Soon after declaring independence, President Abdallah was overthrown by an agronomist named Ali Soilih. The 'revolution' began. Women would no longer wear veils, the *grand mariage* was abolished, and the Moissy, a type of Red Guard, would attack the conservative elders. Mosques were closed except at specific prayer times, and all links with France were cut. But within just twenty-eight months Ali Soilih had gone mad, and ruined the economy. When a fifty-man force of French mercenaries landed with ex-President Abdallah, they met with little resistance, and under mysterious circumstances – supposedly while trying to escape – Ali Soilih was killed. All this was a foretaste of what was to come.

'In Ali Soilih's time it was hard,' admitted Toiliha, hooking his knees over each arm of the chair and rubbing his groin, 'but at least he kicked out the French and tried to establish a Comorian socialism. Now we're back to French capitalism.'

Slowly we pieced facts together. The Mercedes were driven by the *Garde Presidentiel*, most of whom were these same mercenaries who now unofficially ran the country. Their leader was 'Colonel' Bob Denard, aka Gilbert Bourgeaud. This dog of war was born in 1927 near Bordeaux, and was a veteran of Indo-China and Algeria, but he made his name as a mercenary linked with French intelligence in Africa in the 1960s and 1970s, in the Congo, Gabon and Benin (the armpit of Africa) with brief excursions to Yemen and Iran. However, it was here in the Comoros that he had founded his tropical kingdom. He and his men – mainly French army veterans – were the power behind Abdallah, financed originally by France and now by South Africa. The South Africans had some strategic interest in the island and smuggled arms from here to Mozambique.

We spent days huddled from the rain in our 'apartment', Richard still feverish, until boredom forced us out. We hitch-hiked and walked around the thirty mile-long island. It was a sinister place. Where sand had been used to build houses and mosques, beaches had vanished and the black lava beneath was now exposed. It rattled underfoot, a few bits of white coral gleaming like bones.

'That is a bone,' Richard announced.

'It's just goat,' said a young Comorian.

'No, it's a human jaw.' Richard was right. Most of the teeth were still attached.

In front of the mosques on the black seafront the faithful prayed, and shitted. Men, women and children had separate areas in which to perform these two important functions.

'We go back now?' urged the boy.

'No, we go on.'

'Won't you get lost? Aren't you afraid?'

'What of?'

He shrugged. Just afraid, that's all.

Itsandra village squeezed inside its old fortifications beside a grey sea. The houses – huts – were mean, of woven palm leaves or tin, and villagers scuttled in from the rain along the narrow paths without a glance at us. We sheltered in a tiny café. There was nothing there but one table, two brioches and three hunks of goat fat. A youngish man named Issa Ramadan, dapper in a brown mac, was told of our arrival and came running from his house; the restaurant had just been built by his brother, he explained. The brother nodded in agreement, but spoke no French. Corrugated iron sheets had been nailed to a timber frame.

'Phew! *Ça chauf*,' said Issa. I could imagine. The technique was to cover the iron in palm thatch, and that helped a little. The brother's wife lurked in *purdah* behind a partition; occasionally they called to her to check prices and facts and she shouted back through the hardboard.

'Come and see my house,' invited Issa.

He was right to be proud of it – the smartest house in the village, built of coral with a new carved door. This opened onto one long room floored with brown lino squares; a deep sofa and armchairs occupied one end while at the other a cabinet displayed family treasures: plastic flowers stuck in sand, silver cups won at 'basket', a framed photograph of his wife's father. On the walls were a carpet with a picture of Mecca, a souvenir map of Madagascar made of spices, and a clock called 'Westminster Chimes'. Issa displayed it all with dismissive pride, much in the way that he displayed his wife when she emerged shyly from a back room. She was very young, with her hair parted down the centre and rolled into coils over her ears. She wore a flowery nightdress.

'She's six months pregnant,' he said bluntly.

'Congratulations.'

She shrugged, and flopped down beside us on the sofa.

'She doesn't speak French.'

Issa spilled a stack of photographs onto the table.

'We were married last December, at my *grand mariage*.'

'So you already have a wife?'

'Oh yes, but she lives in another house.' Unique amongst Islamic countries, here women own the property, so he had to leave his first wife's home in order to move in with the second.

'I've already got five children,' he added. 'I married her long ago, fell in love, but she wasn't from my native village. A man must marry a girl from his native village, so now that I have more money I have taken this wife.' He was an odd-job man at one of the few hotels in Moroni, so was relatively well-off. He spoke about his wife as if she was not there; she slumped, staring at the photographs, and soon I found myself talking about her too.

'Aren't there problems between the two wives?'

He laughed, and nodded. He was king in his tiny castle. 'I have to be careful. I spend three nights with one, and then three nights with the other. Everyone wants a *grand mariage* once in his life.' So last December he had chosen this eighteen-year-old girl. 'Look! See all the presents.'

Photos showed a table covered in gifts – 200 Benson and Hedges, folds of silk, a gold-plated pen. Over four days all the men of the village were entertained to one hundred goats, chickens, Fanta and Coke.

'It cost me over two million Comorian francs!' Four thousand pounds. He was proud of this. There were scenes of people – including his sons – dancing and feasting, cans of drinks on the tables, but not one of the pictures showed his new wife.

'Oh no, she didn't take part in all this,' he said, disapprovingly. He produced the silk garments he had worn, two exquisitely embroidered *kanzu* and a green shawl.

'And your wife? What did she wear?'

'Her? Just a normal *buibui*.'

She was the result, and not the cause, of the celebrations.

'You must earn a lot of money to be able to afford all this,' I commented.

'Not bad, but I'd earn a lot more if I went to Paris like her brother. So many people go and work in France now. But it's the quality of life, isn't it, not just how much money you have. I'd be living in a room half this size, all alone.'

'Yes, and you'd miss your wife I suppose.'

'No, it's not that. She has her mother to look after her. But me, what if I fell in love with another woman? I'd have to marry her! You can't love a woman without marriage, that's what the Koran says, and I couldn't afford another. You can't go chasing after women. No, I wouldn't want that.'

I thought, poor you, he doesn't care about you at all. She looked bored, but contented enough.

A black and white photograph dropped from amongst the pictures of the *mariage* and Issa pushed it aside, laughing a bit.

'May I see?'

He held it coyly to him, and then laid it on the table. It was a group of very pretty women in military uniform.

'The *Jeunesse Revolutionaire*, the Moissy. In 1978. Of course we don't have them now.' He seemed embarrassed. Ali Soilih was said to have chosen his Red Guards only from the prettiest girls, and to have 'entertained' them in the President's palace. Issa produced a more recent colour photograph of one of the girls holding a baby instead of a rifle. He clearly approved of the change.

'Was life very different under Ali Soilih?' Richard asked.

'Oh yes, very different. We had a society like China!' He was amazed that it could ever have happened. 'They made it difficult to go to the mosque because they said that the prayers interfered with our work. That was hard in a country one hundred per cent Muslim, very hard.' He laughed again. It was all over.

'What about the women's clothes?' I asked.

His expression turned bitter. 'Then women wore no *buibui*, and *short* dresses.' He jabbed at his knees and curled his lip in disgust. 'Even now there are some women –' he looked pointedly at my legs and hesitated, as if noticing for the first time that I was a woman, and then deciding that I did not count. 'There are some women who've been to France and come back in *trousers*. Those big wide trousers, some French fashion. It's not Comorian!'

*

Three hundred years before Robert Newman Hunt arrived, seven Shirazi brothers, said to be descended from the Prophet, set sail from Persia in seven ships. They let the monsoon take them and their religion where it would and it sent them down to the Comoros and northern Madagascar. They shared the islands out amongst themselves. A friend of Rashid, the Zanzibari sailor, was decended from one of them on his mother's side, and we had gone to Itsandra to meet him. He was out, but that evening a man strode into a café and said, 'Hello, Monsieur Richard! Hello, Hélène!' We shook hands, and looked blankly at each other, and then at him.

'Ahmed Alawy,' he announced, and sat down.

He was small with grey curls in his beard and discoloured teeth, and yet later I always pictured Ahmed as a statuesque man.

Conversation was difficult. We sat mostly in silence, and then Ahmed would suddenly giggle. He burst with something that amused him greatly – or was he embarrassed?

'Tell me, er, Richard. Did you ever serve in the Army?'

'No.'

'Hmm.' Another spurt of irrepressible laughter.

I struggled with small talk about the rain and Richard's cold while Richard said nothing. Then at last it came out.

'What do you think of the Ayatollah Khomeini?'

We were both taken by surprise. It was not that we had been consciously avoiding the subject, but until now had met no one willing – or interested – to discuss Islam with us. Islam was not part of the Firm's story; the only reference I had found was an Arabic letter written by Khamis bin Othman which was carried as protection against pirates by all the captains and announced that these were friends (not foe) from an English merchant house and that 'on board is the book of the Arabs'. These days Muslims along the Swahili coast attended mosques but fundamentalists were rare, and only in Zanzibar had we seen one piece of graffiti: 'Allah punish him (Rushdie) and any enemy of Islam!'

Richard and I glanced at each other, and I answered flippantly, 'Crazy man.'

'No! Don't say that. We respected him very much.'

I quickly added, 'Of course, he was a great leader, with an impressive personality.'

Ahmed seemed mollified. 'Yes, so much respect. No one can replace him, ever. His loss is a great tragedy. He was the only one following the true path. Here in the Comoros bah! It's almost anarchy.' And then suddenly he smiled, and bought us all coffee. Grande Comore was the first place where we had seen women fully veiled, but the veils were joyful colours. Men like Issa Ramadan considered themselves devout Muslims, and links with the Arab world were strong – new mosques were being built by the Middle East – but they were cultural not political links. However, when the Arabs fled from Zanzibar some, including Ahmed, came here and reinforced those links.

'I was brought up in Zanzibar,' he explained, 'but my father is Yemeni. Yemen is my homeland. I don't have a nationality,' he added. 'My nationality is Islam.'

He had visited Mecca, met the Ayatollah in Paris, and he despised his fellow citizens in the Comoros who had long since strayed from the true path.

Although he had no job, Ahmed's ancestry gave him stature, and people deferred to him as we squeezed together down the narrow streets, his white *kanzu* flapping about his ankles, to visit his family mosque. His ancestor, a sheik, was buried here. A lacquered coffin adorned with Koranic verses was enclosed in a dark room striped green by the shutters.

'Is she all right?' Ahmed asked Richard as we removed our shoes. 'Hélène. You know.'

'All right?' Richard looked blankly from him to me.

'You know, at this time. The woman. *All right.*'

'Yes,' I snapped. 'I'm *all right.*'

I was allowed in through a separate door, carved with appropriate Koranic verses, at the back. Ahmed shrugged. 'It's our custom.' As we left he said, 'Normally I don't like taking people here because everybody knows me, and they watch, and wonder what's going on. But you're different.' Despite disagreeing with us about everything, he had taken a liking to us, or at least to Richard. 'Monsieur Richard! You are an Arab!' he would announce. 'You have an Arab nose.' He decided that Richard was from a 'good' family.

'Monsieur Richard! I can tell by your bearing, your face.' Richard shook his head. 'Yes, you can tell someone's ancestry even if they are wearing bad clothes.'

'Thanks a lot!'

Ahmed added seriously: 'I don't talk to just anyone, you know, even Europeans.'

How much our lives are shaped by the dead.

Often when we left our room in the morning we found Ahmed waiting for us. One day he invited us to dinner. His family lived in a compound. The largest house belonged to his father, and Ahmed and his brother lived more modestly to one side.

'So you see, Monsieur Richard, I like the family traditions.'

A verandah opened onto a brightly lit room, adorned in the centre with a new and very large computer. A cousin lounged in front of it, trying it out. He looked up at us.

'Hi. It's great stuff this. It can play music, draw in colour, you name it. It cost a fortune.'

Ahmed had no job: it was confusing.

Issa Ramadan lived but a few hundred yards away, yet suddenly that little tyrant with his status symbols and *grand mariage* was diminished. He reverted to being just an odd-job man. Ahmed had of course never spoken to him. Their houses were much the same, however, though Ahmed's was less comfortable. A cabinet at one end housed leather-bound volumes, photographs of Mecca and of the entrance to the bedroom of Mohammed's daughter. There were also unlikely plastic knick-knacks. 'They're left over from my pre-Fundamentalist days,' Ahmed explained quickly. The pure faith had come during his pilgrimage to Mecca in 1973, but with the recent spread of Islam had intensified over the last three years.

We sat outside in the quiet and dark. The cousin, Ali, wore tight white trousers and a white shirt that exposed his abundant chest hair. He had lived in Paris for ten years, first studying electronics, and then living with a French woman. When the relationship ended he came back. His parents were getting on, he said, and there was no one else to care for them.

'Don't you have brothers and sisters?'

'Yes, of course. Eleven. But they are in UAE, Dubai, Tunisia, Karachi, Paris and London.' He ticked them off on his fingers. Itinerant Arabs with ancient family connections stretching all over the world, like a web. On his return to Moroni Ali married, but that lasted a year.

'I'm completely and utterly bored,' he confessed. 'After ten years I'm used to the life in Paris, not this. I can promise you, here there is nothing to do. Nothing. Only drink and women, and now I've given up drink.'

Surprisingly, Ahmed seemed to tolerate his cousin – presumably family loyalties overrode religious fervour – but he was proud when he introduced his younger brother. 'He is very very pure,' Ahmed said, without irony. Large black eyes gazed from the boy's narrow face, skin pale and spotless, cream *kanzu* freshly pressed. There was something ethereal about him. 'Dinner's ready,' Ahmed announced suddenly and led us inside. 'In Europe it's ladies first, but here it's the other way round.' His wife did not appear, and nor was she mentioned; I almost felt I should apologize for being of the wrong sex, and wondered if the pure brother would be contaminated by my presence at the table. And yet absurdly – perhaps because of the general awkwardness – we found ourselves discussing AIDS and birth control. One potentially embarrassing subject led relentlessly to another. 'Le planning family!' Ahmed uttered with contempt. It, like everything he loathed, was a Jewish conspiracy. His leather-bound Koran fell open at the most anti-semitic verses, for this was what Ahmed liked most to read. In a way I hated him, but as a fanatic he was mad and childish, and hard to take seriously. And he would suddenly do something unexpected like anoint our hands with sandalwood oil, or bow humbly and offer us bowls of strawberry jelly.

Unable to understand Ahmed's garbled French, which was even worse than our own, Richard barely spoke. Then suddenly the pure brother gazed at him and said slowly but fervently, in English, 'I want . . . to go . . .*there*.'

Richard glanced behind him. 'Where?'

He wanted to go to London, to study amongst the Muslims.

'Please stay with us when you come,' Richard said, and the boy smiled gently, dreamily.

'You know Ahmed's uncle is one of the leaders of the opposition? He's been in gaol five years,' Ali said, lowering his voice.

'I didn't know.'

'As you see, this is a free country. You can talk about anything, even the government, as long as it's in agreement with the government.'

'Why do people put up with it – the mercenaries running the country?'

'Listen, people here don't want to fight. They have patience, so much patience. Not like you Europeans. They watch, and they wait.' Like Mount Karthala, I thought, bubbling up. Twelve years ago Karthala smothered a village. 'I give this present situation five years. Then it'll all be over.' Ahmed said. Then abruptly he called down the table, 'Monsieur Richard! What about Richard the Lion Heart? And Cliff Richard?'

'He's changed since we were young,' Richard laughed. 'Become a Christian.'

'Oh yes, I know. A bit like Cat Stevens.'

As we left I asked if Ahmed intended to accompany his brother to England.

'No, I don't think you'll see me there. Certainly not for ten years. For the moment I just want to go to the pure countries. I want to go while some of the sages are still alive, even though the Great One has gone.'

Less than four months after we left the coup took place, long before Ahmed had predicted and in quite a different way. President Abdallah was killed. Press reports were confused, but it was generally assumed that Abdallah had been murdered under Denard's orders, supposedly by a rocket fired into his bedroom as he slept. Journalists were threatened and expelled, protesting students clubbed, the interim president held as a virtual hostage, but three weeks later, under pressure from France and South Africa, Bob Denard and his gun-toting, beer-swilling mercenaries were put on flights to Johannesburg where they disappeared. It was over. But the French were back.

CHAPTER SIX

MADAGASCAR – ANTANANARIVO

Neither we nor Robert Newman Hunt were the first to use the Comoros as stepping stones.

Madagascar split from the mainland carrying lemurs and the hedgehog-like tenrec, both remote ancestors of man; and Marco Polo's mythical rukh, with its wing span of thirty paces and the strength to lift an elephant in its claws and drop it to the ground, where it would feast on the bloody pulp. The rukh was inspired by the aepyornis, but has long been extinct; fragments of its eggs – equivalent in size to a hundred and fifty hen's eggs – are still found. Having never been to Madagascar, Marco Polo did make two mistakes, however: the aepyornis cannot fly, and there are no elephants on Madagascar. He was confusing it with Mogadishu on the Somalia coast (under which misunderstanding Madagascar got its name.) No, the island-continent wandered so early that no elephants or other large mammals had yet had time to evolve. But over the next millennia crocodiles and other swimmers did struggle across the 250 miles of the Mozambique channel to Madagascar, and they went via the Comoros.

Not until well after the spread of Christianity did man follow in their wake. One of the first land masses to break away was among the last to be inhabited. But when they did come it was as part of one of the world's great migrations, for the people of Madagascar – only 250 miles from Mozambique – are not purely African. Their faces, language, and customs hint at Indonesia, though the way of life they transported developed, like the fauna and flora, along lines of its own. Anthropologists call the Malagasy 'Malayo-Polynesian'. But how they reached Madagascar remains a mystery. Did they sail across the four thousand miles of Indian Ocean in fragile outrigger canoes? Did westward winds and currents propel them, by chance, to Madagascar? Or did they make their way slowly up the Malabar coast and, like the Arabs and Indians, get swept round the gyre of the western Indian Ocean, via the Comoros, to Madagascar? No one knows for sure.

We were desperate – frantic – to follow them: one week trapped in the rain in Grande Comore was enough, especially when Madagascar was now so close. I like the security of an island, but I like being on its edge, able to escape before it becomes a trap. Yet again there were no boats, because of the weather and dwindling trade, and being the summer holidays Malagasy students were returning home from European universities, via the Comoros, so flights to Madagascar were booked for weeks ahead. Shameless, I would have pulled any string to leave. We told the official at Air Madagascar of my sister's important work for the Malagasy government, how urgent it was that we joined her, but in the end it was four hours of queuing for a stand-by that got us out. La Maman de Dr Said Bakar, Toiliha and Ahmed saw us off.

It was the frilled stain of Madagascar's lifeblood that we saw first, draining off the hills and into the sea at Mahajanga. Gashed land puckered round red arteries which were sluggish with topsoil. This is the way to arrive, I thought, not by boat but from above, able like the giant rukh to see the whole – tragic and marvellous – before its parts.

Deforestation, precipitation, sediment, delta, erosion: the language of geography and geomorphology was transformed suddenly from abstract to reality. Lives shaped by landscape. Months later as we waded knee deep through this reality I had to remind myself of that vision from the air, and reassure myself that the mud was part of a greater pattern, and that it did, somewhere, come to an end. That is the thing about islands.

Black patches were the few remaining trees.

Villages rose towards us, isolated and encircled, though what by it was hard to see. They looked like the mushroom rings that spring up in English fields overnight – but around a whole village?

And then, up on its plateau at 4,500 feet above sea level, the steep house-encrusted hills of Antananarivo itself. Everything was red, red bricks, steep red tiles, red-flowered cacti covered in red dust, the earth as red as the red earth of Devon. And all glowed in the red light of evening. Never have I seen such a light, the colours saturated, pulsating, and not just this evening but every evening.

Laura was waving beyond the barrier, flamboyant in pink silk, long hair flying. Here as a 'Foreign Expert', she had met the press and was staying with the British Ambassador, and now she coolly drove us into town in the Ambassador's Peugeot. But she wasn't really cool; she was in a state of excitement, and frustration that she had been unable to talk about it. Two weeks before leaving England she had fallen in love with a journalist named Johnny and now they had decided (over the telephone) to marry as soon as she returned. Her telephone bill was more than a return ticket.

This dawn chorus was not mosques or birds or radios but whistling. Below our window, in the Avenue de l'Independence, stalls were being clanked into life, white umbrellas raised, and everyone had a different tune on their lips. We wandered excitedly amongst them, stepping over boxes, ducking wooden umbrella spokes and getting in the way.

'*Chocolat au lay-ee*,' called someone with a bucket.

Spontaneously a man broke into song, stamping his feet to the rhythm and clicking his fingers; no one took much notice, they'd seen it so often before. Smiling over mounds of grated carrot and baskets of rice were not only African faces but slant-eyed faces the colour of Caramac. These plateau people with their high hats and cheek-bones, their long plaits and striped *lambas*, could have come from Peru or Tibet. In fact the Merina – one of Madagascar's eighteen tribes – are the most Indonesian of all, and the most powerful.

'*Venez voir Madame! Qu'est-ce que vous voulez? Combien vous donnez? Monsieur? Madaaame?*'

The market sprawled from the grandiose railway station along the tree-lined heart of the city and up the hills on each side, lanes of cotton briefs and of toys made from condensed milk tins stamped with 'Gift of the Italian Government'. Empty plastic bottles of Eau Vive, off-cuts of electrical wire, petrol lamps made from upturned lightbulbs: nothing wasted. Was this where the Newmans sold their blunderbusses and whitewash brushes and cheap tin trays?

Layers of hats kept out the chill of an early August morning, and women lay on straw under stalls with babies and chickens, while others gathered round sweet-smelling vats of steaming manioc. We posed together for a photographer with an ancient plate camera; he thrust his arm under a cloth and up inside the camera, and with the glazed eyes of a gynaecologist fiddled with the developing fluid. We chose our frame, and ten minutes later our images gazed (blotchy and pale) from a TV set. A busker declaimed and people gathered; we peered over their shoulders and saw he was reading braille. A member of the crowd picked a page at random from a book, he found the same page in the large braille book, and the crowd checked to see he got it right. The book was the Bible.

Richard spent days photographing faces, and bargaining for crystal balls. One section of the market was devoted to quartz crystals, and Richard held them up to the light and was entranced by the ghostly constellations of impurities.

I was more intrigued by an old woman who stank of rum and sold piles of folded cloth. She beckoned me over. I pulled out a length of russet cotton. Literally *lambamena* means red *lamba*, but it is also the word for shroud. This, I suspected, was a modern version of the lead-embroidered cloth in the attic in Devon. 'Is it for wrapping corpses?' I asked her. She looked puzzled. 'Is it a *lambamena*?' A small crowd gathered.

'Yes, yes, *lambamena*,' she agreed, eager for a sale. 'We use it to cover the dead but you *vazaha* (you foreigners) can use it to cover your bed.'

'No,' said a woman beside me. 'It's a *lambamena*! It's not for beds!'

The old woman showered her with invective-filled spittle. Now the *vazaha* would never buy it. She turned back to me. 'Even we Malagasy use these for our beds and tables. It doesn't matter.'

The other woman shouted back. I left them to it. The great art of Malagasy weaving reached its height during the nineteenth century and this cotton *lambamena* was crude in comparison. These days few can afford to wrap their ancestors in silk, and some families even resort to nylon. What struck me most, however, was coming across the accoutrements of death in amongst the ordinary products of daily life.

The Zoma was bustling now, but nothing to what it would be on a Friday, which is what Zoma means. Then it was almost impossible to walk. After Zanzibar and Moroni this city was a cornucopia, and we bought kilos of fruit and patisseries. Yet there was restraint and delicacy in the displays, carrots marshalled like little heaps of ammunition, fish on sheets of blue plastic arranged into patterns of threes, tiny pyramids of limes. The *ombiasy* – witchdoctors – sold bundles of medicinal leaves tied with cotton as tightly as they tied their forest secrets to their hearts. I came to see this delicateness as typical of the Malagasy, delicateness and a sort of innocence.

There was cruelty too – the live chickens swung from their feet like bunches of parsnips, and the child beggars who curled up each night in doorways, ragged five-year-olds chanting tonelessly: '*Donnez-moi de l'argent, donnez moi cent francs,*' gazing blankly into the distance, but always there at your knees.

Tiny snot-nosed girls croon '*Vazaaaaha,* whiteeeeey,' and swing about with babies strapped to their backs like misshapen humps; even the babies have learnt to hold out their palms. And mother hovers near by.

'*Madaaame, le petit n'a pas mangé.*'

The undertow of poverty was strong. Lunch at a pavement cafe was punctuated by a small boy who hid behind a pillar and whispered, 'Psst *Madame! C'est bon? C'est bon Madame? Donnez-moi de la monnaie.*' It was hard to know how to respond.

Local residents urged us not to, that it assuaged our guilt and gratified our vanity, but encouraged begging. The women borrowed the babies to tug at our hearts and would never work, however much they were paid. I changed my mind from day to day.

Poor boys trundled miniature lorries and cars made from wood and recycled tin, or pulled a sardine can on a piece of string. Others bowled hoops, like the children who played around the harbour in 1837 when Robert Newman Hunt set off.

Antananarivo had a French sophistication too, bourgeois students home on holiday from Paris in mini skirts and fluffy jumpers giggling over steak *au poivre*, sunglasses on heads. They made us feel lumpen and dirty. They were Madagascar's *nouveaux riches*, and they lived in Ivandry, where Laura was staying with the Ambassador. Here villas were going up with high fences and garaging for three cars. It was the new smart place to live. Their parents mostly worked in 'import-export'. An economy '*A deux vitesses*', people murmured.

In all we spent six weeks in Antananarivo, or 'Tana' as it is known, climbing breathlessly from layer to layer between tall brick houses – yes, *brick* – with carved wooden balconies that clamber on each other's shoulders up the city's vertiginous hills. We took chances on flights of steps that turned out to be short cuts not to the next level but into someone's front garden, full of surprised faces and bougainvillaea. Steep views of fantasy turrets and gables, wrought iron, high eaves and scallop tiles, Renault 4s rattling over cobbles, genteel lacy curtains: we kept thinking of other places, not of Africa but of Torquay or Cork, or San Francisco or Kathmandu – each of them, and none of them.

'I love Tana,' said Richard one day, 'but I hate the smell.'

It was the dry season and open sewers were the one drawback.

We tripped on broken paving between bamboo hedges down ravines filled with orange flowering buddleia, indigenous to Madagascar and covered in butterflies. Poinsettia – here called 'Madagascar' – grew high as houses, and Richard recognized pendulous daturas lilies growing wild. How this would have entranced Uncle Ralph.

In Tzimbazaza Park neat visitors chatted in undertones and stood uncomplaining in queues for the reptile house. On the wall of a mosque in the Upper Town where the few Indians sold expensive jewellery: *'Defense de uriner ici SVP.'*

'You can tell you've just arrived,' complained the wife of a French businessman over dinner. 'You still think it's all wonderful. Michel has to pretend it's lovely because that's his job, but I don't think we should lie to people. We should tell them the truth, how awful it is here. They're savages. They'll steal anything, just you wait, and they can't do anything properly.'

She was gently hushed by her husband, who had heard it all before. She had no job and was bored.

'It's true, Michel. Where can you get a good haircut here? There's no doubt that everything that's good is in Europe. Here as soon as you leave your house, you have to pay for everything.'

'Sounds like Paris,' I joked. She ignored me.

'That's a bit below the belt,' warned Richard.

The pianist played the opening chords of a favourite tune, and Malagasy students around a neighbouring table began to sing; at the other end of the restaurant a man joined in, gazing sentimentally at himself in the mirror; then they all applauded and laughed.

'It'll be the bloody National Anthem next,' muttered the businessman.

'No,' his wife said, 'I will admit that they do have music in their blood.'

Like the eagle (or giant rukh) which was their symbol, the Malagasy royal family made their nests on crags. The Rova, their palace, dominates the city and its baronial turrets rising from the squares of green rice paddy-fields are visible for miles around.

In the middle of the sixteenth century, two hundred years before any European even guessed the existence of the Merina tribe, a highly sophisticated monarchy was growing up. They made their capital on this natural fortress right in the centre of the island, and steadily conquered tribes to north and south until by the nineteenth century they ruled almost the entire island. They were drunken, lecherous and clever and they wore the latest fashions from the courts of Europe.

According to oral tradition, the greatest of the Merina was the first to unite them, King Andrianampoinimerina. (The ridiculous length of his name was as nothing compared with his predecessor King Andriantsimitoviaminandriandehibe.) Fierce and proud, he raised a squabbling group of little princes to the foremost power in the land. He developed a legal system and a system of land tenure, with society ordered into a rigid hierarchy governed by strict rules of intermarriage. His was an entirely Malagasy system in which the old tribal ways were maintained and extended, and he was soon looked back on as a sort of father of the tribe.

But by the time his son Radama I inherited the throne in 1810, his kingdom had entered the outside world. Madagascar was no longer the universe, but an island in an ocean squabbled over by greater powers. In the last years of the Napoleonic Wars the British seized the Mascarenes (though they returned La Réunion to France) and used Mauritius as a base for expanding their influence into the Indian Ocean. Sir Robert Farquhar, the first British governor of Mauritius, set about seducing King Radama, acknowledging him as King of all Madagascar (though this was not yet true) largely so as to keep the French at bay and, more importantly as far as he was concerned, to end the slave trade. His first envoy, Sergeant James Hastie, arrived in 1817 with gifts of horses and military uniforms, a chiming clock, and eventually with an Anglo-Malagasy treaty abolishing the export of slaves. Useful for Robert Newman Hunt was the 1825 treaty in which

British merchants were for the first time given official permission to trade in Malagasy ports.

The French, long interested in the island, particularly in the slaves which they had been exporting to plantations in the Mascarenes, responded quickly. So began the cold war which later developed. A French army deserter became the King's private secretary and not only opened the first (though small and short-lived) school in Antananarivo but also taught Radama I to read and write − in French.

For all his hospitality, Radama remained firmly Malagasy. At one of his weddings, in 1823, the King stood on his balcony and called for silence amongst the crowds besieging the palace. Then he dropped one word: '*Lapa-be*'. There was a fearful tumult of laughing, and at once a most fabulous orgy took place. Slaves took off with the wives of the nobility, and no one could object. When he died five years later, weakened by debauchery and rum, he was buried in a silver coffin made from a meltdown of 12,000 Spanish dollars. Ten thousand more were placed inside to accompany him into the next world, along with eighty British uniforms with feathered cocked hats, golden helmets, silks and *lambas* and muskets. Twenty thousand zebu were killed for the vast crowd, and two military bands played favourite music − waltzes, marches, and British airs.

Almost from its start in 1795 the London Missionary Society had Madagascar top of its list.

Welsh and industrious, the first missionaries arrived in 1818. It was twenty-six years before the first missionary would land in East Africa, and Dr Livingstone was still only five years old. Whatever one thinks of missionaries, it must be said that their achievements in Madagascar, particularly those of David Jones and David Griffiths, were astonishing. Virtually unaided, they set up a network of schools in and around Antananarivo, learnt and taught in Malagasy, taught craftmanship, fought off licentious women, and made conversions. They found the Merina particularly intelligent, able to accommodate Christianity into their own complex religion of ancestor worship and animism. Throughout they were encouraged by King Radama, though he himself never became a Christian. But though they continued their work for seven years after Radama's death, their honeymoon with Madagascar was short-lived.

King Radama was succeeded by his widow, Ranavalona I,

and so began her thirty-three-year reign, much of it a reign of terror. Dumpy and solid, forty years old and childless, she indulged herself in paramours, bloodshed and paranoia.

Fifteen months after her husband's death she bore him a son, named Rakotond'Radama ('Radama's Boy', his powers apparently extending from the grave). In fact the child's natural father was soon accused by Ranavalona of witchcraft and assassinated. His dispatch was not as easy as it might have been: he haunted her dreams. Obeying the dictates of the diviners, she had him exhumed and decapitated, his head moved to his feet and the head of a black dog fixed in its place. When the dreams persisted he was exhumed again, burnt, and the ashes scattered.

He was succeeded by other lovers. Two handsome brothers were particular favourites and their family were, through the Merina Queens, to rule Madagascar for the next sixy-six years. Like the Queen, the brothers were reactionaries. They resented the encroaching Europeans with their arrogance and especially their religion. The London Missionary Society was teaching the slaves that they were equal to the nobles in the eyes of God, equal even to the Queen herself, and while she remained illiterate they were learning to read and write and perhaps to protest.

In 1834 Ranavalona I fell ill; she was forty-nine years old, and even today the average life expectancy is no more. But when she did not die she gave thanks to the twelve fetishes who presided over her royal family. The *sampy* – bits of wood wrapped in silk and a sachet of sand brought from a holy place – gave her renewed strength to fight these outsiders and to return Madagascar to the true path of the ancestors. The missionaries were summoned to a great gathering of the people and warned that they were no longer exempt from the laws of the country. Christian practices were forbidden and though some missionaries stayed for a few months more, most fled. Their schools were closed.

These laws centred on trial by ordeal, principally the *tangena* test, which during her reign destroyed the lives of many thousands of men and women; even if they survived, their health was often ruined. It was used capriciously, the accused charged with any serious crime – murder, being a Christian, being a servant of a missionary, charges often based on the slightest suspicion of guilt. The *tangena* test was conducted by specialists who held in their hands the power of life or death. After being imprisoned for twenty-four hours the accused was stripped naked and made to face east.

'If in reality he has committed the crime, let him die. If he be innocent, let him live,' beseeched his family to the presiding spirits outside the hut. The lethal kernel of the fruit of the *tangena* shrub, the *Tanghinia venenifera* of the dogbane family (which resembles its cousin the oleander), was then grated with an ebony-handled spear (the quantity depending on the executioner and perhaps on how much he had been bribed) and was spread on three fat pieces of chicken skin. These were swallowed with quantities of rice water. Now the accused had to vomit into a shallow basin. If all three pieces of skin were brought up he was innocent. But even that was no guarantee: if before vomiting the fingers of the hands curled inwards, the accused was guilty, even if all the chicken skin was regurgitated. If gagging continued after vomiting, he was still guilty. If guilty, nose and limbs were cut off and the body speared and flung from the precipice below the palace, known as the 'Place of the Hurling'. All his possessions would be seized by the Queen, and his wife and family sold into slavery. If proved innocent, the effects of the poison often led to sterility, to there being no descendants to take care of his remains after death, a punishment worse than death itself.

While Ranavalona was visiting her beloved *sampy* and gathering her strength for the battle to come, Norsworthy wrote enthusiastically to Robert Newman Hunt of future trade with Madagascar. A year earlier Khamis bin Othman had been sent by Sultan Seyyid Said as an ambassador to Ranavalona I. The Sultan's requests for military assistance were accompanied by a proposal of marriage, but Ranavalona turned him down. As a result of his mission Khamis knew the country and spoke the language. He would guide Norsworthy around the coast, introduce him to his contacts, and generally assist Newman Hunt & Christopher in doing business with the natives. It seemed an excellent plan.

Khamis was disgraced and Norsworthy sacked, but Robert Newman Hunt – adventurous and foolish – was still excited by the prospect of trading with this unknown kingdom. In 1837 he continued his journey from the Comoros and landed in Madagascar. He wrote at once to Queen Ranavalona I:

One of my principal reasons for leaving my country and my home was to come to Madagascar, and write to your Majesty for permission to trade with your Majesty's people. The island of Madagascar produces many things which the people of England would be glad to buy, some of them are so useful that many ships full might be sent to England every year, if the people of Madagascar would cultivate and collect them.

His expectations were high, and blithely unaware of Ranavalona's growing dislike of foreigners, he continued with splendid pomposity to extol the virtues of England.

It is by industry and trade that England is one of the greatest nations of the world, and Madagascar could have ships of trade too if the people would learn how to use them. In England we have no wars, all the people are happy under our good King, because we are all employed in peaceful pursuits, and so it would be here if the people knew the benefit of such pursuits.

Newman Hunt could not resist patronizing – much like some aid workers of today – and perhaps homesickness led him to believe what he wrote.

He sent the Queen a gift of knives and forks in a red case, and asked permission to open a House of Business in Antananarivo.

His timing could not have been worse, for now the country entered its darkest hour. As Robert Newman Hunt and Queen Ranavalona exchanged polite thank-you letters, the first of countless Christian martyrs was led to a cliff beyond the palace. As she knelt to pray she was speared to death and flung from the Place of the Hurling to be devoured by dogs and carrion crows.

Over the next twenty years the island was held in the grip of one of the cruellest tyrants history has known. Ancestral traditions were revived including the slaughter of children born on unlucky days, slavery as a punishment for less serious crimes, and the public execution of robbers by an imaginative variety of means. At one gathering 1,237 people who confessed to cattle stealing were fettered together in groups of six with iron collars linked by heavy iron bars and sent off into malarial swamps. As each one died, so the others had to drag around his corpse and irons, until they too dropped. Christians met the same fate; at the height of Ranavalona's reign thousands of people must have been wandering the country in fetters. Those accused of sorcery were plunged head-first into boiling water. The rivers ran red not with topsoil but with blood.

Foreign traders were, Ranavalona announced in 1845, subject to these same laws.

In the Rova, above the Place of the Hurling, Laura was working.

A taxi driver agreed to force his 2CV up the hill, but we were enveloped in black smoke. We leaned, choking, from the open doors, but that made things worse. The petrol tank was a bucket beside his feet with a piece of hose pipe attached to the engine, and he screwed in the gear stick each time he changed gear. From then on we always walked.

The Rova, a museum since the turn of the century, was open to the public during the afternoons, but most of it was closed for restoration; being Laura's 'assistants', however, we were invited in through the neo-classical gateway with infinite courtesy, shaking hands with administrators who welcomed us, formally, to Madagascar. Palaces and tombs in a bizarre mixture of European, Oriental, African and Ancient Grecian styles set the stage for the court's nineteenth-century melodrama, but it was hard to imagine what had gone on here. Up above the city's fumes this was a haven of stillness and clarity. The only sounds were the military band practising for a Sunday concert, black faces under blue caps.

Reigning over smaller chalets was the massive wooden construction of Ranavalona's palace. It was originally built by a Frenchman named Jean Laborde, who in 1831 was washed ashore on the shark-infested east coast. By law all shipwrecked castaways were automatically enslaved by the monarch, but this one was freed and employed to manufacture weapons for the Malagasy army. Engineer, architect, an enterprising and energetic Gascon, he managed to charm the forty-three-year-old Queen to the extent that he survived unscathed in Madagascar, isolated from the outside world, almost until her death. He trod a narrow path: he worked hard, befriended her well-intentioned son, and lowered his eyes on her cruelties. In return he was exempted from the laws of the country. He and Ranavalona were lovers, or so the story goes.

Everything about the palace was on a ridiculous scale. Laborde designed for his Queen a traditional Merina wooden cabin but a colossal five storeys high. Customarily the roofs of Merina houses were supported by one pole; for this palace Laborde needed a pillar of exceptional strength nearly 130 feet high. An army of conscripts between five and ten thousand strong was raised to drag it and the rest of the wood some fifty miles over mountains and rivers from the trackless rainforests of the east. Two thousand men were said to have died in the process.

Here the Queen cavorted with her paramours and chortled over her favourite sport, bulls killing each other with poison-tipped horns. For all her xenophobia she had a taste for European furniture and dress, and she entertained the chosen few to interminable and lavish dinners. Her portrait that hangs in the palace shows a hard-featured masculine woman – almost a transvestite – striding through a landscape. The way it had deteriorated made her look as if she breathed fire.

I hope Robert Newman Hunt made it this far. He would have hovered on the outskirts of the city, waiting for permission to enter on the most auspicious day. When at last he was received at the palace, he would have stood awkwardly in the courtyard, gazing up at the gorgon herself, ensconced on her first floor balcony. She wore a gold crown and a silk *lamba* and liked to remain well above the masses.

The courtyard now lined with dried-up bedding plants, the restored palaces, the sacred fig trees, the balustrade overlooking the city, I see them all with a sort of double vision: how it is, and how I imagine it had been. Even where nothing has changed, the two never quite fuse.

Staircases zigzagged up the five storeys; once Honour Officers of the Palace – obeying orders, plotting, fleeing – tripped lightly up and down these steps lit by flares, but now we had to feel our way in darkness, one foot gingerly following the other, and pause floor by floor in rooms that narrowed like panelled tombs. A Russian doll of a building. The single trunk of palisandre wood loomed overhead like a gigantic mast. Was it really here that Ranavalona breathed and walked and ate, and mistrusted everyone? The restored reception room had been papered with deceptively pretty flowers.

Then at last we climbed out into the blinding light of the roof, and Antananarivo fell away beneath. Cries of children, barking dogs, choking 2CVs: they were as distant as a dream. The city shimmered in a circle of russet mountains. From here they ruled their rocky domain – no wonder power went to their heads.

After her death, Ranavalona's wooden palace – a symbol of

cruelty perhaps – was hidden in a skin of stone. Though Laborde was still very much alive, the British were now ahead in the cold war so a Scotsman, James Cameron, was employed. A carpenter-missionary with the LMS forty years before, he had introduced the manufacture of bricks, which make the highlands so unique in Africa and the Indian Ocean, and built Lac Anosy, the reservoir at the foot of the Place of the Hurling. He was not trained as an architect, but like Laborde (though with less charm) he could do almost anything. Ranavalona II had been delighted by slides of Windsor and Buckingham Palace, and asked Cameron if he could do the same for her. He had to admit that his craftsmen were not quite up to standard, just yet. Instead he simply built the outer shell of another palace around the original, leaving the shingle roof peering over the top. Style-wise he was equally inventive, mixing neo-Renaissance arches with the odd Byzantine window and four square baronial turrets which might have been lifted from Glasgow and dropped, like the rukh's elephant, onto this crag.

Perhaps the Christian missionaries, the main chroniclers and historians of Madagascar, exaggerated the horrors of the murderous Queen. Today the Malagasy sympathize with her attempts to preserve their culture and keep foreigners at bay. For as she had warned, with the return of the missionaries and traders after her death, the country was now wide open to exploitation by foreign powers. By the end of the century the British had lost interest in the island, and while they kept Zanzibar the French also conquered Madagascar.

Laura worked behind a pair of heavy blue doors in what is known as the Silver Palace, because of all the silver fixtures and fittings with which it was once decorated. Polished parquet, sun streaming through high windows, tapering hessian-clad walls hung with bad oil paintings. Was it here, in front of his wife and less than two years into his reign, that Rakotond'Radama, now Radama II, was dispatched to join his ancestors with a silken cord around his throat?

'Come in!' Laura was on her knees with pins in her mouth amidst waves of velvets and silks. Headless pink dummies stood to order in French Empire dresses, once worn by Ranavalona I and her successors. Laura was excited: though mice, rusty pins, bright light and previous attempts at restoration had taken their toll, the quality was even higher than she had expected.

'Look at this.' She lifted the collar of Ranavalona I's state cloak. It was royal red, and encrusted with gold, 'It's not just gold-coloured thread, you know, it's pure gold. I don't want to lift it off the floor because the weight of the gold will rip the fabric. It's that delicate.'

The lavishness was astonishing. There were velvet crinolines given by Queen Victoria and Empress Eugenie of France when both countries were courting Madagascar, and silk tail coats copied from Parisian fashion plates years out of date. Malagasy women embroidered the jackets with silk flowers and so made them into a style of their own. These jackets were worn by the most cosmopolitan of the Malagasy princes.

Even more than the lavishness of the gold thread or the rarity and beauty of the textiles, it was anomalies like these which fascinated Laura. European-style jackets and waistcoats were woven from the stripped membranes of the raffia palm. A flowery coat, again in European style, was made from a bast which Laura suspected was banana fibre. European silks had been made into what appeared to be slashed silk bloomers – Elizabethan? – and red cotton into Arab djelabas of enormous girth.

The fabrics were lustrous despite years of neglect, but problems had been caused by the dummies. They were imported by the French, but the French physique bears little relation to that of the Malagasy, and the clothes had been altered to fit the dummies rather than the other way round. All this had to be undone.

Also here were tattered red umbrellas, carried only by the nobility. The broader the umbrella, the higher the rank. Red umbrellas featured on the Newmans' cargo lists: surely these were they.

Until the Europeans arrived the Malagasy generally wore nothing but *lambas*; wrapped about them like a toga. These were woven from silk or cotton in complex patterns, and sometimes from raffia. Since the largest *lambas* were used to shroud the ancestors, *lambas* in general had acquired an almost sacred aura for the Malagasy. Even now upper-class matrons wore their cream-coloured silk *lambas* – reduced in size and colour since the heyday of the nineteenth century – around their shoulders with pride.

Those that filled the Rova were of the highest quality. Many had been folded, and had rotted along the folds; Laura rolled them in acid-free paper. And they resembled the two *lambas* we had found at the Pool, woven from raffia and from lead-embroidered silk. Perhaps Queen Ranavalona I herself had given them to Robert Newman Hunt.

Richard was disappointed to find that although most Malagasy people wear hats most of the time, there were no hats here, and nothing even resembling a crocodile eating a fish. No insignia, no family crests, no carvings. We would have to look elsewhere.

For five days he photographed the objects while I was his assistant and Laura worked. Her Malagasy fellow-restorers were shy. Sammy wore cowboy-heeled ankle-boots and had malaria. Madame Eulalie shared confidences with Laura in an undertone. They were quick and skilled, as was Laura, whom I had never seen in her professional capacity. We were all impressed as she tested the UV and whirled her whirling hygrometer. Everyone we met seemed to know of her work; it was only thanks to her that we were allowed inside these back regions of the Rova.

One object that to us seemed barely worth keeping was a *lamba* of stained russet silk, torn at the edges. Laura watched Sammy curiously as he unrolled it.

'There's something odd,' she muttered. 'He seems to be . . .' She walked over from her table and touched the fabric. 'These stains. I think they're blood.' She glanced at Sammy. 'Is this a *lambamena*?' Sammy nodded.

'Whose?'

'I think Andrianampoinimerina.'

No wonder they held it so diffidently. Ancestors are sacred, but most sacred are the royal ancestors, and above all Andrianampoinimerina, almost the presiding deity of the royal family and the Merina tribe. This was one of the eighty *lambamenas* in which his corpse was wrapped, and to touch something that had touched his remains seemed to Sammy at once repulsive and thrilling, and almost sacrilegious.

Displayed in the Besakana, an earlier King's palace which was later used as a royal mortuary, were more objects found in the royal graves. Ranavalona I's sacred possessions included several pieces of large and English-looking silver cutlery. In the files at the Pool was the following letter, written in curling Malagasy script and, in a contemporary translation on the back, in English:

Dear Robert Newman Hunt,
We inform you that her Majesty has received the letter you wrote to her,
as also the present you gave her, consisting of twelve knives and twelve
forks in a red case. She is obliged to you for them.
    May you live long
    Saith
    Ramiaramanana and Rahaingio
    11 Honour Officers of the Palace.

The red case had gone, but surely this was the same cutlery.
Nobody knew.

Beneath the Rova's parapet plunged Madagascar's Tarpeian
rock, the Place of the Hurling, Ampamarinana. In 1849 eight
men and six women were brought here and blindfolded. Refusing
to foreswear Christ and acknowledge the *sampy*, they were flung
two hundred feet to be dashed on the rocks below. One man
asked for his blindfold to be removed so as to survey the scene for
the last time, then fell, singing a hymn, to his death.

'I hope it was worth it,' Richard commented. The bodies were
burnt at Faravohitra, a neighbouring hill, along with four living
Christians, members of the nobility, one of whom gave birth in
the flames. The baby was pushed back into the fire. Among
many other horrors, there was a description in 1857 of a
Christian woman who was led to the market place, where her
backbone was 'sawn asunder'.

After Ranavalona's death Christianity surged back and in due
course Protestantism became the official state religion. The
London Missionary Society was quickly followed not only by
French Catholics, but also by a multitude of other Protestant
groups. Lutherans from Norway arrived in 1866, and after some
squabbling over territories confined themselves to parts of the
Betsileo tribe's domain in the southern highlands. American
Lutherans from a Norwegian settlement in Minnesota went
down to the far south, and Quakers and Anglicans fitted in
between. Hospitals and schools were built, and while most of the
missionaries were fairly tolerant of Malagasy customs, some of
the more brutal aspects of ancestor-worship such as the *tangena*
test were abolished, under pressure from them.

Meanwhile the British missionary-architects took off, and now
churches mark the sites of the martyrdoms, dominating Tana
and sucking in colour at dusk. The untrained faithful laid bricks
they had baked themselves and learned by experience how to

construct a roof with often elaborate and bizarre results – beams all over the place. We persuaded a guardian's child to open the door at Ampamarinana; the church was entirely panelled and smelt of bats. Mid-week only the Catholic Cathedral was lively, redecorated recently for a visit from the Pope. We switched on the lights and the Virgin Mary announced in neon letters: *'Je suis L'Immaculée Conception.'*

The touching LMS graveyard told the tale of missionary struggle so far from home. Within just a few years of arriving these simple men from the Welsh hills had not only created the written language but had translated the Bible, and now Amen was the only familiar word. But fever and accidents took a heavy toll. Mothers and babies died within days of each other, the wives still in their mid twenties. Some of them might have been brought here in Newman ships. Even now many of the white faces in Madagascar were those of missionaries; we met them at embassy cocktail parties.

Berjules Raminoarivony was a preacher from the LMS (now amalgamated with other Protestant churches) had been to theological college in Selly Oak; we went with Laura to hear him preach. His red brick church was built by an LMS missionary on a windy hill near Tzimbazaza zoo. Cotton dresses, silk *lambas*, blazers: for the first Sunday of the month 600 Protestants filled the pews. They watched as we were led to the vestry to meet the vicar: being with Laura elevated us to VIPs. The deaconesses were robed in white and had wrapped two plaits together at the nape of their necks, just as modest Christian women were taught to do by the missionaries one hundred and fifty years ago.

We were led to pews of honour at the front, six hundred pairs of eyes on our backs. Laura was introduced to the congregation, and the word 'Expert' aroused applause. The choir was young but barely needed: each member of the congregation sang with full voice, instinctively taking parts in harmony. This must have been a joy for the Welsh missionaries.

Reverend Raminoarivony lurched towards the microphone, arms gesticulating, voice resonating into every crevice in the old church, then leant back to survey the congregation, and whispered seductively. I wondered how sermons like that went down in Selly Oak. When we shook hands in the porch his face was running with sweat.

'The church was closed for sixteen years. He's built up the congregation all by himself,' explained his wife proudly. 'But I don't know how many really believe. It's a social event, and everyone loves to sing.'

The Reverend, the missionaries, the palace administrators – I told each one about the letters in Uncle Ralph's attic, but they shook their heads. The name meant nothing. I was beginning to feel irritated by Robert Newman Hunt. He seemed to have had surprisingly little effect on the country, and was changing from an elegant gentleman paying courteous respects to Her Majesty to a ginger-haired fellow with white eyelashes – a bit of a wimp.

There was one missionary who seemed interested. I shall call him Mike, for he would hate me to use his real name. Without being sanctimonious, he said that the only name he wants to publicize is the name of Jesus. Mike was burly, his features too large for his face, his accent still betraying traces of the West Country after nearly thirty years in Madagascar. One day after the war when he was working in his family's estate agency in Newbury he suddenly stood up and left. He had a bicycle and a train ticket, and no other possessions in the world. Even now he had only as many belongings as would fill two suitcases, no home, no pension (though he was in his seventies), and no way of knowing where his next meal would come from. He was a respectable Christian version of an Indian *sadhu*, wandering the world relying on the goodwill of others. He was a friend of a friend, and we saw him often. Wherever we went he was greeted with warmth. People loved Mike, and even paid for his ticket back to England once every few years. He still had a sister in Newbury.

Mike said that Newman sounded a familiar name. 'I've definitely heard it before. Perhaps there are some Newmans living in Tana. After all, there are Robinsons and Johnsons and none of them have English blood.' Most of these were named after missionaries whose schools they attended. We searched the telephone directory: predictably, there are no Newmans. But one morning a note arrived at the hotel: Mike had found something in the Archives that would interest me. It was a letter from Queen Ranavalona to Robert Newman Hunt, thanking him for the gift of two Arab horses, and it was proof at last of his presence here. He could not have given me a better gift, but it was in old Malagasy which Mike had difficulty translating.

We took it and a picture of the crocodile bowler to one of the descendants of the rulers of Madagascar who still lived in

Antananarivo. We had an introduction to her through the Rova administrators, and we hoped she could shed light on the firm's connection. Madame Rasoanaivo's ancestor was the flamboyant prime minister Rainilaiarivony, who after disposing of the debauched Radama II sensibly married in succession two of his widows — daughters-in-law of Ranavalona I — and then a third Queen. Through them he ruled Madagascar until in 1895 he was ignominiously exiled by the French to Algiers, where he died in 1896. Ranavalona III followed him in 1897.

On the edge of town his white country villa with tall green shutters still stands in a garden of ancient mango trees and poinsettia. It was not early but Madame Rasoanaivo was still in curlers and slippers; she had been delayed, she apologized, her maid's mother had died that morning and the maid was being comforted on the verandah. Yet she was elegant, with arches of pencilled eyebrows, light skin and eastern features. She wore a pale blue blouson jacket and we — Laura, Richard, Madame and I — stood in the dining room on parquet. The walls were festooned with silk wallpaper that hung in tatters, light shafting from Georgian windows into darkened rooms. She sighed for the old days.

'I knew everybody. Everybody came here. Ambassadors from all over the world — English, American, Scandinavian. Look, here they all are in the *Livre d'Or*.' She opened a leather book to show us the signatures. 'Even President Tsiranana — that was before the present regime of course, but even then ... Well, we have nothing to do with politics, we just want everybody to like us, and we like everybody. But in the old days — oh! Life was marvellous. We went to Europe. I've been twice, in the 1950s, and I loved it. Everywhere we went we were fêted. It was marvellous! We had tea with the Queen, and met the President of the French Republic, and at soirées people used to come up and touch me, and say, what have you put on your skin!' She laughed, a theatrical tinkle. A black and white photograph showed a pretty young woman with wide cheek-bones and full lips, and the stiff hair of the 1950s.

'Was your husband an ambassador?' Richard asked.

'No, he was a civil servant but it was because of our ancestors that we were invited everywhere.' She guided us round the house. This chandelier was given by Queen Victoria, that plate by Emperor Napoleon.

'How long have you known this house? Since you married?' I asked.

'Oh no, all my life. My husband and I were cousins so I always came here. Cousins marry each other so as to safeguard the inheritance.'

'So has nothing changed since your ancestor lived here?'

I thought of the Pool. Nothing ever leaves this house. Like my Uncle Ralph, she lives immersed in her family past.

'Nothing. I did give a few things to my brother-in-law but the house is still the same.'

'Haven't you even added a bathroom?' I felt very bold – rude almost – asking a Malagasy such a direct question.

'No!' She was vehement. 'We go outside, in the Malagasy way.' She looked at us for a moment. 'I *had* a bathroom. My husband installed it when we celebrated our silver wedding and the Crown Prince of Germany came. But we suffered misfortunes, and one day there were the most terrible noises from the cistern, bam bam bam.' She punched the air. 'I knew at once that the ancestors were angry because I had changed things. So I took it out.'

She sighed in front of a portrait of her illustrious forebear. It was on marrying his second Queen, she explained, that he became a Christian and so was forced to divorce his first wife, a *Hova* like himself, by whom he had had sixteen children. He loved her, and the marriage had been happy; he had no children by the three Queens.

'What could he do?' asked Madame. 'It was politics.'

His sons were so outraged by the divorce that they threatened to poison him.

We were interrupted by a young servant girl. Tea was served on the verandah amongst the pot plants. We sipped from porcelain and the chairs wobbled.

'I've got something very special to show you,' I said, producing a photocopy of the letter.

Her pencilled eyebrows lifted in surprise. 'It's from Queen Ranavalona I but it's not written by her. She was illiterate. Look, here it's signed by Rainiharo, the Queen's prime minister.'

'Is he a connection of yours?'

'Of course! He was Rainilaiarivony's father. As soon as I saw the letter I recognized the writing – it's the writing of our family.' She read the letter and told us that with typically Malagasy subtlety Rainiharo accepted the Arab horses – presumably brought from Zanzibar – but avoided being indebted. It does not matter whether it is from the English or the French, he wrote; it is the spirit of the giving that matters – a souvenir of Robert's visit – rather than the gift itself. Robert Newman Hunt as an elegant gentleman was resuscitated.

'Perhaps you might also know something about this hat,' Richard suggested, producing the photograph.

We suspected by now that the hat had belonged not to Ranavalona I but to Ranavalona III, the fourth wife of the prime minister Rainilaiarivony. It was tiny enough to have fitted her: not for nothing was she known as '*La Petite Reine*'. Her portrait shows an anxious face on which the hat would have added humour. After her death her effects might well have travelled from her place of exile in Algiers across the Mediterranean to the South of France, where it was bought by Richard's grandmother. But Madame Rasoanaivo knew nothing of crocodiles or hats.

Suddenly, sipping tea on the verandah, I saw us all with our ancestry, Richard with his crocodile hat, Laura and I with the Newmans, Madame with her prime ministers: proud of them, ashamed or indifferent, it didn't matter. There they were, invisible, elusive, yet inescapable, fixed to our heels and stretching out behind us like shadows.

'And do you use these rooms now?' I asked.

'Oh yes!'

But I wondered if she understood my question. She was a widow, and her only child lived in Saudi Arabia; I could feel her loneliness. The Wednesday Club of ambassadors' wives occasionally met here to sip tea and play cards, but that was all. And now the house belonged to the state who were trying to move her out so that they could turn it into a museum.

'The parties! You should have seen them. In the Prime Minister's day – before my time of course – two hundred people would have been here, roaming from room to room, out on to the terrace, the dresses, the uniforms . . . they danced, the musicians . . . palanquins were always left at the gate.'

I saw in my mind the ladies in their crinolines on the red velvet chairs beneath the palm fronds, fluttering behind their fans.

'Of course that was before the French arrived in 1895.'

She had no time for the French colonialists who, like all colonialists, relegated the native people to second-class citizens. 'In those days everybody spoke English. Even my grandparents, they lived in Paris, but they *never* spoke French. Only English. I have a huge English Bible which was brought out here by one of the missonaries,' Madame added. 'And this house. It was built by Cameron, you know.'

Even after independence in 1960 the British never regained their former presence. Cut-backs by the Callaghan government closed the British Embassy in 1975, and were taken as a slight by the new Christian-Marxist government; there was also an embarrassing incident involving a diplomat and smuggled dinosaur bones. Now relations with foreign countries were governed largely by how much aid they provided, which meant that Britain was not high on the list. Laura was an attempt to change that.

Madame was thrilled to hear of Laura's work.

'Most of the clothes I think belonged to your ancestor the Prime Minister.'

'Oh yes! He had marvellous clothes. Hundreds of them. Very smart.'

Laura (but not us) was invited to sign the *Livre d'Or*.

She led us into the garden, first to the old bread-making hovel, now lived in by her servants. She referred to them as 'descendants of slaves'. They lay on the ground, and struggled to their feet as we appeared. The lawn was ringed by ancient fig and mango trees. A strange thing happened there not long ago, she said. It was ten o'clock in the morning – bright sun – and she suddenly noticed a man standing beneath the largest and oldest of the trees. He was wearing uniform, and instinctively she addressed him as Dadabe, grandfather.

'How are you, Dadabe?' she asked. He was angry, however, because one of the sacred figs had been cut down.

'Who did this?' he demanded. She explained that it was her brother-in-law, and that she was very sorry. 'Where is your husband?'

'He's inside having his siesta.'

'Go and fetch him then.'

'Yes, Dadabe.'

Madame Rasoanaivo went towards the house and hid for a while on the verandah. Then she realized she could not lie. She went back to the man.

'Forgive me, Dadabe,' she said. 'In fact my husband is dead.'

'I knew it anyway.'

'Then he told me not to cut the trees, not to do this, not to do that. He blessed me, and said, "You are the last. You must keep the place beautiful because the ancestors do not like the dirt." With that he vanished. I was crying and wailing,' Madame laughed. 'A burglar! Come quickly, a burglar! The descendants of slaves came running. They looked everywhere but couldn't find anybody. They thought that Madame had not yet had her morning coffee, that must be it. They took me inside and when I saw his portrait I knew it was him. The Prime Minister Rainilaiarivony himself. No one else had seen a thing.' That's why, she concluded, she could not change the house. Dadabe was watching.

Richard asked if he could photograph her, and her hands flew to her scarfed head.

'Oh no, not in my curlers, oh no, excuse me, I couldn't. Do you mind? I'll go and take them out. Wait a minute.'

She brushed out her hair, surprisingly dark for her age (Laura pointed out later that it was a wig). She put on high heels too, and sat grandly but a little self-consciously in the red velvet throne, her hands in her lap.

'Thank you so much,' we said.

'No, it's for me to thank you.'

In the afternoons Richard and I escaped to the blue hill of Ambohimanga, twelve miles away. Past ancient walls of baked red earth and the vivid green of newly-planted paddy rose another rock, though being sacred this one was still clad in its deciduous primary forest. Here Andrianampoinimerina lived before conquering and transferring his court to Antananarivo. We came here often, and each time our moods lightened; no wonder the Queens used this as their summer palace, and built themselves an exquisite (though now crumbling) chalet. There is an almost Japanese delicacy. It came as no surprise to learn that this is Imerina's spiritual capital.

Both King Andrianampoinimerina and Queen Ranavalona were buried here but were moved to Tana by the French in 1897 to prevent Ambohimanga from becoming a centre for anti-French feeling. But even though the bodies have been gone for nearly a century, the site of their grave remains sacred. We often saw the remains of sacrifices – chicken blood, feathers, honey and chalk – scattering the ground where people had asked the royal ancestors to grant them favours. A child perhaps, success in exams. Even bourgeois Malagasy came, but often early in the morning so none of their friends would see. They would ask for money. Other people took away handfuls of sacred earth. Sometimes this meant that they were going abroad, and would take the red earth of Madagascar with them. Their link with their country would be in their pocket, and they had to bring it back some day; they had to return. Some people would take earth from their own family tombs, but if the tombs were too far away they would come here and take earth from the communal ancestors instead.

One day we interrupted a family who had travelled here from Antsirabe to thank the royal ancestors for restoring a child to health. They stood silently around a pool where King Andrianampoinimerina and his successors took their ritual new year's bath. In Madagascar ancestor-worship needs no temples, and the *sampy* were long ago destroyed, so it is sites like these that are sacred. With a witch doctor who had accompanied them here, the men wrapped red cotton *lambahoany* around their waists, and lowered themselves into the now stagnant pool to fill bottles with water which they would take home to use as medicine or to wash their wounds. They placed the bottles on their heads and quietly prayed to God and to Andrianampoinimerina while the women and children stood silently beside them. A child played with the zip on his jacket and the women hung their heads in prayer; it was a ceremony moving in its humility. The royal ancestors were then offered honey and sweets (which would be snapped up by the guardian or by local children when this family had gone). Holy water, thanking God – it was so pragmatic the way the Malagasy took what they wanted from religion. When it was over, the witch doctor had to hurry away to mass.

Another evening when the light was golden and we thought we were alone among the sacred rocks in the wood behind the palace, we came across a family singing to their accordion and dancing, waving a coloured *lamba*. Way below were churches and small red villages, and hazy in the distance the towers of the Rova.

'Join us,' they called.

But we did not want to intrude. Theirs was a private family matter, one of asking the royal ancestors to grant a child to an infertile couple. They had aimed pebbles into small holes in the rocks which were ringed in chalk and filled suggestively with wax and honey. The eye-shaped hole was for a girl, the round hole for a boy.

Instead we sat in the garden of a café on the hillside and drank citronelle tea from a Provençal jug, and took photographs of the moon in the trees, thin as a fingernail clipping.

At a party at the English language institute I met Jeanne Rambinintsoa, *Directrice* and a professor of English at the University. She wore a sturdy suit and short straight hair and I liked her forthrightness.

'I think the British and the Malagasy are quite similar,' she observed. Her father had been a diplomat in Britain, and she had spent two years at the French Lycée. 'For one thing, we are both island people, and that's very important. We belong with Africa and yet we're apart, a bit like you and Europe. People here hate to be called Africans. We're independent, and proud of that.' She dragged on a cigarette. 'Our reserve too. That's something that made it much easier for us to get on with the English than with the French. We hate to say anything too direct.' She was one of the few exceptions. 'Many people think the English are hypocrites, but at least they are not so direct. We'd rather be wrong than have an argument. The other thing is that we're both still very chauvinist, and obsessed by class.'

'But this is a Marxist country.'

'I know, but things haven't changed that much. Our *Andriana*, our nobles, still expect to be addressed as such. It's quite ridiculous. Do you know about our hierarchy?'

'Not really.'

'It's very strict. Nobles, like your aristocracy, then the *Hova*, the middle class, and then the *Andevo*, the descendants of freed slaves, then *Mainty*, the descendants of actual slaves, at the bottom. *Mainty* means "black". They're the darker-skinned people.' Jeanne's skin was honey-coloured: it was not hard to see where she belonged. She disliked the hierarchy, and yet she was part of it: she had her shadow at her heels like all of us. 'It's almost impossible to change from one class to another here. If a noble marries outside his class then he and his wife can't be buried together. She has to go back to her family tomb. That's very significant for us. And as for inter-tribe marriage – almost never.' Unusually, she herself was unmarried.

'I suppose it's still like that with us, though less so,' I said. 'Classes tend to stick together. Accents, ancestors, it's all much the same really.'

'The British are terrible like that.'

'Yes. But why do you say Madagascar is chauvinist? I see men holding babies, and there are women like you with powerful jobs. It's quite different from say, Zanzibar, or many Muslim countries for that matter.'

'Yes, it's true in a way. You'll have noticed that all but two of the English teachers here this evening are women.' She was right: women in sensible shoes preparing to go back to their provincial towns to teach.

'Sixty per cent of our magistrates are women. My mother was a judge. People do describe Madagascar as a matriarchal society.'

'And you had a succession of very powerful Queens.'

She agreed, and added: 'This is the only African country where excision has never been practised.'

I looked blank.

'You know excision?' She smiled slightly. 'Female circumcision. We've never had it here.'

'Ah hah.' I nodded.

'Men are considered the weaker sex because they are so easily tempted, so women have always kept the family money. But how is it that we have only one female minister and one woman MP? It's pretty much like you. A few Queens don't make for an equal society.' She lit up again. 'Yes, we're still pretty backward.' She hesitated, blowing out smoke, and gave me a sidelong look. 'You know, of course, that most people here still worship their ancestors?'

'Yes. Don't you?'

'No. But my family is not at all typical. My parents are devout Protestants and don't really approve. Of course, in a way you do it too.'

'You mean family photos?'

'Yes, all those old portraits you British have on your walls. It's only another form of ancestor worship.'

We both laughed.

'We don't exactly worship them,' I said. 'And not everyone has family portraits, not by any means. It's really a class thing. If people do have them, they often don't know who they are.'

'Even so, with this quest of yours . . .'

'Yes, I see what you mean.'

'But I don't suppose you would practice *famadihana*.'

'*Famadihana*?'

'You've heard of our exhumation rituals I suppose?'

'Yes, a bit. I mean, it interests me very much.'

She looked at me curiously, expecting me to disapprove.

'*Famadihana*. I hate this. The rotting bodies, the smell.' She shuddered. 'You know that corpses are exhumed until there is nothing left? People actually dance with their dead.' I had picked up snippets already – the *lambamena*, the outlines of ancestor worship – and the more she told me the more intrigued I became. Tanindrazana: Island of the Ancestors.

'Are these traditions still going strong?'

'Strong? I should think so. Amongst the Merina it's part of daily life.'

'Even though most people are Christians?'

'Oh yes, they don't bother about that. Only recently I received an invitation myself to a big exhumation, but I wouldn't dream of going, never.'

'You mean you get sent an invitation like you would to a wedding? Monsieur and Madame So-and-So invite you to the exhumation of their father? Like that?'

Jeanne smiled ruefully. 'Yes, like that. Weddings here aren't specially important. It's incredible, I know. Most of my friends do this. But when someone dies I do feel obliged to offer condolences. We give a small amount of money in a ritual way at sunset, so sorry and so on. We give the money with both hands and then say, it's getting dark, we have many other duties so we must go now. In the old days people used to have very lavish what's the word? They do it in Ireland.'

'Wake?'

'Yes, wakes. But now you often see in the papers "No wake." People can't afford it. It's all ridiculous, I know, but I'm still proud to be Malagasy.'

'Of course.'

'There's no other country like this one. We're completely isolated, completely apart. France means more to us than Africa. As you know, many of our customs are Indonesian. But none of this religion means anything to me. You see, I don't believe in God.'

She hit the 'd' aggressively, intending to shock, and here in Imerina, in the highlands, it was certainly unusual. God of one sort or another was at the forefront of most people's lives.

André Ramanantsoa was the round and endlessly courteous administrator at the Rova. He invited Richard and me to dinner.

'I'll pick you up,' he said. 'I'll come early because the streets get so dangerous. Thieves. You've got to be very careful.'

All Malagasy were afraid of Tana at night. There were tales of tourists being held up – physically – while their shoes were removed. We felt unafraid, yet Laura had had an unnerving experience while driving through the *zoma* on a Friday. As she paused at traffic lights a youth crouched at the open window and wrenched a gold hoop from her ear and ran off through the traffic.

As we negotiated the broken slabs of paving under the arcades of the Avenue de l'Indépendance we told André of an incident at our hotel. We had a room at the end of a gloomy corridor, the sole advantage of which was its view over the market. Next door was full of junk – old beds and mattresses – forgotten but not unused. Each night there was scuffling and whispering, footsteps, girls washing their legs with the bathroom door open. Late one night Richard fetched the doorman.

'There's no one in there,' the doorman insisted.

'Open it. Go on.'

He pushed it open. A dishevelled couple shrieked, squeezed past and ran away down the corridor.

'While we remain here,' Richard said, 'that room remains empty.'

The doorman was contrite. 'Yes sir.' But it was soon happening again.

André looked uneasy. 'I don't know. Prostitution. Drugs.' Proud and reserved, he hated to hear of this. 'There are a lot more drugs than there used to be.' Yet Tana lacked the frightening edge of Bagamoyo or Dar, or London.

'Hard drugs?'

'Oh no! At least, not yet.'

'It seems a lot safer than many places.'

'Really?' His voice shot up in surprise. 'We have the feeling that Tana is one of the worst in the world.'

*

It was Thursday night. Streets that were normally deserted soon after dark were busy with families staking out sites for stalls in tomorrow's big market. Most had come in from surrounding villages and huddled together under blankets, and all night metal poles and trestles were manoeuvred into place in the flare of petrol lamps. Men pissed openly in the streets, and the pavements were awash.

André led us up an alley-way no more than a yard wide. Chickens squawked out of our way and neighbours watched.

'*Vazaha,*' they whispered.

André took no notice. He tapped at a narrow door.

'*Bonsoir! Entrez.*' His wife, Maxine, stood in the doorway and we squeezed past her. She was slender and beautiful, every feature tiny – perfect little nose, miniature ears, feathery eyebrows – yet strong. She was a receptionist at a big hotel.

'Excuse the small apartment. It's not our place, it belongs to a cousin. We're just staying here while Maxine does the early shift.'

The housing problem was notorious. Shanty towns were growing up along the canals on the outskirts, mostly lived in by students who could find nowhere else to go. Students who did get a university room sometimes had their entire families living with them. (The university itself, known as Beirut for its bombed-out look, was bankrupt.)

This was more of a passage than a flat, but it was clean. We sat on narrow sofas round a table with a vase of dried flowers; on the wall hung a clock in the shape of Africa, a souvenir from one of André's visits with the boy scouts. Maxine produced freshly squeezed strawberry juice and we chatted about plans. Was it our British and Malagasy reserve that made us feel awkward? Or was it the growing desperation that we sensed everywhere? We spoke of their problems in making ends meet, even though both have good jobs and not yet any children.

'You may have noticed that there are people here with cars and houses that you could never buy on a Malagasy salary.' André spoke bitterly.

'Yes. It's a mystery.'

'Is it?' He raised an eyebrow.

'What about the elections?'

André and Maxine glanced at each other, and chorused in English, 'Fed up.' Nothing has changed, prices rise, people are bored with the whole thing. 'Most people didn't even bother to vote. It was all fixed anyway.'

In 1960 Madagascar freed itself from French rule and under the Presidency of Phillibert Tsiranana became the Malagasy Republic. But links with France remained strong. The French still dominated the economy and trade, exporting the profits from vast French enterprises in sugar cane, sisal and tobacco; they maintained their military bases on the island, and retained a strong influence over education and intellectual life. In return the French committed themselves to a substantial aid programme. But towards the end of the 1960s the economy stagnated and students rose up against the pervasive French influence, and in May 1972 called a student strike, which was taken up by workers, civil servants, peasants and the unemployed urban youth. Protestors set fire to the town hall (which seventeen years later remains a shell on Avenue de l'Indépendance). Security forces opened fire and killed about thirty people, injuring 150 more. Tsiranana handed full power over to the army. Eventually an interim government was formed in which one President was assassinated after only a week in office. This was succeeded in 1975 by the 'Christian-Marxist' President Didier Ratsiraka, a naval Lieutenant Commander, who ended the special relationship with France, nationalized the French enterprises, produced a 'Charter of the Malagasy Socialist Revolution', and re-named the country the Democratic Republic of Madagascar.

The day we flew in, President Ratsiraka flew out to visit his friend the Stalinist Kim Il Sung in North Korea. Midi *Madagasikara*, the leading bi-lingual paper, reported Ratsiraka's departure but did not hunt out what was under everyone's breath: economic chaos and corruption.

The ousting of the French left a niche for the Russians to fill, and now Aeroflot was the only foreign airline allowed into Madagascar. Fat pale Soviet women could often be seen buying souvenirs in the market, and the USSR was building a massive embassy complex. However, independence was all, and a party named 'Christian-Marxist' was not so much a contradiction in terms as an attempt to keep both capitalists and communists at bay.

But things were looking bad. Economic growth has failed to keep up with a rapidly expanding population (now twelve million people, 60 per cent of whom are under fourteen), and the country was on the verge of bankruptcy. Ratsiraka had fallen into the trap of being seen as a classic African dictator (though small scale compared with some) with all the attendant charges of nepotism, and *folie de grandeur*. His gigantic new presidential palace, the building of which supposedly caused a national shortage of cement, dominates the road south. Recently minor uprisings during the presidential elections had been quelled by the timely visit of the Pope, and the week we arrived a coup was announced: armed students had taken over the national radio. But within three hours it was quashed. The public noticeboard in Place Colbert showed bloody pictures of violence in Tiananmen Square, but the pictures were not of the students but of the 'heroic' soldiers who killed them. I suppose they were meant as a warning.

Now, however, under pressure from the IMF and the World Bank, a sort of *perestroika* was underway. Censorship of the press had officially been lifted, though it was still only in the privacy of their apartment that André and Maxine could speak so openly.

'We can't be bothered with politics any more,' André said wearily. 'All we can think about is daily life, just making it from one day to the next.'

André was a Communist, but simply because his boss was a Communist. This and family connections were the only ways of getting work.

The kitchen was more of a scullery, with a big old sink and bare walls. Maxine squeezed round the table to serve rice and chicken. She had laid an embroidered table cloth, and made the best of things. I asked them about the social hierarchy.

'Oh, it's still there,' André said with disgust. 'Amongst the Merina if you have curly hair and marry someone who looks more "Indonesian" it can be a problem for the family. It can even hinder you both in getting a job.' He spoke bitterly, and I noticed that his hair was slightly curlier than Maxine's, his skin a shade darker.

I asked about other customs, but either they knew little, or did not want to discuss them with a stranger. Perhaps they were not interested: simply living was more important than anything.

'What about the exhumation rituals?' I persisted.

André looked up in surprise. '*Famadihana?*'

'Yes, I'm very interested.'

'Yes?' André's voice rose in boyish surprise. He hovered

between being slightly ashamed of this archiac ritual, and flattered that anyone should be interested. 'It is the season now.'

'Is it?'

He watched me for mockery or ridicule, but there was none. 'Yes, the dry season, from June to October. When the crops are in and all the children are home from school.'

'I'd love to see it.' I wanted this almost more than anything, but I trod carefully, afraid that I might tread on *fady*, the complex system of taboos that still governs much of Malagasy life, particularly in relation to the ancestors. It varies from village to village and from family to family, and might decree that you do not work in the fields on a Thursday, or that you do not eat pork, or that you do not allow *vazaha* to witness a *famadihana*. To act against a *fady* or to offend somebody would incite retribution from an ancestor or another person in a system similar to the Hindu *Karma*. '*Hitodianny atao*,' say the Malagasy: what is done will return. But unlike Jeanne – who turned out to be the exception in disapproving of *famadihana* – André slipped from shyness to enthusiasm, and offered to take us to a *famadihana* the following Saturday.

André collected us in his battered VW Beetle. Before we had even reached the outskirts of Tana we were blocked by musicians in knee-length shirts and boaters playing not African or Indonesian instruments, but drums, flutes, trumpets, clarinets, horns and accordions; around them thronged cotton dresses and fluttering hands. Bounced joyfully above their heads was a coffin.

'That's it!' André exclaimed, drawing into the pavement to let them pass.

'*Famadihana*?'

'Yes. Why don't you take some pictures?'

'Won't they mind?'

'No, go on, I'll wait.'

Richard got out of the car.

'*Vazaha, vazaha, vazaha!*' Children yelled with excitement and the crowd halted while they danced for his camera. They grinned and stank of rum. A few yards on we came upon another, and then another, some with eight-piece bands, some with only six.

'I said it was the season now, but I didn't expect as many as this,' said André.

We had arranged to meet someone who would guide us to his family's *famadihana*. We parked in a village in a tiny patch of shade, but as we waited it receded, and we were soon glued to the seats. Mopping his face and keeping watch for our friend, André explained.

Madagascar is home to eighteen different tribes, each with their own customs and identity, but what unites them is their language, their use of *fady*, and their respect for the ancestors. For the Malagasy almost all aspects of life depend, paradoxically, on their dead. 'Think of it like a river,' said André. 'The source is the unborn. The river is the river of the living, and it flows out into the sea, the sea of the ancestors. Then, as in the natural world, the cycle begins again. And again.' The infant is not a reincarnation of the dead, but receives its gift of life from them. I remembered the family tree at the Pool: he begat she begat he begat she in ruled lines. In Madagascar it was quite different, not linear but circular. Rivers flowing, and returning to source. Past, present and future are one.

'We have God too of course,' André added. 'Zanahary, the creator.'

He unclipped a fountain pen and drew a pyramid divided into five sections. At the apex was God, then the ancestors. These were in the realm of the dead. Below came the sovereign, then the Andriana, the Hova, then the masses, who were subdivided into the free and the slaves (or their descendants). These were in the realm of the living. It was Jeanne's hierarchy, ordered into a diagram. So far it seemed clear, not so different from the Divine Right of Kings and Medieval Christianity.

'What you've got to remember,' André added, 'is that for us "*Ny fanahy no olona*." Man is a spirit.'

I saw suddenly that the shadows were not the dead but the living, shadows cast by the ancestors, by the Light of the World. No wonder the LMS found the Malagasy so receptive.

Although each tribe respects its ancestors, it is only the Merina and one or two other tribes who practise *famadihana*. Literally *famadihana* (pronounced *famadeean*) means the turning of the bones, ancestral bones. Burial is not once and for all. During the dry season the bodies of ancestors are exhumed, wrapped in new *lambamena*, and returned to the freshly swept tomb. Not morbid but practical: the living and the dead succour each other, the living easing the spirit's path to becoming an ancestor, propitiating it, keeping it sweet; in return the dead nourishing the rice fields and providing an abundance of healthy babies. Significantly, only in South Sulawesi in Indonesia is there a similar practice, the *maqneneq*.

More *famadihana* passed by – a mass of black arms and bleached straw hats – but without a sign of our friend. André got out and explored the few houses that made up this village. Nothing. He had not turned up. We tried not to show our disappointment for André's sake, but he was angry for ours. We sat in the car a while longer staring at the road. Suddenly there was a tap at the window; a toothless grin: he'd been held up in the *zoma*, Michel explained; he sold knitwear there each Friday. He got into the back with Richard and we set off on the terrible red road west to Ambohimanana.

The land opened into a treeless plateau, light and shadows shifting, clouds low. Steep, thatched adobe houses lined the crest of a slope; we parked outside the largest and Michel's elderly parents took our hands in both of theirs, bowing slightly. They were expecting us but spoke no French. Lowering heavy lids his pale-skinned mother gestured us to follow her upstairs. Wedding photographs and Protestant texts dotted the living room walls. She swept red dust from the neighbouring room for us and we sat on a straw mattress.

'She says that tomorrow will be the first *famadihana* since 1967. It's going to be a good one,' André informed us.

'What makes them do it now, after so long?'

'They thought it was time to bring all the family together. There'll be about three hundred people here tomorrow.'

'But why now?'

'Don't know. Maybe one of them was visited by an ancestor in a dream; perhaps the ancestor complained of being cold, wanted new clothes. Or perhaps the family has been having a run of bad luck. A *famadihana* would appease the forebears. Anyway, they'd go to the astrologer, and he studies the signs and selects the most propitious day. Having done that they fatten up the zebu for the feasting because fat is a sign of largesse, and then they find the money.' They were artisans – knitters – descendants of a noble but poor. 'They've probably been putting it off for as long as possible. They could be crippled by the expense – the musicians, the grave-diggers, the feast, the new *lambamena* – but it's good for prestige. And it's an investment,' André added. 'With any luck it'll bring huge returns from the ancestors.' Like many people, André disapproved of the extravagance which often left families hungry for the rest of the year. 'The end of the dry season is known as "the time of crisis" because by that time many people have spent all their money on their dead. The middle classes, though they're much richer, are far more modest at their *famadihana*.' André paused. 'I say "they" but of course I mean "we",' he admitted in a rush. 'I'm Malagasy after all. We do it too.'

André left soon after, hoping to reach Tana before dark. Abandoned, we were unsure what to do next. We still had the evening to fill. Richard wanted to sit in the sun on the verandah and read, but so many astonished children gathered in the yard below that it was impossible. At first they had been afraid – *vazaha* eat children, don't they? – but now they found us hilarious. Our hosts, busily preparing for tomorrow's three hundred guests, felt as uneasy as we did – were we comfortable? did we eat Malagasy food? – so we escaped to the spiked grass of the opposite hill. Banana leaves rattled and a man called to his zebu, every tone distilled. Villagers in bright clothes straggled up the track and two boys toiled behind with blackened cauldrons dangling from shoulder poles. Excitement was brewing.

Two fat sisters were leaning against the balustrade when we returned.

'Hello!' they called, as if they were really pleased to see us.

It was a relief, and they spoke French. They were the granddaughters of our host, Michel's nieces, and they had walked here from Tana, they said. They did it once or twice a year, but their grandfather did it once a week, thought nothing of three hours on foot. Haja was twenty-one, studying to be a technical secretary, the smaller and, initially, the quieter of the two; Holy was nineteen and moustached, her eyes filled with teenage anxiety. She wore the Maoist peaked cap of the compulsory National Service, in which she taught literacy to grown-ups in Tana. They linked their arms through mine.

'Listen! It's a *famadihana*!'

We ran downstairs to join the cortège. Held aloft, a Malagasy flag twitched beside a shrouded corpse.

'It's a cousin,' Haja shouted. 'He's being brought home from Tana.'

'Why?'

'If the family can afford it, everyone must return to where they come from. Even if you die abroad. One day, even if it's years after death, you must return home. *Roots*. They're very important to us.' The body was carried into a house and the music stopped. 'That's where he'll spend the night, in his own house. He'll be reburied tomorrow.' Far from being frightened or disgusted by having a corpse in the house, the descendants were honoured and excited.

We lay on the straw mattress in the candle-light. Wind rattled the shutters and all night we heard relatives arriving with much shaking of hands and exchanging of gossip. They bedded down where they could. We felt guilty that we should have this large room to ourselves when some forty people were squeezed into three other rooms, but no one disturbed us, and we were too tired, and spoke too little Malagasy, to make our guilt understood. Perhaps they preferred us to stay out of the way. Anxiety about tomorrow kept us awake: I was more worried about intruding on this private family affair and offending all the different *fady* that I suspected lurked unseen around the tomb than I was about seeing decayed human corpses, but that was rather a daunting prospect too. Before coming to Madagascar I had not anticipated getting quite this close to anyone's ancestors.

At dawn we found the action behind the house. Each member of this massively extended family would have to be fed and ten cauldrons, mostly rice, bubbled on flames. Two hump-backed zebu had been sacrificed the previous day and now an oil drum of beef and innards boiled in fat and stank. Barefoot men grinned at us and stirred the pots, and scooped rice into baskets to heave them into a neighbouring house where guests were already eating in shifts.

'Everyone must eat something,' Haja warned. She had shining eyes. Perhaps to protect me from embarrassment, this morning they were both wearing trousers. We were the only women not in skirts, and later I discovered that it is insulting to the ancestors for women to wear trousers.

'Us too?' I asked, dreading the food.

'Yes. It's a terrible insult if you don't.'

We were guests, privileged to be here: we had to do it. We climbed rickety stairs past busy helpers and sat on newly laid mats around the walls. Rice filled one enamel plate and meat, fat and inner tubes and bits of stomach were ladled into another. I prided myself on being able to eat anything, but the long black hair was too much. I knew I had to make at least a token gesture but my spoon, dipped briefly into a bucket of cold water between diners, was coated in congealed grease. Later I heard that poor families make the food as oily as possible so that guests are sickened and eat less. When Holy (perhaps out of sympathy with us) objected to a second curl of intestine the serving boy scooped it up and swallowed it himself.

Music! We could escape. The rest of the family was returning from the tomb of their noble ancestor having asked for his blessing, and they danced into the main square waving eucalyptus leaves, straw hats bobbing, joy on their faces. The corpse that arrived from Tana yesterday was brought out of his house and laid on a table of honour.

For the next ten hours the musicians never stopped. It seemed odd that at such a very traditional Malagasy ceremony the instruments should be European, yet this was just another instance of the two cultures blending to create a hybrid of their own. In 1820 Governor Farquhar arranged for young Merina men to go to Mauritius to learn military band instruments and King Radama's favourite British airs. These tunes were their descendants, as was the style of playing, for we noticed that the clarinets were tilted upwards, and the reeds were upside down. Perhaps one musician had developed this style of playing and it had become the norm; in any case it enabled them to compete better with the trumpets and drums.

In front of the ancestor on his table of honour the dancing began. Before opening the tomb we would dance in front of the corpse, not with it. Despite our protests, within minutes we were pulled into the ring, my hands grasped by our hostess, Richard's by Haja. 'We flutter our hands like this,' explained Haja, fluttering her hands. We danced on and on in the hot dusty air. When we stopped, people grasped our hands and thanked us for honouring their ancestors. With music and dancing the spirit is summoned back from the realm of light, the ocean of the dead, to re-inhabit its corpse and so to appreciate what is being done in its honour and we, it seemed, had helped. Sometimes the old women danced alone, twitching arms and shoulders, shuffling feet, minimal movement but always rhythmic. They were thin as boards, breastless, elegant.

At a table beside the corpse guests handed over 500 francs Malagache (fmg), 1,000 fmg, their contribution to the huge cost of the event. Name and amount were noted in an exercise book.

'That book'll be the most important family treasure,' Haja

said. 'Everyone must give something, and it must be more than you were given at your last *famadihana*. If someone gave you even a million fmg you must give them one million one hundred, even if it bankrupts you. You *must*!'

By mid-afternoon there was still no sign of the tomb being opened and latecomers, more members of this vastly extended family who had gathered here from far away, ate on. I was struck by the politeness with which even the adolescents greeted each other, and by the close bonding of the family. The men disappeared behind a shed to swig *toakagasy*, their illegally brewed hooch, and the dancing livened up. At last we paused (incongruously) for the Malagasy National Anthem, hats raised, and then a few speeches of thanks. Shrouds were appearing, and rolled mats on which the ancestors would be exhumed.

'I think we're off,' Haja shouted, and drums pounding we surged towards the outskirts of the village.

The tomb was a pillbox of concrete, hairy with unkempt grass but a house for the dead far more substantial than a house for the living. Why waste money on a house you live in for only a few years when you are in a tomb for eternity? By the time we arrived the musicians were already installed on the roof, the dancers in full swing (one or two so drunk they could barely stand), and the elders – the men – heaving stone slabs from the entrance. We were hustled to the lip of the tomb. A red tunnel yawned in the earth. Steps led down a dry throat to shelves: on these lay the corpses. Nervously, wondering if it was *fady*, Richard raised his camera.

'Yes yes! Photo!' Frenzied drunken people were pushed aside to clear his view. I was grasped by a toothless woman.

'It's a joy for us, this,' she cried, 'a joy! But later we'll weep – you'll see. Ooh la la – how we'll weep.'

Already the intense happiness of some faces was mingling with grief at the prospect of being reunited with loved ones – a parent, a child.

'I'm a *métis*,' the woman explained, 'Swiss-Malagasy. So I know both systems. You see, for the Malagasy just a few flowers on the grave isn't enough, but I prefer the *vazaha* way. I tell my children but they're horrified. Maman, how could we just abandon you like that, they ask. It wouldn't show enough respect. But this is too traumatic for the people.'

'Helena, look!' Haja pulled me towards her. Like a chrysalis being born out of the earth, a long thin bundle rolled in a mat was heaved up to be greeted with clamours of excitement. 'Who is it?' the crowd shouted. A name was called and the closest relatives jostled through the scrum to get close, to touch it, and with the corpse held high above their heads danced away through the crowd, bouncing the corpse up and down as if giving it birthday bumps.

'That's my grandmother,' breathed the drunken Michel. He had gold teeth and clutched me sweatily round the waist before joining the mêlée, waving his hands in the air. More remains emerged and were met with the same euphoria.

A corpse was laid in the laps of some women. While the men were busy in the tomb, here the women gathered. They seemed anxious, absorbed. One danced over the body – I guessed this was her husband – while others appeared to caress the mat. Then the mat was opened. Though still wary of intruding I came nearer and caught a sweetish fermenting smell but whether this was rotting flesh or rum on breath I couldn't tell. In Tibet I had seen a newly-dead girl being butchered and fed to vultures who flapped off into the sky: the Sky Burial. There, only if all parts of the body were consumed, if it left no trace, was the spirit free to be reincarnated. Here it was the opposite: only if the corpse was cared for, cleansed and purified, would the spirit be at peace. Ancestors: not only where we come from, but where we are going. Past, present and future are one.

This was the theory, but I had never been so close to a corpse before. In Tibet I was kept at a distance. For all my preoccupation with ancestors, the romance, the detective work, man as a spirit, here was the gruesome reality. I glanced at Haja – touched base. She nodded, amused, and I moved closer. Inside the roll were what looked like clods of earth mixed with decayed *lambamena*. The remains were even the same red colour as Malagasy earth: earth to earth, land of the ancestors, literally. It bore no visible relation to a human being. The odd bone was visible but little else: previous *famadihana* and termites had broken it up. In any case it is rare for a *famadihana* to take place before at least three years have passed. Anthropologists talk of the flesh separating from the bones, the wet from the dry, the polluted from the sacred. Another corpse brushed against my trousers leaving a rusty patch, but there was nothing horrible, I noticed with relief. The old lady dropped in morsels of beef fat while another woman in an ecstatic state rubbed a handful of the remains round her teeth. I waited for her to swallow it – if she did, would this be cannibalism? She spat it out.

The clods of ancestor mixed with the old decayed *lambamena* were then patted and kneaded like dough, tidied into shape, rolled out of the mat and into a new rust-coloured *lambamena*. This was wrapped around the corpse and made into a parcel, as carefully as if they were going to post it, and tied up with strips torn off the *lambamena*. It was far simpler than the shrouds in the attic at The Pool House, but at last I saw the use to which they should be put.

I noticed that two men were squabbling over the now discarded mat. They were tugging at it, angry and drunken. I learned that the mat, soiled with the remains of an ancestor, is a potent symbol of fertility, and to make love on it is highly prized. To have sex on the putrefied remains of a corpse and for new life to arise from it could seem abhorrent, but in Madagascar even birth is a gift from the dead. To me that day it seemed quite normal.

Some of the bundles were larger – a husband, wife and children wrapped together. As identities are forgotten, remains are combined until nothing is left. In any case it hardly matters who they were or what they did, they were simply ancestors afloat in the ocean of the dead.

'What happens if one of your ancestors is a murderer or something?' I asked Haja.

'He would be excluded from the tomb, so he would be forgotten after death – a far worse punishment for us than prison. But otherwise he would be treated in the same way.'

'So just a normally bad person would be given a *famadihana*?'

'Yes. Otherwise he or she might get angry and seek revenge.'

I couldn't tell if she was smiling. But I liked this idea. It no longer mattered that my ancestors traded in ivory, and black ivory; I no longer need bear any moral responsibility for their actions; they were simply ancestors, dead but with tremendous presence in my life.

'What do you think of our Malagasy customs?' A man with a pock-marked face pulled me aside. In the excitement and heat it was hard to know how to reply, but throughout Madagascar we would be asked this. 'What do you think of our Malagasy *fomba*?' There was always a mixture of diffidence and pride in the question. I liked the idea of keeping the dead alive and not shrouding them in silence, pain and slow forgetting. Keeping the dead alive, not just as a vaporous soul ('whomsoever liveth and believeth in me shall never die') but as a physical reality with whom one can speak and dance and almost have a relationship. Ancestor worship: it could be a conservative force with customs maintained simply because they were the ways of the ancestors rather than because of any intrinsic value. But here ancestor worship was not arcane mumbo-jumbo; it seemed to move with the times. The tomb was built with concrete, and there were guests with degrees in hydraulics and law, yet they saw nothing odd about *famadihana*. Perhaps that is the strangest thing about it, how vibrant it is and how normal.

'For us, *famadihana* is a duty,' the pock-marked man explained. 'We must do it. Our ancestors have given us our rice fields and we must honour them in return.' That seemed only right, far preferable to consigning a parent or grandparent to a cold and solitary grave, or worse, to some numbered plot in an anonymous cemetery. And dancing with the dead, was it so strange? Perhaps it was a metaphor for my own ancestral quest.

There was something else too, the link with a place. At the *famadihana* I saw how entwined are birth, death and the land. Where the tomb lies is where the family fields lie, and is where you come from and to where you will return. Families can be stifling, and perhaps some of the revellers here secretly longed to escape, but I envied this family's sense of identity and of belonging somewhere that many of us have lost. These days of the 'Global Village', the breakdown of local life, have left many people restless and without the confidence of a clear identity. I want to belong in Dartmouth, but perhaps I belong more where I was at school, or where my parents live, or where I live now – or nowhere.

There was a shout from the tomb. 'Whose are these?' A man clutched two greenish-grey skulls. A moment's pause; Haja stifled a giggle. The old woman thought it might be her husband's. She touched it – did those teeth look familiar? – and decided it was. The parcel was unwrapped and the skull placed inside. As soon as it was ready it was snatched from the women and danced off through the crowd, seven times around the tomb, before being reinterred. I stood on the tomb and the landscape, unaffected by this writhing knot, spread away. A kestrel attacked a buzzard overhead and, on the horizon, Antananarivo glittered on its rock. When we sought our hostess to say goodbye, she was so engrossed in her work she looked through us. Nothing mattered but the ancestors. Some thirty bodies were disinterred that afternoon.

André picked us up later. We drove to a church and sat on a wall while the organ played. I was glad of the rest. The flutes and clarinets still shrieked in my ears, and we had eaten virtually nothing all day. But only when the familiar funeral march played did I realize what was going on. The doors opened and a woman was led by her daughters to a hearse. It was her mother she mourned. She wept, barely able to stand in her grief. The hearse was decked in wreaths, and the mourners wore black. It was all so familiar: but for the dust and heat we could have been in any British village. But in three or four years these same dignified people would be cavorting with her body. It was hard to envisage. Yet through *famadihana*, the Malagasy are more able than we are to come to terms with death; Irène had told me that they have no word for 'anguish'. Far from being taboo, after a few years death for most people becomes something to celebrate.

This funeral was unusual, however. By chance, the astrologer had decreed months ago that today should be the *famadihana* for this dead woman's husband, who had died three years previously. The stars were incontrovertible, so at the same tomb the bereaved would have to dance with his body while mourning over hers.

'Don't the cultures clash?' Richard asked André.

'Not at all,' he said, surprised. 'There will often be a priest at a *famadihana*, and most people there will be Christians. Today I expect the *famadihana* will be very low-key. Sometimes people do this deliberately so as to save money on opening up the tomb.'

People said the radon gas given off by Tana's granite cliffs made them weary. Perhaps it was that: it was certainly time to move on. We bought maps of the remote west coast. No roads were marked, but we would get by somehow.

At Irène's party at the English Language Institute I had met a young Englishman named Simon. At once I liked his open friendliness. We discovered by chance that he had been to private views at Richard's gallery, but we had never seen him before. After eight years of working for a smart London art dealer he had abandoned his job to come and live in Madagascar. 'Pursuit and escape, a bit of both,' he said, by way of explanation. I visited him at his Quaker school where for the moment he was teaching English. He had a tiny room and dysentery but he was passionate about Madagascar. His pupils, all pretty young women, asked politely what I was doing there. They had read about Laura's work in the newspapers, they said.

'I am especially interested in *famadihana*,' I added, slowly and clearly. A woman put up her hand. 'My parents have just received an invitation to a *famadihana* and they cannot attend. It is a very big *famadihana* in Ambositra. A King. Maybe you would like their invitation?'

'Do you mean it? Of course I would.' Ambositra was a highland town at the heart of the Betsileo tribe's domain, 170 miles south.

'I am sure the family would be happy to receive you and your husband.'

'When is it?'

'In three weeks' time.'

Richard was keen to change our plans.

'But we've bought the maps now,' I said.

'So what? We can't not go.'

It was then that we met Christine and Brunoh. Walking along Avenue de l'Indépendance, looking at the displays of East European drabness in the shops under the arcades, we got chatting to a woman who was studying English at the university. It was a relief to speak English. Christine was pretty with wavy short hair and wide eyes; her husband Brunoh was unusually tall and had a glass eye. Though still in his thirties he had been invalided out of the army (without a pension) and Christine bore the burden of supporting the family. Unable to find work, they had retired to till their small plot of family land. They spoke heroically of the masses escaping from the corruption of the cities, but really they were desperate, and had come to Tana to sell their remaining possessions. We were both moved by their bravery. We saw them often, and liked them. They were proud, reserved people who had seen better days.

Their four-year-old son, Mbola, was to be circumcised. Circumcision is important to all Malagasy tribes, probably stemming from early Arab influence. Originally it was a communal celebration carried out every seven years but now it is in most places a more private affair, performed on all boys under the age of seven; death beforehand means exile from the tomb and an eternity in a hungry and unloved limbo. Like *famadihana*, circumcision takes place during the dry season, and is almost as much of a social occasion. At lunch one day Brunoh described some of the more peculiar rituals which would take place, rituals which had been laid down by the ancestors.

'Substitutes for the boy have to go and steal sugar cane and water from someone else, and they have to get caught and have a fight.'

'They have to steal?'

'Yes, it's part of proving their manhood. And the father has to eat his son's foreskin on a banana.' They both laughed. Neither of us believed them but they swore it was true.

'Why don't you come?' Christine said. 'It's in fifteen days.'

It would take place in their family home, in Ambositra. It was almost as if some 'other' force – the ancestors perhaps – were propelling us to Ambositra. Simon, who was also a friend of Christine and Brunoh, would join us there.

Before leaving Laura gave a press conference in the Rova and that evening in a restaurant we saw her on the television news. A Malagasy woman recognized her and thanked her for what she had done. The next time I saw her she was a married woman.

CHAPTER SEVEN

DOWN THE EAST COAST

The train east left at 6 am. Full of renewed energy, we heaved on our packs and strode up the still dark Avenue de l'Indépendance, empty but for black trees and men hunched around braziers drinking coffee. Ambositra was 170 miles south, but we had fifteen days in which to get there, so we would go the long way, around three sides of a square, east then south then west. Only now in the dark and bustling station was our adventure really beginning.

It was a long time before the Rova disappeared from view. Women with impossible loads on their heads chugged past; we saw houses marooned in paddy fields. Twisting off the red highlands and down the eastern escarpment, this railway is a turn-of-the-century engineering feat, a French version of the Uganda Railway carved through forested mountains from Antananarivo to the east coast port of Tamatave, causing many deaths in the process. Years before the railway line was built this was the route along which diplomats, traders and missionaries all journeyed to Tana, and left it. The road was kept deliberately bad to deter foreigners, and if they made it to Tana they dreaded the return with its drop back into the 'most pestiferous regions'. We were swallowing nivaquine but the mosquitoes were said to be immune.

The journey had improved. The plastic seats reclined and wore antimacassars. It was not long before a passenger balanced a synthesizer on his lap and played jazz; at the other end of the carriage another plucked a guitar. Their talent made their evident poverty all the more poignant.

As we wound downwards rain folded in and swelled the rivers with earth from the hills: our worst fears of deforestation were quickly realized. Smeared windows gave on to dismal clumps of Australian eucalyptus, the dreaded import that grows fast and provides firewood but sucks all nutrients from the soil. No wild-life survives. Denuded hills, where once jungle grew lush, sprouted hummocks of grass and the fanned leaves of the Ravinala palm, the traveller's tree indigenous to Madagascar that traps rainwater in its broad stems for thirsty passers-by. It is one of Madagascar's symbols, but ironically it is a sign of destruction since it comes with secondary, not primary, growth. When Robert Newman Hunt arrived, Ranavalona crowed in the knowledge that she was protected by her two favourite generals, General Jungle and General Disease, but now the first general was being conquered. Slash-and-burn agriculture is one of the ancestral practices brought from Indonesia; it made the journey a depressing one.

At Perinet, where a small patch of forest remained intact, we got out. The old colonial Hotel de la Gare was full, so a forest warden offered us the choice of the laboratory of his fish farm – abandoned through lack of funds – or the room behind his 'office'. We chose the office. It was a dank hut with rats' dropping scattered over the mattress like seeds. Cobwebs looped the walls. The warden lifted a log that bridged a ditch: a boa constrictor knotted round itself. We touched its firm body.

'It eats the rats,' he said, reassuringly.

He produced a bucket of water and a candle, and indicated the earth closet behind a bush. Then he said goodbye.

We were alone on the edge of the forest.

Rain dripped from the canopy. Suddenly the air ran with a mournful cry.

'Indri!' whispered Richard.

The sound seemed not to travel in a line from one source, but to spread wide, as if all the indri in the forest clamoured instinctively at once. That day it haunted but evaded us. The indri is Madagascar's largest lemur, and is among the earliest mammals to resemble man. Lemurs died out in most other parts of the world, but Madagascar, cast adrift, was free of predators so they evolved here along paths of their own. The Malagasy call the indri 'father-son', believing it embodies the spirits of the ancestors, the cry of our oldest forebears.

We locked our wooden hut and slid along rutted tracks; the olive-green trees were not majestic like Indian jungle trees, but delicate, typically Malagasy. We sat on a bridge listening to the silence which gradually filled with insects, frogs and kingfishers quietly but efficiently going about the business of living. The forest seemed subdued.

Feeling adventurous we set off up stream, brushing through undergrowth, rain dripping on to tree ferns. The forest which had looked small on the map stretched into infinity. I was afraid but Richard's sense of direction was finely tuned. Soon an angry brown lemur sneezed at us, tail lashing, pug face furious. It jumped from branch to branch, determined to make its presence felt. We met another, red with a white chest and shorter tail, and then another, but the indri had gone quiet.

It was then that we noticed the leeches. They slid up our legs seeking gaps between socks and trousers. We flicked them off, revolted, and suddenly the rainforest lost its charm. We hurried back to the bridge and Richard lay with his head in my lap in a brief patch of sun. Absurdly, we began to speak of our house in England, aware that when we returned to it we would remember that bridge in the sun in Madagascar when we dreamed of England, and that we would dream of returning, or of setting off on some new adventure. An escape route without end.

The forest was too wet to light a fire so the time came, after over two months, for the great moment of trying our new meths stove that we had carried all the way from England. Balanced on a bench outside the hut it worked fine. We fried onions and salami with noodles. But when I lifted the frying pan Richard shouted, 'Look out! You've got – *Jesus Christ!*' The stove had stuck to the base of the pan and dropped, spraying flaming meths over the pine needles and the bench. At once I feared a forest fire, and stamped on the flames. Richard was shouting '*Jesus Christ, Jesus Christ*' and I thought he was over-reacting a bit until I saw him flapping at his chest. He was on fire. Immobilized, I stared while he jumped about waving his arms, trying to flick the fire away, but he was protected by his water-proof jacket and managed to put it out. He was very good about it.

We picked pine needles off the remains of our meal and began again. It tasted delicious. We ate in darkness, our torch batteries having died. A tiny sliver of moon shed no light as we felt our way back to the lake; visible only were the glitter of puddles and the shine of Richard's white trainers. Insects wheezed, the dam roared; I heard voices, engines and footsteps, but it was only city noises I had brought in my head.

Our candle guttered low and by seven o'clock it was too dark to read or do anything but lay out our sleeping bags and tuck our mosquito net firmly around us to keep out the rats. Richard hung a pine branch above the candle sending antlers of shadow up the wall; we risked another fire but the singed needles smothered the smells.

I don't remember sleeping.

As the river Vohitra broadened, the hills flattened, and we continued by train to Tamatave. We bought banana fritters from the window, slept and read intermittently as red brick houses became thatched huts, and pines and eucalyptus became palm groves sprouting ferns like Afghan coats. At once we could feel the change of altitude, and took off layers of damp clothing.

Cross French tourists with waxed legs complained when we blundered on board with dripping rucksacks. Though it was August – high season – we had seen few foreigners in Tana, just the odd scruffy naturalist. They must have been secreted in the Hilton and now converged at Perinet. They were too big, too pink, too glossy, and too many.

We escaped into the night in Tamatave, port of riff-raff and pirates. An aisle of hungry *pousse-pousse* drivers fought for our fare. We took one each, half lying, half sitting, rucksacks in our arms, and were pulled through the streets on unsprung seats. Heavy breathing, flat bare feet flapping on tarmac, tiny candles wavering, metal wheels, muscular thighs: above all, laughter. *Pousse-pousse* (from the French for 'push-push') are common in most Malagasy towns. I never got used to having a man tow me to my destination but sometimes there was no alternative.

For a port, Tamatave was oddly silent. At 8 pm the boulevards and avenues of colonial palms were deserted. On the terrace of the smart Hotel Joffre a white couple sat drinking, alone. Even the next morning the market was hushed. Villas of wooden weather-boarding and tin roofs were spaced apart by gardens: a generous, pleasant, rather full place.

Here Robert Newman Hunt, Norsworthy and all the captains landed. They were thankful to come in safely over the reef. The bay was beautiful, a sweeping arc, but hills lowered on the horizon and they knew that up there power lay. They stepped ashore, swaying still after days at sea and nervous of the dark-skinned Betsimisaraka who ran down to meet them. Though the sight of a church mission was reassuring, Robert Newman Hunt was dismayed by the port itself. There was simply nothing going on.

Today there were three ships in dock, not much for the largest port on the world's fourth largest island. We wheedled our way past the guard and stood dwarfed by soaring hulls, engines churning, pumps regurgitating. Chinese immigrants do much of the trading, a port official explained, but port tariffs are too high. A ship was leaving, and with a great unbuckling processed into the open sea, smoke threading overhead, rump riding the waves, one hoot its parting gesture. Who knows where the cargo – coffee, vanilla, graphite, mica, minute parts of Madagascar – would end up?

We had no time to waste. We wanted to head south but had been warned that there were no roads. The annual cyclones have destroyed most of the bridges. A boat was the answer. We went to SCAC, the shipping company.

'We only deal with sea shipping, and nothing's going south at the moment,' said a surprised and friendly man. 'I don't think what you want to do is possible, but you could try the "*port fluviale*".' (Parallel to the coast for over 280 miles runs a network of waterways called the Pangalanes.)

'That sounds a good idea.'

We bumped over pot-holes out of town. The *port fluviale* was a brand-new construction, acres of empty tarmac and a hangar-sized warehouse. More were being built with French Aid. It was empty, though in the distance a few barges were being unloaded on the quay. They sat in a solid mat of water hyacinth.

'No no, it's impossible,' the dockers said, and pointed us to the 'tourist' boat, a motor launch, long unused and draped in tarpaulin. 'In any case, no boats are leaving until Thursday.'

Today was Saturday. There was no way we would get to Ambositra on time if we sat in Tamatave for five days. We had to leave today or tomorrow.

'And,' they added, 'none will take passengers.'

'I knew it was too much to hope for,' I said to Richard, pessimistic as ever, staving off what now seemed inevitable disappointment.

'Don't let's give up yet,' he replied, optimistic as ever.

We pleaded, but the No was final. We had failed on this journey already. It was not just the circumcision and the *famadihana*:

I hated the thought of future regrets, of the journey I didn't make, the journey that went on without me.

Then I explained about my ancestors; they traded here, I said. We were following their route. The foreman looked more sympathetic, and translated for the rest, who were amused by the sight of these two desperate *vazaha* in their sleepy port. A hundred and fifty years ago, I added encouragingly. Surely they would do something for us.

'You must go and see the boss. Maybe he can help.'

'OK, anything, thanks. Where can we find him?'

More discussion. A map was drawn on the back of an envelope. People added bits. It looked complicated.

'It's hopeless,' I insisted.

We hung around a while longer, not sure what to do next. Even if we found the boss's house he was bound not to be there. We sat glumly on the quay.

'There's the boss!' Two men got out of a land cruiser, one in a suit. 'The one in the shorts.'

'The *vazaha*?'

'Yes.'

Monsieur Gallois, a fair-haired Frenchman, owned all the boats. He employed two thousand people in sisal plantations in the south-east and in a large graphite mine near Vatomandry, seventy-five miles down the Pangalanes. Again I explained our story. He too seemed amused.

'Those boats,' he said, pointing to rusting metal lighters lying below us. 'They're going to Vatomandry. They're taking rice to my workers.'

'Could we go on them?'

'Are you serious? You'd be crazy. Look at them – there's no cabin or anything. They're not cruisers.'

'We don't mind, we'll take anything.'

'It would be two or three days.'

'That's OK.'

'Even if you get to Vatomandry you'll be stuck there. There's nothing after that. No roads. You just can't get through. You could be there for weeks. And there aren't any boats south of Vatomandry either – the canals are all choked up.'

We unfolded the map. 'A road's marked here.'

'That's completely out of date. There's nothing left.'

'We could always walk.'

'It's the lagoons – you can't walk across them.'

Richard and I looked at each other.

'You're welcome to go on my boats if you really want, but it's a big risk.'

'We'll take the risk,' we chorused.

'OK then. But you'll have to be quick. We're leaving in an hour.'

Yelling with delight, Richard took my hand and we ran back across the tarmac to the road. When we raced back to the port with our luggage and extra supplies from the market Monsieur Gallois was still shaking his head in disbelief. 'You'll regret it,' he warned. The Malagasy port official, plump in a crisp white shirt, thought we were mad. The boats were still being unloaded of sacks of shimmering graphite.

'It's mostly sold in Scotland,' Monsieur Gallois explained. 'Attention!' he shouted as a man almost lost his head under a crane. 'These Betsimisaraka, they're imperturbable. Imperturbable.' He shrugged. 'Nothing bothers them. All they want to do is lie under a tree and dream. It's almost impossible to get them to do any work.' During the colonial era this was a common French complaint.

'So the Betsimisaraka are quite different from the Merina,' I observed.

'Yes, the highlanders are the workers, and the *côtiers* are not.'

'But President Ratsiraka is Betsimisaraka, isn't he?'

'Yes.'

The Gallois were among the few remaining colonial families. He had been born here, as had his mother, yet he had never learned Malagasy. Things were deteriorating, he said, especially in the last few years.

'Before 1975 there was no thieving for example. Nothing. Now you have to be careful all the time. And how can you blame them? The minimum wage is 40,000 fmg per month, and a kilo of rice is 500 fmg. Each man eats a kilo and a half of rice a day, and has to feed his family . . .'

'It's impossible to live.'

'Yes. And have you heard the latest? All the best pilots have just been offered jobs by Air France with a salary four times what they can earn here, so they've all gone. There aren't any pilots left who are qualified to fly the Boeings. So they've all been grounded. There's only the small planes left. So now you can't get a seat on a flight. Hopeless. Hopeless collapse. It's sad. And then look at this port. What's the point of it? There's no traffic on these canals, so what's the point of that enormous warehouse?'

'Is it empty?'

'Completely and utterly empty. And always will be. That's aid for you. You can bet that someone did very nicely out of it, thank you.'

There were so many Aid stories. There was the one about stocking Lake Victoria with Nile perch, a carnivorous fish that ate the native fish. The locals did not like Nile perch, and the new fish was so oily that it had to be smoked rather than sun-dried for transport to the cities, increasing deforestation round the lake. Then there were the cashew plantations at Mtwara in southern Tanzania. The factories were built, experts employed, only to find that cashews cannot grow in Mtwara. Now this canal project, wasted money with people being given what they 'ought to have' rather than being asked what they need.

Gallois was explaining our plans to the Captain, a smiling old man who shook hands.

'He doesn't speak French.'

The Captain was in charge of a tug named *Dauphine*. This would pull four lighters, one of which carried the fuel. 'You can go with him, or you can choose another boat, whichever you like.'

Dauphine would be noisy and smelly. We chose *Touraine*, the last of the lighters, the furthest away. We lowered ourselves on deck, the dockers gathering round for a laugh. The metal surface was almost untouchable in the heat, and crumbly with rust. *Dauphine* started up, pumping filth, and we forged through the water hyacinths. Monsieur Gallois waved. 'Good luck,' he called.

'Thank you, thank you,' we shouted. We were jubilant.

Hoping to have the boat to ourselves, we had barely left the port when we stopped beneath a bridge and dozens of women and children appeared. They carried baskets and cooking pots and hesitated when they saw us, but the captain nodded and they ran down the bank. A plank was pushed out and they wobbled aboard, and vanished down a trapdoor into the holds. Soon we stopped again; this time six dug-out canoes loaded with bananas were roped to our stern. We were not the only ones looking for a ride. How much did Monsieur Gallois know?

The canal opened on to a lagoon, protected from the sea by a narrow spit of sand along which ran the Tamatave-Tana railway line. For all that day we would retrace our route, though a good deal slower. Into the distance spread flat expanses of green and blue. Reeds and *vali* leaves, broad as bananas, water and sky. Fishermen lay low in the water, slipping unseen through stockaded bamboo traps that zig-zagged from shore to shore leaving a channel only just wide enough for us. They must have seemed sinister hazards to Robert Newman Hunt and his captains. Robert Newman Hunt wrote to Queen Ranavalona asking if he could send all his goods up to the capital, but in those days no canals linked the lagoons so at each bank the boats had to be unloaded, and all the cargo and the boats themselves lifted out and carried overland to the next lagoon. It was a laborious affair.

The distant highlands swirled with cloud.

It was hard to distinguish passengers from crew; they shared the steering and took turns to cook. A man chopped wood and lit a fire in the bottom of an oil drum with cut-away sides. Rice was washed, sifted, and cooked, and a man lathered his head with soap, then rinsed his head and the decks with a bucket of canal water. They were more African-looking than the Merina. Just twenty years after Robert Newman Hunt arrived, a stalwart Austrian lady named Ida Pfeiffer determined to explore Madagascar even though – or perhaps because – by then there were no other white women on the island. All the missionaries and their wives had long fled. She arrived in Tamatave and had nothing good to say about the natives:

They have wide mouths and thick lips, broad flat noses, protruding chins, and prominent cheekbones. Their complexion varies through all shades of muddy brown, their hair . . . is marked by a peculiar hideousness, it is coal black but as woolly as the negroes, and much coarser and longer, sometimes attaining a length of two feet. When the hair is worn in all its native luxuriance it has a horribly disfiguring effect. The face seems quite lost in a virgin forest of thick frizzled hair, standing out in all directions.

I liked the sound of this, but these days the women had tamed their virgin forests into plaits and the men wore theirs cropped short.

*

One by one children emerged from the hold to gather round us, shy but curious. We felt shy too: none of them spoke a word of French. At last I would be forced to try my Malagasy, which I had studied for three months in London. The wife of the pastor of the French church in Soho was Malagasy, and for several evenings a week entombed beneath the church off bustling Oxford Street, she tried to instil in me something of the complexities of the language.

Malagasy provides one of the strongest proofs of the origins of the people. It shares its roots with Maanyan, a language spoken in south-east Borneo, but has links even further afield. *Vahiny* means guest or stranger in Malagasy, while *vahini* means girl in Tahitian Polynesian, suggesting that settlers travelled both west to Madagascar and south-east to the Pacific, and that for some reason 'girl' and 'guest' should be linked.

At least it has a Roman alphabet, thanks to the LMS missionaries. Previously, where there was writing the Arabic script was used, but it was Messrs Jones and Griffiths who in the 1820s were responsible for the written language as we know it. Radama I had insisted on a phonetic language, but to mollify the French faction at his court and to end furious disagreements between the Welsh, one of whom threatened to include the Welsh 'w' for the 'oo' sound, he proclaimed that the consonants should be pronounced as in English and the vowels as in French. It must be the fault of the Welsh that most words are so very long.

English and French words for things that had never existed here before were absorbed too and, typical of the Malagasy, made their own. The English word rabbit became *rabitro*, but *ra* is a word of respect, not permissible for a mere rabbit, so the first syllable was dropped. Book became *boky*, pencil became *pensily*, school – *sekoly*, bible – *baibole*; *du vin* was translated as *divay*, *français* as *frantsay*, and *du thé* as *dite*; there is *seza (la chaise)*, *latabatra (la table)*, *lalimoara (l'armoire)*. Thanks to the worthy LMS the English words are mostly education words; French words are mostly food words, and home comforts, which is just as it should be.

The language works on two levels, one simple, the other the elaborate tradition of oratory. The latter is filled with sophisticated metaphors and elliptical parallels. The indirectness of the language, so expressive of their reserved character, is something of which the Malagasy are proud. English – and French even more so – they find shockingly blunt. In the bilingual newspapers any criticism of the government is always expressed in Malagasy; the journalist can hint with far more subtlety.

Even on the simple level when I came to adverbs of place I was already defeated. Every relationship had a word of its own. *Ety* – I can see the object and touch it. *Eto* – it is a bit further away, I can still see it but not touch it. *Izatsy* – I can see a bit of it, but not all. *Ato* – it is next to me, but I can't see it; *atsy* – I can't see it but I know it's there; *aty* – it's very near but I can't see it (i.e. it's inside me). There are dozens of such words. The Malagasy need to situate themselves exactly in the cosmogony, not only in relation to each other, but also in relation to rocks and streams and stars; if you know where you are, then you are less likely to put a step out of place and offend *fady* or the ancestors.

My first sentence was nothing special. 'What is your name?' I asked a pretty girl with hair wrapped in two knots at her ears. She looked blank. Though all Malagasy speak the language, there are many dialects. My teacher spoke Merina. I tried again. Her name was glorious: Philomena Boly.

'Where are you going, Philomena Boly?' I hazarded.

She and her father Georges were going just a few miles south. Georges took our phrase book and map, and pointed to words he wanted to hear in English. They all found the curt sound of English hilarious.

Georges's care for Philomena Boly was touching. He folded a sack for her to sit on. 'She's hungry,' he complained, awaiting his turn for the cut-away drum. 'Hungry and cold.' It rained frequently and we all retreated into the hold at the stern. Here a sort of bed had been rigged up, a sheet of cardboard across the metal ribs of the lighter. It was not much; dark, rusty and home to cockroaches, but once we clanked shut the metal doors at least it was dry. I wrapped Philomena Boly in my shawl.

At 4 pm we moored at Ambavorano, a village hidden behind trees. Each house was identical, a single room built of bleached woven palm stems and bamboo, raised on stilts two feet off the carefully swept sand. They stood in rows, each house facing the same direction. This was in accordance with *vintana*, or destiny, a complex system rooted in Islam that together with *fady* controls the lives of most Malagasy. The world is conceived as rectangular, and all these houses are miniature worlds, built in relation to the four cardinal points of the compass. They stand on a north–south axis, with the door on the west. *Vintana* and spacial organization are interrelated in an esoteric way. Different areas of the house represent the minutes of the hour, the hours of the day, the days of the lunar month and the months of the year, so the new year resides in the north-east corner nearest the rising sun. As it travels around the house, *vintana* gives each of the days and the months its own character and destiny, some good, some bad. According to the day or month's position in the rectangle of the house the different *vintana* agree or disagree. A man and woman born on a day or a time situated on opposing sides of the house will have opposing destinies and should not marry. A child's *vintana* may be opposed to her father's and so be a threat. Certain actions must take place in certain parts of the house, and establishing the exact position of the *vintana* at any one time may be vital in deciding when and how to act. It is essential for the Malagasy to know exactly where they stand.

It was not until later that we saw *vintana* in action. Here we were struck simply by the ordered neatness of the houses, not aligned by planners or architects but by the ancestors.

Women looking like East Africans with coloured cotton around their waists pounded rice, beating human-high pestles on to wooden mortars. Their bodies were shaped by their work: narrow hips and jutting buttocks. They called me over to have a go, and were disgusted at the feeble amount of effort I put in. Richard came around the corner and his look of surprise caused even more hilarity but young children fled screaming at the sight of us. How much more frightened they would have been 150 years earlier when the first white travellers came this way! I suspect the watchful faces were more shy than hostile, but a nineteenth-century gentleman from Dartmouth might have found them intimidating.

Some passengers gathered in a tiny shop, which was obviously a regular stop, to buy sweets or a single cigarette. The men already stank of rum. A family of plump women, clearly better-off than the others, wore make-up and gave me suspicious looks. It was hard to know how to break the ice. I felt self-conscious and disoriented, but perhaps it was just a combination of too much sun and not enough food. Everyone was preparing their meals; it was time for us to do the same. We set up our cooker on deck.

There was a look of amazement, a shout, and soon men, women and children clattered over the boats to watch, our every action increasing their mirth. Luckily the rain saved us and they vanished.

The plump women rigged up a plastic sheet and lit fires. They were on the petrol boat. *'Liquide inflammable'* warned a notice. Ironically their boat was named *Ny Aina* – life.

We were invited to sleep on the oily floor of the *Dauphine*, the most comfortable place in the convoy, between the steering cable and the water barrel. The Captain produced a mat and a candle, and as he shut us in for the night searched for words and came up with *Bon voyage*. Off on our ship of sleep.

The plump women played hymns on the radio and clanked saucepans and pounded overhead. But even when the party subsided we could not sleep. The floor was too hard, there were fleas, and we were too over-excited. Beyond a narrow partition lay a man, woman and child whispering unknown intimacies. Richard peered through a hole and found himself inches away from a shiny black face dragging deeply on a cigarette.

Rain drummed on deck before dawn and splashed my face. It got light fast, and we left at 5.45 am, no waiting around, just up and off. It was a clear, cold dawn, the sun rising over the invisible (but always audible) sea. At once a whistling chorus began, especially effective through gaps in missing teeth which enabled the whistler to split the notes into chords.

The Pangalanes widened into a vast lake flashing with white water and the odd paddle blade. They were stealthy these canoe-ists, creeping up banks, and for some reason not using sail as they do on the backwaters of India. Sometimes a group circled round a shoal of fish and beat them with sticks and cries into their nets. At the sight of other motor boats, coming perhaps from Monsieur Gallois's mine, all the passengers fled down their holes like rabbits, emerging only when the coast was clear.

Then the waters narrowed again, and our fleet snaked between empty jungles where orchids flowered, the odd lonely hut visible on shore. Secret villages were revealed, and then out to the stumpy deforested hills again. All day long the water expanded and contracted, winding its laborious way south.

Philomena Boly, still wrapped in my shawl, snuggled close and gazed up with hopeful eyes. She was thirteen years old, but like most Malagasy children looked much younger than her age.

'Take her to England,' her father joked. He was suffering from his night of rum and was angry when we refused him our malaria pills. They got off at the next village without saying goodbye.

Slowly – almost as slowly as our flotilla moved – time passed. I cut Richard's hair which entertained people for a while. Then that was over, and it was still only 10.30 in the morning. At first the enforced idleness was a relief: responsibility for getting south was out of our hands. But gradually time stretched.

We had read our books and left them in Tana. All that remained was *Taboo*, a study of Malagasy customs by a Norwegian named Jørgen Ruud. It listed every sort of *fady* – plant *fady*, animal *fady*, marriage *fady* and sex *fady*. Every tribe, every village, every family worked with different complex restrictions derived from past incidents or divination. We carried it throughout our journey, hoping it would keep us out of trouble in the villages, but it turned out that Ruud had made his study between 1934 and 1954 and with people moving around the country in search of work the old ways were breaking down and *Taboo* was considered long out of date.

Our helmsman was a rough-looking fellow with the hooked nose of an Arab. His skin was black and crinkly as a lizard's, and he grinned pink gums stuck with three yellow stumps. He wore a tattered boiler-suit split across the backside. Mostly he sat on a tyre at the stern wrapped in a blanket, hand on the tiller, staring at the flat watery nothingness, or lying on his cardboard table. A boy boiled haricot beans for all his meals. He was bemused by us and by my Malagasy. Then one evening he produced a plank strung with metal wires, knelt on rusty old *Touraine* to grip it between his knees, and began to play. It was light, delicate music, the music of water and of Madagascar, not mysterious like Indian music, or dangerous like African, but gentle and fresh.

Dusk turned yucca plants to silhouettes clawing the sky; now there were no lights, no houses, no villages. Our engine intruded – reassuringly – on the emptiness.

Our helmsmen gestured for us to sleep in his cabin. We lit a candle, and instantly a row of faces lined the crack in the partition between us and the rest of the hold where the other passengers slept on graphite sacks. We waved, and they vanished, only creeping back later. We tried to ignore them. Incarcerated down here all noises were magnified. Small waves banged against the sides, and when we brushed the banks it seemed the world had ended. The rain was deafening. We laid our sleeping bags on the cardboard.

'It's like lying on a bier,' Richard murmured. 'Being drawn through the night.'

When at last we moored we heard shouting, disco music. There was excited chatter and footsteps. At 5 am it was still going on. We hauled ourselves out and found the disco in a large thatched building. People shuffled blankly over the earth floor, lights flashing, youths in jeans, patterned shirts, white trainers. To our helmsman's delight (the story was retold several times) Richard had a bit of a dance. Around the hall huts with rusting tin roofs stood on stilts behind picket fences. It was a ramshackle strip between fresh water and salt, littered with rotting coconut husks. Beyond, the Indian Ocean crashed on to the beach misting the air. We didn't linger: like most beaches, this was the village shitting place.

Suddenly, at the stroke of six o'clock, the disco vanished. The lights went out, the music ended, and small groups in the dismal early light queued for vegetables. The flashy shirts became tattered rags, the high heels bare feet, and the disco a market. The dream was over. The rather haughty plump girls returned to *Ny Aina* to clean their teeth over the side and put on make-up; none of our fellow passengers on *Touraine* had danced.

'Too expensive,' they said. It cost 300 fmg, about 12p.

Richard brought back fried cakes made from minced manioc, a woody root vegetable, and a kilo of rice wrapped in a banana leaf. At once the shout went up: the *vazaha* has bought rice! You eat *rice*? Even the most sophisticated Malagasy could never get over this, as if rice was something peculiar to them. When we explained that many people in Europe ate rice once or twice a week, they looked disbelieving, suspicious even. Rice belonged to them, not us. We ate bread. That was the principal difference between Malagasy and *vazaha*. Rice was their sacred food. 'Rice and I are one,' King Andrianampoinimerina had declared.

The passengers gathered to watch us cook. They thought little of our methods. For a start we did not eat enough, and we mixed it with tomatoes and sardines. This was almost sacrilegious. As the hours droned by we took to watching them, and began to realize what rice means. At dawn the plump women begin their pounding, even as the boats move. For three whole days they cannot be without their mortars, reverberating through the metal hulls. Then comes the winnowing in a broad flat basket, and the family pick out stones. More sifting, then washing, meanwhile the fire is lit, and the rice loaded into huge cauldrons, lid on. Three-quarters of an hour later it is whisked down into the hold and devoured with tablespoons, often not accompanied by meat or vegetables but just a little salt. The rice must be a solid lump, and burnt on the bottom. After the lengthy preparation, the actual eating is not an elaborate ritual but a brief, private affair.

Then comes the rice water, poured over the burnt crust and heated. When I first tasted *ranovola* I thought there had been a mistake – how could anyone drink burnt rice water? – but we both came to like this hot smokey drink and even to brew it ourselves. The sodden crust is the finale, the favourite part. Then comes the washing-up, scrubbing the spoons and plates with handfuls of sand. By that time it is midday, and the whole process begins again. And then again for supper. Every day the same. Life is about eating enough rice.

Our helmsman's mate rarely worked on the boat, he was too busy caring for his family. His wife had sullen looks and a shiny purple dress. She wrapped an orange *lamba* round her chest and tucked in a baby. Slightly older babies played on deck, and washed their own clothes and helped the eldest daughter cook and clean. When the husband cut his foot blood slid on to the rusty boat, but the wife took no notice. She looked hard. But later, through the crack in our partition, we glimpsed them lying in the hold in a single pool of light, him in her arms, while she lovingly picked lice from his hair.

We too lay about – trying to get comfortable on the iron-hard deck – and from a distance watched the life of the convoy. It felt odd to be so detached, but a relief too. Participating, trying to communicate: after two months it had become exhausting. I sensed we had failed, had not been entertaining or friendly enough, but Richard never minded that sort of thing. He often got fed up with talking, and sat dreaming or gazing at the light on the reeds.

In mid-afternoon *Ny Aina* stuck on the mud. Nothing would move her. The *Dauphine* tugged, engines whining, and the crew stripped off and waded in, prodding around the hull with sticks. I had visions of Ambositra, and of us not getting there. We could

An Indian Bohra mosque overlooking the old dhow harbour in Mombasa. Only a few dhows remain, but when the Newmans arrived in the 1830s this coast was bobbing with Booms, Sambuks, Ghanjahs and Zarooks. Steps down to the harbour below the mosque were built by the crew of **HMS** *Leven*, who under Captains Emery and Owen landed in Mombasa in 1824 and declared it a British Protectorate. It is possible that the Newmans heard about the potential for trade here through this expedition.

Omanis, Africans and Omani-Indians in Zanzibar. We were travellers
in a travellers' world.

After the revolution in 1964, most of the Omanis who had dominated
the island for 130 years fled back to Oman. Their palaces were gutted,
and poor squatters from neighbouring islands moved in.
(Below) Wooden lorry no.10 took us south to Makunduchi.

A mosque door in Zanzibar, its carving a typical blend of
Indian and Arab.

Advertisements for clove products decorate the wall of the first British Consulate in Zanzibar, where a plaque commemorates the visits of Burton and Speke before setting out in search of the source of the Nile. Just as the Newmans arrived in Zanzibar, Sultan Seyyid Said decreed that for every three coconut palms, a clove tree must be planted, and so laid the foundations for Zanzibar's wealth. The harbour is still filled with sacks of cloves, mostly destined for Indonesia as clove cigarettes.

Turkish baths at Marahubi Palace in Zanzibar, built in 1882, where Sultan Barghash was attended by his ninety-nine concubines, mostly slaves from Nyasaland.

(Above) Beside the Friday Mosque a successful headmaster ceremoniously announces his *'Grand Mariage'*. In line with Comorian tradition, he will leave his first wife and family to marry a younger, prettier wife and begin again.
(Below) Ahmed in his family's mosque, Moroni.

Fishermen set out at dawn from Maroantsetra in north-east
Madagascar. Their boats have barely changed since Maroantsetra was
a haven for European pirates who cruised the shark-filled waters of the
Indian Ocean during the late seventeenth and early eighteenth
centuries.

FAMADIHANA, THE EXHUMATION OF THE DEAD
IN THE HIGHLANDS OF MADAGASCAR

(Left) Musicians summon the spirits of the ancestors to reinhabit their bodies so as to appreciate what is being done in their honour.

(Below) The extended family dances towards the tomb on the outskirts of Antananarivo. The rolled mat is for lifting the corpses out of the tomb. A coffin carries an ancestor who has died far from home; where the tombs lie is where you come from and to where – if the family can afford it – you will someday return.

(Left) The tomb is opened and the corpses re-emerge like chrysalises from the ground. Only the family elders are allowed into the tomb.

(*Left*) Wrapped in a mat, the corpse is seized by its closest relatives and danced around the tomb. Later the mat will be squabbled over: dusted with the remains of the ancestor, this is a potent symbol of fertility, and to make love on it is highly prized. Putrefaction leads to procreation: odd, and yet not odd in Madagascar, where birth and death are entwined.

(*Above*) Little remains of the corpse except old rotted shrouds.
(*Above right*) Wrapped in a new shroud, the ancestor is danced seven times around the tomb before being reinterred, clean and well clothed. There is nothing macabre, just an overwhelming sense of joy.
(*Right*) Bulls are sacrificed to the ancestors, and cut up to be boiled in fat for the feasting. Everyone must honour the ancestors and the family by eating something.

Antananarivo, Madagascar's capital. The hill-top church at
Faravohitra marks the site where in 1849 four Christians were punished
for their faith by being burnt alive. Below are spread the white
umbrellas of the market.

Fish, some of which are reared in the flooded paddy-fields, are displayed in the market. The delicacy of the pattern is typical of the Malagasy.

Near Antalaha on the north-east coast of Madagascar, a man bundles his pods of vanilla for export to the USA for ice-cream. Vanilla is an orchid from Mexico, and along with coffee and cloves has become one of Madagascar's main export crops.

Over half the world's species of chameleon live only in Madagascar.
(Below) Stepped paddy-fields near Maroantsetra in north-east
Madagascar. The Indonesian origins of the Malagasy can be seen in
their cultivation of rice, which plays a central part in their life and culture.

Wading across the Masoala Peninsula between Antalaha and Maroantsetra.

be here for hours. But by chance the *Dauphine*'s sister tug passed – the only other boat we had seen all day – and managed to push the lighter free. Passengers were being transferred from boat to boat, and suddenly our captain shouted at us to collect our things. This new boat would go not to the graphite mine but direct to Vatomandry, and there was room for us on board. What? Us? *Now*? There was barely time to say goodbye.

We bounced joyfully into Vatomandry. We had made it to our first stop and it felt good to use our legs. Now our journey could begin again.

'I wonder if there's a hotel,' I said.

'Who cares?' Richard was elated. 'What does it matter? Adventure. This is what it's all about.'

The town smelt of flowers. Every house was smothered in them, and birds sang. There was a hotel, a bungalow with huts in the garden. Like most of Madagascar, it had come down in the world. Our hut had a bed but the shelves were thick with rat shit. Richard tried to pretend it was old, or that it was bats, but when I found teeth marks on the soap I knew better. Richard complained but I insisted on packing up everything again and changing huts. On the verandah we drank excellent Malagasy beer. Four men in suits discussed prices of coffee and cloves, Madagascar's export crops, and the dire state of the economy.

We studied the map, already falling apart having been unfolded so often, and measured kilometres. It would take one day to get to Mahanoro if we could find the transport (lorries were said to go that way) and if Monsieur Gallois was wrong about the bridges. Otherwise we would have to walk and find boats, which would obviously take much longer. But at dawn we found a taxi-brousse with its engine ticking.

'Mahanoro?'

'Yes, Mahanoro!'

'Really? Rich, do you hear that? You have room for us?'

'There is always room.'

They had just arrived from Tamatave, and were leaving in ten minutes.

'You're lucky,' said John, the driver. 'We only come this way once a week.'

It was an old Bedford van with rows of seats so cramped together that no one's legs could fit between them. 'Do not drink rum or speak to the driver' ordered a notice. Both were ignored. We could barely see the road for the bags and bodies (I soon had a child asleep on my lap) and the rain which streamed through the screw-holes in the roof, and through ill-fitting windows.

'It's a reservoir,' observed a woman sitting beside me, pointing at the red mire beneath our wheels. We lurched through clove and coffee plantations and stopped at a river bank. A small 'hotely', a hut, produced tea in enamel mugs and steamed manioc tasting of chestnuts, while we waited for the ferry, which arrived on time: so far so good. But after thirty kilometres and five hours we stopped at our second river. This time there was no ferry.

We stood around the taxi-brousse chatting. A beautiful Indian *métis*, a young man with a straight Indian nose and slanting Malagasy eyes, eulogized about Madagascar. 'Will you be going to Nosy Be?' (A tropical island off the north-west coast.)

'I expect so.'

'*Aah. C'est du paradis.*' He sighed. '*C'est presque Paris.*'

I became aware of an elderly man hovering nearby. He wore shorts and a stetson and he trembled as he spoke. 'Excuse me, may I ask why you are here in Mahanoro district?'

'We're just travelling.' I explained about our rendezvous in Ambositra. It might have seemed odd that we were hurrying to reach a circumcision and an exhumation, but he merely nodded, and then frowned.

'But where is your guide?'

'We don't have a guide.'

'How can you find your way?' It seemed incomprehensible to him. Again and again we encountered this sort of anxiety on our behalf.

'We like to be free, and go where we want.'

'Ah, you're doing a tour of Madagascar then?'

'Sort of.'

He seemed pleased by this, but I felt uncomfortable. Our easy tourism beside his poverty. He had served in the French Army so at least he had travelled to Tana and to Diego Suarez in the far north, but he would never see as much of his own country as we were to do. It was not just his lack of money that held him back, it was also his fear. Lurking beneath the Malagasy charm and good humour was almost always this lack of confidence. As if to offer an excuse for our 'free' wandering I explained about my ancestors. He was delighted by this, but even more delighted to hear we were English.

'It's incredible.' His lower lip quivered. 'You are English so you must be Anglican?'

'Yes, well sort of.'

'This is incredible, because I too am Anglican. I can't believe this.' He laughed and shook my hand, and told the people standing round us the story. 'You're Anglican and I'm Anglican. We're both Anglican.' He shook my hand a second time. 'The vicar of my church in Mahanoro speaks excellent English. When we get there I'll take you to meet him if you like. We'll go together. Would you like that?'

'Yes, very much. Thank you.'

'It's incredible. In fact, I want to invite you to my house. You can stay there. You can stay as long as you like. And then I'll take you to the Presbytery. It's because we are both Anglican that I say this. I would be honoured to show you my Bible.'

I tried, rather guiltily, to remember the last time I had been to an Anglican church. As we sauntered over to a hotely where the *métis* and his friends were seated round a table, my new friend explained. There were smiles and handshakes all round. They moved up to make room for us. A bottle of sugar cane rum was produced.

'Try it, come on.'

It tasted good. Then came sugar cane 'beer', brown and yeasty. I noticed that the Anglican swallowed both with excessive haste, and flared briefly when someone took the bottle from him. His trembling grew less. With each new arrival in the hotely our story was explained again, and we shook hands again. Fish cooked with ginger and rice were produced from a smoke-blackened cave.

'It's wonderful that you come in these hotelys with us and eat rice like that,' the *métis* enthused. 'I've never seen a *vazaha* eat rice before.' In their drunken state they wanted to embrace us in warmth and comradeship. After the awkward feelings on the convoy, the lack of communication, I basked in it.

'We are companions in travel!' they cried. 'We share the hardships, and we must share the rum too.'

Rum flowed to the Anglican's heart. 'I've never spoken to a *vazaha* before, and you're so nice!' His eyes were moist. 'I want to introduce you to my wife. She is also very nice.'

'Thank you, I'd like that.'

An hour passed, but still no ferry. The Anglican went to seek news and returned ashamed and cross.

'I can't believe it. It's broken down. We'll have to spend the night here.'

We got out our map. Time was short. We could find a canoe to paddle us across and continue the journey on foot. We would enjoy that. This is *living* we said to each other, being on the move, plunging in each day without knowing where we would end up or how we would get there. But for the sake of speed we waited for the ferry. The Anglican invited us to visit a sugar cane 'factory', so we wandered up the path away from the river.

'I want to invite you to my house,' he repeated. 'What I eat, you eat.'

'Thank you.'

'It's nothing to me. I want to do this.'

'Thank you, you're very kind.'

'What's mine is yours.'

'Thanks.'

'By the way, what do you think of this system apartheid?'

'Apartheid? I detest it.'

'Good. That's why I want to invite you to my home. And because you're an Anglican.'

Richard walked apart, looking at the flashes of orange and scarlet birds that sprung up from the marshes around us.

'Listen!' Over the trees echoed a hooting, a descending scale of bubbles of sound, mysterious, calling us to the jungle. We wanted to stay still and just absorb it, but the Anglican kept on. 'So it's really the first time you've been to Mahanoro?'

'Yes.'

'It's incredible. You really don't know anyone there?'

'No.'

The delay of the ferry brought out all his frustrations about the country, unleashed now that we were out of earshot. The flood of warmth was turning to bitterness. He kicked at the earth.

'You come all this way, and now you have to wait and you have your rendezvous in Ambositra. It's too much.'

'It's all right,' I murmured, soothingly.

'This place!' He almost spat. 'I only came back here because my parents were old. It was better in the army.' He was now a technical adviser to a local commune. 'It's hopeless here. The roads are so bad, we're all so poor. Nothing works. Last month there wasn't even a taxi-brousse so I had to do the whole journey on foot. I walked for eleven hours.'

The sugar cane factory consisted of a mangle in a shed.

'The owner is a big boss, Malagasy but a big boss like the people in your country,' the Anglican explained.

In his experience all Europeans were bosses. He asked a child to pick wild oranges for us but they were so bitter we threw them in the bushes when the Anglican looked away. From a table balanced at the river's edge we bought satsumas in exchange and pressed them on him.

The *métis* drunkenly appeared with – as if by magic – an aubergine and sardine speciality. 'We brought it just for you! We wanted you to taste it. We must share everything on this voyage.' We tucked in with tablespoons.

'Thank you. It's delicious.'

'We hired a *pirogue*. Over the river is a Chinese restaurant.' We stared at the jungle. It seemed unlikely, but this delicious salad was proof. 'We three will go round Mahanoro together. I'll find you a hotel, and a lorry for the next stage!'

'Yes, yes,' we placated him.

I glanced up and saw the Anglican standing in the doorway. His face was dark.

Eventually there was a shout. 'The ferry's here!' A new engine: smiles and laughter all round. We chugged slowly against the current as the rain set in again. The *métis* asphyxiated me with his rum breath.

'I bet you don't have roads like this in your country.' I had to admit that we did not.

'But we have too many roads,' I added quickly. I wanted to make it up to him in some way. 'We don't have enough countryside like this any more. Roads everywhere. Pollution.'

'Ah, but I bet the ferries aren't like this.' He was determined.

'They are. Exactly the same. Perhaps they don't break down so often, but they look the same, at least they do in some towns.' The Dartmouth–Kingswear ferry, with its separate boat pushing it across the river, was almost identical.

He did not want to believe me. He thought wistfully of Europe, of Paradise. So many immigrants arrive with the same vision.

'You know, in England there's lots of unemployment, life is

very hard for some people. It's not all perfect. They get a small
amount of money from the state but it's not enough to live on.'

'Well, at least they get something. Here it's nothing. But the
real problem here is that however hard you work you can never
make any money. There's no possibility to improve. The problem every day is simply how to get enough rice.'

The Anglican drew me aside. 'You must make a decision. Do
you come with me, or go with him?'

I did not want to start a fight.

'The first thing we have to do is find our transport for the next
stage of our journey.'

He nodded.

Through more dripping coconut palms and coffee plantations,
and neat Betsimisaraka villages lined up in rows beside the road,
and after the ritual breakdown, we arrived in Mahanoro,
President Ratsiraka's birthplace. It was late afternoon. John the
driver, an intelligent and sensible man, had also offered to help
us find our next vehicle. We knew we could trust him, and as we
unfolded ourselves from the bus the *métis* veered over, eyes red,
hair tousled. The enthusiasm had worn off. 'You're all right
about the lorry, aren't you?'

'Yes, yes. John is here.'

'Good. Bye then.'

We shook hands and he wandered off. I waited for the Anglican. We would find our transport and then spend the night with
him, I thought. But he did not appear. In the crush of bodies it
was difficult to tell where he had been sitting, but somewhere
along the route he must have got out.

'He was probably regretting it, once he'd sobered up,' said
Richard.

'But he didn't even say goodbye.' I felt puzzled, and ridicu-
lously hurt.

'You know what it is.'

Each of these towns was much like the next, with a central
market square dominated by a stone celebration of
Independence carved in the shape of Madagascar. The squares
were surrounded by wooden boxes on their sides which were the
shops. We bought biscuits and torch batteries, and hot prawns
fried in batter from a woman squatting on the road over a
charcoal stove.

'OK, Richard, Helena, you're off!' John had persuaded a friend to drive us the eleven kilometres to the next village on the banks of another expanse of lagoon.

'Thank you very much, John.'

'Don't mention it.' He was unusually efficient and energetic. We wished we could have known him longer.

We raced through the night, the road scattered with nightjars that swooped from our headlights amongst fireflies, and drew up by the water. Some brisk negotiations, and we had a canoe. It was a dug-out trunk with planks laid across as seats, barely wide enough for one, and we were low in the water as we wobbled off into the night beneath the moon and stars. Plants reared up around us. I hardly dared move for fear of capsizing. *Chop-chop-chop* – paddles knocking against the sides of the canoe, the silence of the empty landscape, and we entered a lagoon. It seemed endless, just a black line of trees in the far distance protecting us from the violence of the sea. Rain clouds loomed; the paddles chopped faster.

'*Vite! Vite!*' the boatmen shouted to each other. We watched the clouds' ominous approach. But it was not the rain that worried them.

Later people asked, aghast, 'You went across that lake? At night? Weren't you afraid?'

'Of what?'

'Of the ancestors.' Spirits lurked here.

After half an hour we beached at the village of Ambodiharana. The boatmen shook hands, relieved to have made it, and we heaved on our packs and set off.

'Wait! Where are you going to stay?'

'We're going to go on, and put up our tent.'

They looked doubtful, but we were still full of energy and the momentum of travel: we had been on the move for fourteen hours. Now we were longing to escape from people, and also to try out our tent. The village stretched along a broad track, tiny houses in rows, some candle-lit, with children singing and clapping inside. We longed to relax in a warm home but could not face the prospect of being stared at, and of more talking. A child ran screaming as we loomed through the night, humpbacked and huge.

As we reached the outskirts the deluge started. Idiotically, instead of seeking shelter we chose that moment to put up the tent. Richard hurled himself at the task, shouting orders, me shouting back: both of us furious with each other and ourselves.

'It was you who wanted to camp,' he yelled, stabbing metal poles into the earth.

'If you didn't want to why didn't you say so?' I was struggling inside the tent.

'When you get an idea in your head you've got no idea how determined you can be.'

'Bullshit. You only needed to have said.'

'Well now you can shut up and just get this fucking tent up.'

Within minutes we, our bags, and the tent were awash. There was no way we could sleep here. Angry and humiliated, we took it down and returned to the village. All doors were firmly shut against the rain, but at last a figure materialized and led us to the President of the village. Richard stepped up on to his verandah and tapped at the door.

A tiny old man appeared in bare feet. He was on his way to bed. A young wife lurked in the background.

'We've come from Vatomandry.'

At that all the women in the surrounding houses tumbled out laughing, as if they had been expecting us. We were ridiculous. The President showed us to a hut.

'It's not much,' he shrugged.

It was bare but for a table, a mat on the floor, a toothbrush pushed between the palm leaves of the roof, someone's certificate of confirmation in the Anglican church, and two narrow doors made from the same woven palm fibres as the house. They lifted aside. Someone swept it out, and then left us. It was perfect.

We hung up our soaked clothes and the tent. All our possessions including Jørgen Ruud and our passports were sodden. We lay on the floor in the candle-light under our mosquito net and comforted ourselves with tea and biscuits. At least the lighter still worked.

The village woke. Farmyard noises and human murmurings, then the rhythmic thud of pounding rice. Smoke seeped from chimney-less roofs and hovered, like lilac haloes, and firelight glimmered through cracks in walls. The President produced a bucket of water, and accepted our thanks and 1,000 fmg with a wicked gleam. We heard an engine and thought vaguely of a tractor, but as we knew there was no way of reaching Masomeloka except on foot, we took little notice until an anxious face appeared round the door to say it was going. What, we did not know, but we followed the woman through the village to find a cargo boat casting off. 'Hurry up!' A plank was lowered.

We were both slightly disappointed that there would be no epic walk, but at least this way we might make it to our rendezvous. The *Jupiter* was running gasoline to the headquarters of the Pangalanes' reconstruction company.

'You're lucky,' said the captain. 'Normally we never stop here, but we had some problems last night with the engine. It's not normal this rain,' he added. 'This is the dry season. It must be something to do with global warming, weather patterns changing, pollution in the developed world, all that. I hear you've got a drought in Europe.'

He stood beside me in the bow, dignified and intelligent, dark-skinned with dark glasses and a much-coveted denim jacket. We exchanged the usual information. He was in his late thirties, and his wife had died the month before, leaving him with six children.

'And you, is that your brother?' This was a regular question. Is it that all *vazaha* look alike?

'No, he's my husband.'

'And no children!'

'No.'

I changed the subject and explained how we had got here.

'Ugh, there's so much stealing from Gallois,' he said, disgusted.

'Stealing?'

'Everyone takes his cut on every transaction, from the highest to the lowest. Gallois is so rich that either he doesn't know or he doesn't care. Lots of people are rich because of him.' I disliked the idea of our benefactor being ripped off. 'The point is that people are forced to do this, otherwise they can't live. Life is hard. We do it too. Look at this boat.' It was packed with people. 'We don't earn enough, so we take on passengers, do a bit of business on the side. Life is hard. What is so sickening is that it's the same throughout the country, even the President. He has so much money abroad, foreign bank accounts, houses.' He repeated the criticisms of the government that we had heard before, though not often from a Malagasy. He gripped the hand-rail. 'I can only say this to you. I can't say it to a Malagasy. He tells someone who tells someone else, and before you know it . . .' He crossed his wrists, handcuffed.

President Ratsiraka stared, slightly cross-eyed, from the wall of the wheelhouse.

'Here, if you show your head, it gets cut off.'

Again the fear.

In almost the same breath he spoke of the ancestral spirits that lurk in the water. 'One mustn't joke about these things. For example, only the other day –' We were interrupted by the rain. I was bundled down into the cabin. Four berths with thick mattresses, freshly painted walls, knick-knacks: it was a different world from Monsieur Gallois' pitch dark rusting hold.

Here there were posters of Golf GTI convertibles, French models and pop stars, and 'I LOVE YOU' stencilled on the wall. On the window-sill lay intimate essentials of Malagasy life: toothbrushes, French comic strips, an old sardine tin serving as an ashtray, a pack of cards, a torch, a bundle of medicinal leaves.

'Come in, sit down.' A crew member patted his berth beside him. We didn't want to intrude. 'No, make yourselves at home.' He was in his thirties, toothless but still handsome. Stretched out behind him, wrapped in a *lamba*, was his wife. 'She's six months pregnant,' he said. She smiled weakly. 'She's my second wife. I've already got four kids in Tamatave.' He was divorced. This was their home; a thin curtain their only privacy. He produced photographs of himself posing on the *Jupiter*, himself in Mahanoro, himself with the ship's crew, himself as a young Catholic chorister in Tana. There were no pictures of his wife.

'That's my father.' A man in army uniform and a beret stood smartly in the port at Tamatave. 'I failed the army exams.' I sensed the disappointment – familiar now in Madagascar – of someone who had come down in the world.

'And who's this pretty girl?'

'That's my daughter.'

'How old is she?'

'She was eight then. She's already dead.'

'Oh. I'm so sorry.' What could I say?

He shrugged and put the book away.

As rain poured through the hatch, the hold filled with shy children who clasped smaller children in their arms. A mother in a straw hat and neatly plaited hair got chatting in an undertone.

'How many of these are yours?' I asked politely.

'Five.'

I made the usual expressions of delight.

'No, it's too many.' The youngest was only two years old, and her husband had died the year before, aged only forty-two. Death was everywhere on this boat. No wonder the ancestors are so present in their lives. 'I'm thirty-seven. I'm old. How can I live?'

'Do you work?'

'I'm a teacher in a primary school. But I also have to work the fields, grow rice and manioc to feed the children. Life is hard.' *La vie est dure*: this became a sort of chant. She sought sympathy and I gave it, but she was resigned to her hopeless situation.

Like most people, she assumed we were French, not because of our perfect accents, but simply because here *vazaha* were always French. '*Vazaha*' is said to be a corruption of '*français*'.

'We're English.'

She looked as blank about England as most English do about Madagascar. Then she lit up. 'Oh yes, you drink a lot of tea and wear hats. That's what we were taught at school I remember.' (Typical French teachers, I thought.) 'Excuse me, but I find you so modest.' Modest: this was a great compliment from a Malagasy. 'It's unusual in a *vazaha*.' She wanted to 'correspond' she said, but in a way that I was now getting used to, when she left the boat she did not even turn and wave. Perhaps they feared the consequences of their friendliness, like the English do after striking up conversations on trains and quickly regretting it.

She spooned clods of cold rice into plastic plates for her children, and her space was taken by an old man with grey prickles on his chin and a waterproof over-shirt woven from raffia. The raffia palm flourishes here on the east coast. He had attached his *pirogue* to the stern.

'Life is hard,' he said.

He was not whining, or begging, but simply stating a fact that was on everyone's mind.

'We can hardly live.' He was a peasant, and he spoke of the annual cyclones which destroy his crops. 'Every manioc, every blade of rice, every house – all lost. Every year. And as for the price of rice, oh! Most people earn 1,000 fmg a day, and eat 500 fmg's worth of rice a day, at least. So if you have a family of ten, as I do, you have to spend about three times what you earn every day.' It didn't occur to any of them to have fewer children. They were devoted to them, and they helped with the work; besides, family planning was non-existent.

By late afternoon we had reached Masomeloka. The hotel was a long thatched hut partitioned into bed-sized rooms, the bathroom an enamel basin on a chair behind the huts. The loo was the bushes on the outskirts before dawn.

'Mmm, *presque Paris*,' said Richard. Most residents ate their meals on a rough table by the back door of the family house; we were shown into the best front room, chairs quickly dusted. It was an old bungalow with hardwood floors which a servant girl was polishing by skating around on a coconut husk on one leg, the other flailing along behind.

Mademoiselle Georgette was the spinster daughter of the house. She was plain and anxious and she shooed the chickens out. She and her parents were all of a fluster at our arrival.

'Good? It's not good!' she exclaimed when we praised the simple but delicious grilled fish and rice, cooked in a tin shed on a charcoal fire. She tutted at a boy who accidentally brushed my arm. Bobbing with deference she produced her best (though often mended) china for the citronelle tea. On the walls hung mats woven with Malagasy sayings and a crucifix. They were devout Catholics: perhaps that explained their humility.

A magician from the east coast island of St Marie had been with us on the *Jupiter*. He was illiterate and his voice high-pitched and monotonous, his slant eyes blank, and his teeth big and yellow. The teeth were his livelihood. In fact he was a Grand Master of the Teeth on a nationwide tour. He lodged next to us, and Mademoiselle Georgette was thrilled.

'Have you heard what Monsieur Jean-Claude can do?' she whispered. 'He can pick up a muscular man with his teeth! And a motorbike! Through his powers he transformed a bottle of water into fruit soda, and crushed a coconut with his head.' The Grand Master erected a red flag in the square and rang a bell which drew an instant crowd of children. He would perform in the morning, he announced. They peeled off shrieking with anticipation. Mademoiselle Georgette was open-mouthed.

Late into the night Jean-Claude and his assistant drank and sang. All down the east coast we had heard this song; the children on the *Touraine* had sung it again and again; it was whistled in markets and played on the radio. It was a love song. Much later we would stop and say: 'Darling! They're playing our song.' By midnight in Masomeloka we had heard enough.

'*Monsieur le Magicien! S'il vous plaît! C'est assez!*'

In the morning Mademoiselle Georgette cringed. 'You were disturbed. Excuse us. We are used to it but *you* . . . I'm very angry with them.'

The rats had disturbed us more, circling our mosquito net along the rafters just above our heads. And these days I was so full of this journey, of planning the next stage, of worrying about not reaching Ambositra on time, that I rarely slept at all. The circumcision and the *famadihana* had assumed enormous import- ance: we *had* to get there. Richard was always more relaxed. He didn't really mind if we made it or not.

At 6 am the town gathered. The drum rolled, the assistant waved a flag. A boy was selected, seated on a chair – abra- cadabra – and hoisted in the Grand Master's teeth. The crowd loved it, especially when the Grand Master strode away across the square, the boy passive and unsmiling on his chair up in the air between the Grand Master's jaws. But when he lifted an oil drum with his teeth and swung it around, the crowd were unim- pressed. There was no applause, and people wandered off.

We visited the *gendarmerie*.

'Come in! Sit down!'

They said it was fairly dull here, just petty crime, until the '*Fête des morts*', All Saints Day, in November. The Betsimisaraka have no *famadihana* but once a year the families gather at the tombs to clean them and to feast and drink.

'That's when the problems start,' said the gendarme.

'What sort of things?'

'Murders. Lots of them.'

'*Murders*? These polite people? How many?'

'Last year – let's see.' He glanced at a list on the wall. 'At least a dozen.'

'In this tiny place.'

'Yes. It's the drink. And of course that doesn't count all the people who were wounded but didn't actually die.'

Fady, vintana, the ancestors, the law: their lives were controlled on every side. No wonder violence exploded from time to time.

Nosy Varika, forty kilometres south, was our next destination. At last a walk looked likely. We pulled ourselves over a river on a bamboo raft with a liana as a rope. The road was a sand track along the newly re-built canal, and soon the trees vanished into acres of deforested nothingness. The development project had done its worst, and left the land barren but for a few stray periwinkles. Of all the places to walk we had chosen the most bleak. Struggling through the sand in boots was hard work so we walked barefoot. The going was slow.

It was two hours before we heard our first vehicle: a land cruiser churned beside us. A Frenchman with red hairy arms offered us a lift. His name was Claude Garcia and he was the mechanic for the canal project. 'I'm only going to my base, mind you, not to Nosy Varika,' he warned. We rocked over log bridges to a settlement of huts, on the edge of which stood his wooden cabin.

'You see. I have everything I need. Here are my orchids.' The verandah housed his collection which he had gathered from the forest. 'In the evening I sit here with a drink and I'm almost drowned in the scent.' There was a fishing rod, his other passion. To our obvious astonishment he showed us his double bed with a gingham bedspread, dining room with television (we had not seen electricity since Tamatave), and pine table and chairs and – *bathroom*. Red and white check curtains – a tiny piece of Provence – fluttered on a landscape of desolation. He invited us to share his lunch.

'I've just got to go and do a bit of work so make yourselves at home. Have a shower – I've got a generator so we've got plenty of hot water. You can watch a video if you like. Have a drink. Anything you need just ask François for it.' François was his chef. However tempting, the effort of undressing and washing seemed too great. The bathroom was too spotless for the likes of us. Instead we sat around drinking cold beer.

Claude Garcia was in himself an oasis. In his fifties, he was huge and strong and filled with *bonhomie*.

'Try some Malagasy whisky,' he said.

'Is it good?'

'No, that's why the bottle's full!'

Yet there was an odd feeling of displacement. He was Spanish-bred but Marseille-born, now domiciled in Texas but unable to speak a word of English. His wife had stayed home.

'What could she do here for six months?' he said, waving towards the wet desert. 'Nothing.'

As we sipped cold drinks a truck arrived with a white, gleaming Italian fridge-freezer. It was like a messenger from outer space. Claude barked orders in an accent thick as *bouillabaisse*. In seconds the Malagasy employees unloaded it and Claude connected it up. He chucked a packet of Gauloises at them and they scrapped over them good-naturedly, like children scrabbling for sweets.

'That fridge was with us on the *Jupiter*!' Richard exclaimed.

'Good, so you escorted it here,' said Claude.

Baguettes, butter, wine, mineral water, *crudités, côtelets du porc, fromage et fruits*. 'Thank you, François, you've surpassed yourself,' said Claude, patting his belly.

'You look after yourself well,' I commented.

'*Il faut, hein?*'

Everything he required – food, furniture, clothing, videos – was driven from Tana to Tamatave and shipped from there. He had lived all over the world and knew how to make himself at home. When he revealed that he had spent most of his life in the merchant navy, it fitted. The good humour, the practicality, the rootlessness, the great ham-like forearms: he was clearly a man of the sea. I explained our story.

'So you've been to Zanzibar, I suppose?' He said. 'Wonderful!' A few months back he had met a man from Tamatave descended from a European pirate. He relished that.

'I suppose some of the pirates here must have come from Marseille,' I said.

'I hope so.' Claude topped up his beer with a pint of wine. 'I won't serve you, mind! You've just got to help yourself.' The bottle was quickly emptied.

The canal project, he said, was futile. It would be impossible to maintain because the banks were made of sand with nothing to hold them up.

'But I don't care. I'm the mechanic. I have my job to do and I just do it.'

I saw him suddenly as a latter-day pirate, retiring from a life on the sea to settle in for the good life. But he had his wife to return to, and he would not choose to stay. The country was falling apart, he said.

'Some of my lowest-paid workers used to be teachers, drove cars, and now they're reduced to this. Labouring here in the middle of nowhere, living in stone age huts. It's pathetic. But most of them are like children anyway. Can't look after themselves. Even the qualified engineers. Kids.'

I thought he was being patronizing, but later a Malagasy

approached him, humbly requesting Claude to repair some part of his boat's engine. I barely recognized our friend, the captain of the *Jupiter*. Claude's massive confidence and size diminished that dignified man, turned him into a child. Treat people like children and they behave like children. It would have been the same for sixty years of colonial rule.

Hours later, well behind our schedule, Claude kindly arranged for someone to drive us on to Nosy Varika. He wanted to load us with bread and bottled water – 'Anything you want, please just say' – and seemed offended when we turned him down. We wanted no more weight on our backs. But we would miss his hearty generosity.

Claude insisted that there was no road from Nosy Varika to Mananjary, the next stop. The bridge had collapsed, and there were never any boats. 'It'll take you two days for sure. Count on three.' Our vision of Ambositra faded yet again. But on arriving we saw a blackboard outside a Chinese shop chalked with the almost unbelievable announcement that a boat would be leaving for Mananjary in three hours.

'Does it go every day?' I asked in the shop.

'No, not even every week, just occasionally.'

It would take eleven hours.

The Chinese shop stocked Chinese blankets, camping Gaz, digestive biscuits: this family controlled the town. If a shop or hotel was well-run, it often turned out to be Chinese-run. Yet the Chinese are not resented in Madagascar as the Indians are. They blend in better, have mixed marriages. The year before, Nosy Varika had been destroyed by a cyclone; little of it was left except foundations; the people had sheltered in the church. The only other building left unscathed was the Chinese shop: it was almost as if they controlled that too.

The boat was a small passenger ferry with benches for us to lie across.

'It's a family trip,' said a lady with jade earrings. 'I've put rice and fish on board for you.'

Steering was haphazard, the only light a torch flashed sporadically at a bank we were about to hit. (There were no Chinese aboard.) We spent the night moored off the village of Ambohitsara. Mist hung on the water, and when the engine stopped our ears filled with insects and the clap of the Indian Ocean. A moonlit sandbank gleamed overhead. We waded up, footsteps muffled, and found a silent village of identical houses pale in the light. Their stilts were in shadow making them weightless, as if they hovered here. Nothing had any solidity. Without obvious windows or doors they were blank.

'They look more like houses of the dead than of the living,' Richard murmured, and he was right. Silent sarcophagae. Houses like tombs and tombs like houses: the living and the dead interchange.

Three youths heading for an evening piss were distracted by the sight of us.

'Come over here,' they whispered. We followed them behind a sprouting picket fence to find an elephant carved from stone. It was hollow and stood four feet high on stout legs.

'The legs go down another four metres below the sand,' they said.

Lichen gleamed on its back. The tusks and the tail had gone, but genitals and trunk were intact; the trunk was outstretched, trumpeting over the sea, perhaps back to India or Indonesia or wherever its creator came from. How old was it?

'Thousands of years old,' the boys said. 'Its history is written on it.'

The moonlight was not bright enough to read by, but in the morning all we could read was graffiti. 'J. Bardot 1864'. Perhaps Monsieur Bardot was a pirate from Marseille. His name was cut deep; he must have lived here for some time, just three years after the death of Queen Ranavalona I. Old, but not that old.

The mystery is, of course, that there have never been elephants in Madagascar. No one knows its origins.

Sleeping on the boat's benches was made more difficult by the boatmen who swilled *toakagasy*, illegally brewed spirits, and stumbled over us to vomit and then to snore. Breakfast was sticks of sugar cane pinched from fields along the bank for some, soup bowls of *toaka* for others. It was between 80 and 90 per cent proof, they claimed. They squatted in the bows and spooned last night's burnt rice into their mouths, and then sat on the tin roof in the sun flirting with two floozies with orange nail varnish and thick legs. They patted the larger girl's backside and leered at Richard.

At Mananjary the Pangalanes ended, and we would leave the

coast to cut west back up into the highlands to Ambositra. Mananjary was our first proper town since Tamatave. We had suddenly re-entered the world. There was a busy taxi-brousse station and a floating shanty town of rafts, and a line of government buildings beween the canal and the sea shore. Perhaps it was confirmed with hindsight, but even at the time we sensed a new atmosphere of aggression. There were beggars, many of them well educated but desperate, and there were gem-sellers who sidled up to unfold brown paper twists of emeralds and garnets. They beseeched us to buy them, but we were not interested and could not pay.

The only thing of importance about Mananjary is the *Sambatra*. This takes place every seven years, when every boy under the age of seven is communally circumcised. Festivities are said to go on for days and nights, but it was not due until 1993.

There was something new to preoccupy us: Richard had dysentery. We had only four days left in which to get to Ambositra, and he was not well enough to travel by bus. My sympathy alternated with impatience, and guilt when he apologized for holding us back, as if he could help it.

I left Richard – feverish now – in the empty French motel and wandered the streets. Knots of men collected on corners and watched me approach. It felt uncomfortable to be alone after all these months; I was not frightened but self-conscious. They called 'Bonjour Mademoiselle' and sniggered behind me as I passed, and I realized (not for the first time) how much more fun it was to travel with Richard than without him. I missed him already. I had thought that by being alone I would see more, be more alert to my surroundings, more open to other people, but in fact it was the opposite and I saw only myself. I had also thought that making decisions would be easier alone but it was the opposite. Shall I turn left and explore there, or go straight on? Another person's wishes create a reason for doing one thing rather than another. Alone it was hard to make it matter either way. Especially when alone what I saw was more in my head than on the street.

After a night of Flagyl and motel luxury Richard felt a little better. Perhaps we would make it to Ambositra after all. He felt well enough to move into our tent on the beach. We would save money and were happy to be camping at last. On our final night on the east coast we could be alone and gaze out to sea like the elephant. It was dark by 6 pm so we went to bed; we lay naked in our sleeping bags and unzipped the doors so as to enjoy the breeze and the moon.

'I hate taking out my contact lenses. It makes me feel so vulnerable,' I said.

Around midnight we shut the tent against mosquitoes. I woke to find Richard slapping frantically at the doors and shouting, '*You bloody shit.*' It was a primordial shout, a shout from the belly. I shot up, blindly. 'It was nothing. A dog or something.'

Despite trembling hands I managed to put in my lenses. Richard was involved in some long story about a dream of someone tearing stamps.

'What's going on? What's happened to the door? It's all slashed.'

'It's nothing. Don't worry.' Richard was swathed in a blanket of calm.

'Tell me! What's happened?'

The tent had been slashed with a knife. Through the holes Richard had seen a man hesitating, knife gleaming, uncertain whether to continue or to run. He ran.

We crouched in the tent, windowless and exposed. Anyone could be out there. Periodically Richard flashed the torch and saw no one but every sound set our hearts pounding.

'I think we should move. Let's pack up the tent,' I said.

'No, he won't come back now. Besides, it's raining, so the tent will be wet. We can't pack it wet.'

'We can leave the tent, just take everything out of it.'

A twig cracked. We moved.

The motel's guardian was asleep under a blanket on the floor. We shook him awake and explained. He did not understand and was more worried that we should report his sleeping to the boss but he let us stay on the concrete verandah. Here, under the spotlight, we were sure to be safe but the night turned impenetrably black around us. By covering our faces we managed to sleep a bit; in the morning a camera lens, an expensive penknife, a waterproof jacket and a film had vanished.

Madagascar turned bleak and grey. We sat in the taxi-brousse feeling shattered. How could someone do this to us, I kept repeating to myself. Illogically, I took it as malice, personally directed at us. All the Malagasy in the bus were to blame.

Eventually we took it out on each other.

We wound our way up through the crags of the eastern escarpment, bananas and coconut palms giving way to eucalyptus and stepped rice fields. Opposite me sat an exquisite child with golden skin and perfect neat feaures, eyebrows like feathers. She wore an orange cardigan and dispelled my fractious mood. I longed to give her something but had only bananas which were not appropriate. The taxi-brousse was branching south to Fianarantsoa, we were going north; by early evening we reached the crossroads, and our driver flagged down a lorry heading our way. With apologies for the discomfort to come we were bundled into the back. I quickly made a nest in my sleeping bag between sacks of coffee and shut out the world. We all wrapped our faces in scarves against the choking fumes and dust.

Later – I lost track of time – we paused in some highland town. It was cold. I blinked out not at bamboo huts in rows but at high brick houses, paved streets, men in long cotton table-cloth shirts, swathed in *lambas* and carrying staves. They were proud and fierce and sat on their sacks of oranges. They were heading for the *zoma* in Tana. Later still we were dropped outside the Grand Hotel in Ambositra. We had made it.

— CHAPTER EIGHT —

IN THE HIGHLANDS

After weeks of travel and exhaustion, the last thing we expected happened: Christine and Brunoh were not at home.

'But they invited us to Mbola's circumcision!'

Brunoh's sister shrugged. She knew nothing of any circumcision. She had not seen them for months.

We discovered that the children at least were with Christine's parents in Sahamadio, a village a few hours drive north. No one knew their address; all we could be sure of was that Christine's mother was also called Christine, and that she was a teacher. A taxi-brousse would leave but not for four or five hours, we were told. At our dismay a man shrugged and said, 'Oh well, if you don't have the patience to wait . . .' It was a rebuke. Impatient bossy *vazaha*, always complaining.

The taxi-brousse went as far as Fandriana, from where we walked. A coffin lay on the roadside with a Malagasy flag on top. Someone had died away from home and had been brought back in a taxi-brousse to the family tomb. At this time of year it was often hard to get a seat on a bus for all the people escorting corpses home. We walked on past not taking much notice: we were used to it now.

The land undulated up an open terraced valley with red-walled villages and large red churches capping hills: we could have been in Tuscany. Beside the track men were moulding mud bricks to be fired in ovens – *Salama tompoko!* – and women slapping clothes on rocks in irrigation channels paused to wave. This tribe, the Betsileo, are renowned for their rice-growing skills and their hard work. People chopped wood, carried water, ploughed fields: it was medieval Europe, Breughel. Other walkers joined us, offered to carry my bag, showed us short cuts and then went on their way.

Wrought-iron gates led to a bungalow and a neat lady. She

had bright eyes and a white smile. Yes, she said, amazed, she was our friend Christine's mother. Would we come in? We sat on a leather sofa. The living room was fresh and airy; it was a relief to be in someone's home after months of hotels, with ornaments that meant something to the family – a Mahafaly tribe's *aloalo* (a carved wooden stele) and a massive shark's jaw which Christine's father had caught off the south coast. He emerged from his siesta, dark and frail and looking older than his fifty-five years. He, like Brunoh his son-in-law, had a problem with his left eye. We shook hands and explained who we were. Mino, Christine and Brunoh's twelve-year-old daughter, ran in to say hello. She had a mischievous face.

'They're here, you know,' Christine's mother said.

'Christine and Brunoh?'

At that they opened their door, muzzy with sleep, and laughed, astonished at the sight of us. Christine tried to straighten her wiry hair, and tucked in her clothes. Little Mbola, grave as ever, dutifuly kissed us. I did not take in its significance at once, but he was wearing a dress.

'We had the circumcision last week, you know.'

We had battled to get here on time. For nothing. I tried to swallow my disappointment.

Fresh milk was produced – a rarity in Madagascar – and we went for a walk. Christine and Brunoh told us all they knew about the area and its customs, trying to compensate for what we had missed. We had also given them some money and a radio-cassette (which they had asked for) and they felt they owed us this information in exchange. I disliked our relationship becoming not a friendship but a deal, but we were grateful to them too – we had so many questions. They agonized when they didn't know the answers, unable to fulfil their part of this unspoken bargain. This bridge is where people summon crocodiles to ask for a special favour; no, no one has ever been eaten. People who live north of the bridge cannot marry people who live south, because they will be seen to be going *down* in life not *up*. All marriages should be from within the same *karazana* or clan so that the land and tombs can be kept together. No, Brunoh comes from another clan but at least his is also a noble family, so it is all right. Their nobility was important both to them and to their families, as was their tribe.

It was a beautiful afternoon, the sun golden and gleaming on the drowned rice fields.

'This is a village of intellectuals,' said Christine, bright-eyed as her mother. 'Everyone likes very much to study.'

She pointed out the house of an airline pilot, of someone in the government (hence the rare electricity pylons) and of Manandafy, the leader of the opposition, all related to her family in some way. The track swayed with workers in straw hats returning drunkenly from ploughing; their zebu were inflamed with rum too which made their work easier. They sang on the road but paused respectfully as Christine passed, and greeted her. Most of the fields were owned by her family and always had been. This was where she belonged.

Her ancestral village, a few miles from where her parents now lived, was encircled by a ditch over twenty feet deep. Most villages had been fortified in this way against marauding clans: these were the mushroom rings I had seen from the air. Christine's was now a sheltered garden for sugar cane, coffee, tea, peaches and bananas. The village within it was little more than a hamlet, a few hovels clustered on a hill around scratching chickens and a pig.

'As nobles we never ate pig before, but as there was so little else we had to get a special dispensation from the witch-doctor.' Any transgressions of *fady* might bring down the wrath of the ancestors. A man who had built a new house facing the view but not the correct direction as dictated by *vintana* ignored the witch-doctor's protests on behalf of the ancestors. 'So it kept burning down,' Christine said. She laughed, seeing how extraordinary it must seem to us.

'What happened?'

'He had to abandon it.'

Christine's cousin returned from the fields and invited us in. His house, like most, was thatched, built of bricks and rendered with mud. Her grandfather had lived here, and his father before him. Downstairs was for the animals, with a steep staircase up to a large sitting room with small glassless windows and wooden shutters. In the smoke-blackened kitchen I stumbled on hens; a heap of sticks was the stove. There was no electricity, no plumbing. Up a ladder to the loft: here the rice was stored and a rat was flattened in a trap. I could never equate Christine with her English degree and tasteful – if rather well worn – clothes with these pimitive living conditions. She, however, was not ashamed;

far from it, she was proud of her ancestral home.

As for her cousin, he had spent six years studying cybernetics in East Germany. But there were no jobs in Madagascar. Besides, he said, he wanted to work his ancestral land.

'Nowadays many intellectuals are returning to the land,' Christine chipped in, still full of Marxist idealism from her schooldays in the seventies. But her cousin seemed bitter, and having had six years' experience of whites in East Germany was also wary of us. Yet he was drunk and in his drunkenness all was forgiven, we had to stay for a meal, he begged us to stay, it was very rude not to accept, all visitors should be given rice. He pursued us down the hill repeating apologies and wanting to shake hands.

Christine laughed but was embarrassed for us and begged him to understand that we had to return to her parents now and would come again another day. She was always polite.

We teetered back along narrow banks between the rice fields, four-year-old Mbola trotting silently on bare feet. We had walked several miles but he never complained, never cried. 'He's used to it,' said his parents. Like many of the children he was placid. I wondered if it was shock after the circumcision, or if it was from eating too much rice. 'Perhaps he's weighed down by starch,' I suggested.

'No no!' Christine was shocked. 'Rice gives strength. He's just like that, that's all.' He had no toys, no books, nothing, and yet he never asked for anything, never whined that he was bored.

For eight years Christine and Brunoh had tried to have a second child. The exhortation at Malagasy marriages is: 'I hope you have seven sons and seven daughters.' The more children the more solicitous attention you will be paid after death. When at last their son was born they named him Mbolanirina which meant 'We still wish for another'. Poor Mbola, I thought, not being enough in himself. It was not a name I would have chosen. But now Christine and Brunoh were trying to accept their fate, and said that in any case they could not afford more. These days, they said, the marriage exhortation had become: 'I hope you have only one son and one daughter.'

I liked the system of inventing names, usually a wish for yourself or for the child. It was not necessary to take a parent's name. Christine herself was called Voahangy which meant Orange in the coastal dialect, signifying something good. Orange: it was preferable to Christine, which was her French name, used with us but not with the Malagasy. Their daughter was Minosoa, meaning 'To believe in the good things'. Christine's niece was called 'Money'. A man we had met in Vatomandry was called 'Sweet'. 'Hello, Sweet,' I kept wanting to say. 'How are you, Sweet?' Some parents searched the calendar for names, which meant that there were not only Maries and Nicholases and Pierres but also children called Tous Saints and Fête Nat.

Children were always given nicknames, for fear that pronouncing the full name might attract the attention of evil spirits. Nicknames put evil spirits off the scent; they guarded their full names with silence.

Back home we gathered on beds under blankets around a colour television. There was a theatrical version of a *famadihana* which was popular with the children, and Indian government propaganda which was not. 'Make yourselves at home,' Monsieur Valson, Christine's father, kept saying.

Her mother produced a feast. A chicken (a stringy old bird) had been specially killed, and the best red rice, rice of the ancestors, was pounded and husked and cooked in a great red mound. They were proud of their rice and of the amount they, the Betsileo tribe, could eat. Richard will never be forgotten for asking for more. Lack of space pushed the children into exile beyond a hatch, from where they watched us and giggled, especially when sheets of typing paper were distributed as napkins.

Monsieur Valson said grace (the family being devout Norwegian Lutherans) and then served himself. I was struck by the respect he was shown. On every subject he was quietly deferred to. The hierarchy of age is as important as the hierarchy of class – I suppose the older one is, the closer one is to becoming an ancestor. In some tribes, we heard, it was *fady* for children to address their fathers directly, or to wear shoes while they were still living. Not only was Monsieur Valson head of the family but he was also President of the *Fokonolona*, the village council.

'It's like being the mayor,' he said. He had to arbitrate in disputes, preside over meetings. He was looking forward to the approaching end of his five-year term. He was tired, and he did not look well. We spoke of *famadihana* and he asked us about funeral arrangements in Britain. At the time I had rarely come into contact with death.

'I think we mostly employ undertakers to look after things,' I said.

'You mean you pay someone else to do it?' He looked aghast.

'I think so. Don't we, Rich?'

Richard shrugged. He knew as little as I. Monsieur Valson shook his head in disbelief. It was the disrespect, the lack of care for the ancestor in question. I tried to explain that for us it was often too painful to deal with directly, that we didn't have the same easy attitude to death. He shook his head again. We moved on to the church in Britain, and he was horrified to hear that churches were often half empty on Sundays. His disappointment made me want to pretend it wasn't true.

Hot water was boiled specially for us – our first warm wash since leaving England. We carried the buckets into the stone-cold bathroom; wet knickers hung from a string. The wash was chill but worth it. Then we unrolled our sleeping bags in a room full of African violets. As we were going to sleep Christine knocked on the door. She held a chamber pot. 'You won't want to go outside tonight because there are so many sorcerers.' She smiled, but for all I knew she meant it.

Shutters opened on layered mists and smoke seeping from high houses. Eucalyptus hovered, without trunks. A ragged group of locals passed by singing hymns and carrying a coffin. Another *famadihana*. Christine joined me on the verandah; her head was wrapped in a blue jersey.

'I wanted to apologize about the circumcision. About having it early.' The words came out in a rushed undertone.

'Oh no, it doesn't matter. We're very happy to be here anyway.' This was true.

'No, I must explain. It was the witch-doctor. All the signs said it was better last week so we changed the date.'

Over the next two days we heard what had taken place. Better that we were not there: it had been a private and rather painful family affair. First the men (Brunoh and Christine's father) had stolen the requisite sugar cane and water from a neighbour, had staged a ritualistic fight over it and won, thus establishing Mbola as a man who could fend for himself. Then a doctor arrived at the house and the women left. It was *fady* for them to stay, and they wanted to escape as far from Mbola's cries as possible. If they felt pity for the boy, the wounds would not heal. He was sat on Brunoh's lap, his arms held. He knew what was coming and was frightened, tried to squirm away. Knives were produced; no anaesthetic allowed. It all seemed unnecessarily cruel; no wonder he was now so subdued.

The operation lasted ten minutes and then came the great moment: Monsieur Valson ritually challenged Brunoh to eat the foreskin. It was a challenge he was not allowed to refuse. So he wrapped it in carrots and gulped. He rushed outside, ready to vomit, but managed to hold it down. Had he vomited, he would have had to fish it out and begin again: the foreskin must be digested, forging an actual physical link between father and son.

Monsieur Valson joined us on the verandah and Christine left to help her mother prepare breakfast. A woman passed with buckets of water.

'We'll take extra today, thank you,' said Christine.

Monsieur Valson said. 'I suppose in your country you can just turn on the tap and get water.'

I admitted this was so. 'But in most places we can't drink tap water because it's so polluted.'

'Yes, that's what I've heard.'

Chickens pecked around our feet. The garden was full of flowering fruit trees and vegetables; they grew almost everything they needed.

Richard joined us. 'It's lovely here,' he said. The place brought out all his longings to live in the country.

'*Oui*,' Monsieur Valson sighed, looking down the length of his ancestral valley, '*c'est agréable . . . c'est agréable . . . c'est agréable.*' He said it eight times. He felt it deeply. They had lived here only ten years; for much of his life he had been posted to the primitive arid south to work amongst the Antandroy as a punishment for his opposition to the Tsiranana regime. Now he hoped to stay here until he died.

Breakfast was a repeat of dinner – rice, chicken, omelette – but breakfast rice was wetter they said, easier to digest. We drank good strong coffee. It was interrupted by two anxious men with a message for Monsieur Valson. His aunt had died in Tana. We all expressed our sympathies, and breakfast continued. Later Christine said: 'You see how we treat death? It's just a part of our lives. Nothing special.' But perhaps they were just being polite in front of guests. Or perhaps they barely knew this aunt – they had so many aunts.

Surely Christine would not be so glib about her own father's death? I remembered the funeral we saw, the woman crumpled with grief.

'No,' she insisted. 'We miss them of course, but we are happy that they have become ancestors.'

Mino and Vola, Christine's nieces, put on pink track-suits, turned on the radio and disco-danced around the house. Monsieur Valson smiled affectionately at his granddaughters. They had no books, no toys, yet they seemed happy. Throughout the morning little treats were produced. Freshly-roasted peanuts, stewed manioc, haricot beans. When we left our bags were loaded. Monsieur Valson saw our hardwood stick with a sharp bone point that we had bought as protection against thieves in Ambositra. He seemed taken aback.

'It's sacred wood, you know. From Tulear. Normally only very respected elders like *ombiasy* carry it.'

'Is it *fady* for us to have it?' We did not want to do the wrong thing.

'No, not for you *vazaha*. But if you were to even raise it against a thief he would be terrified. To be hit by it would almost kill him.'

He gave us a map of Madagascar carved from the same wood as a souvenir. We were sad to say goodbye.

Five of us walked to Christine's mother's rice fields, several miles away over pine-covered hills. Brunoh had twenty-five kilos of rice seed on his head, and Christine trotted at his side, taking tiny steps in her old flip-flops but never tiring.

'We're used to it,' they kept excusing themselves as I scrabbled over rocky short-cuts, barely able to keep up. Brunoh offered to take my rucksack as well as his twenty-five kilos, but I couldn't let him. Christine's nimble mother never faltered. She wore a sturdy skirt and an unbleached silk *lamba* tossed around her jacket, her hair neatly plaited and rolled at the nape of her neck, shielded by a wide-brimmed raffia hat: she was the essence of respectable Malagasy womanhood. She pointed out different crops (pineapples, cassava, asparagus) shredded recently by hail, and desperately skinny zebu suffering from winter's lack of fresh grass. We came to a red church with a tin roof.

'This is where we pray to God each Sunday,' she said.

'Why do you come so far?' There were many churches closer to home.

'Because this is the church of our ancestors. This was where Christine's father was educated, where his father taught, where we were married, where Christine and her children were christened.'

It was more than family tradition: this was where the ancestors had decreed they must worship.

She pointed out their family tomb, a house-sized concrete box with a metal grille for a door. Its exact siting was vital. If its shadow fell on a house it would bring the taint of death, and if it was oriented the same way as the houses the spirit might get confused and return to the wrong home, inflicting its presence on the living. According to the rules of *vintana*, tombs are built askew to the cardinal compass points, and oblique to the house. Christine's family were planning their own *famadihana* for the next few weeks, when they would transfer the dead from a tomb they had outgrown to this new one.

A half-built tomb of a government minister swarmed with labourers. 'It's going to cost over 20 million fmg.'

I did a quick calculation. £8,000. In a country where the majority earned 8op a day. The minister's old family house, mud and thatch, stood beside the new edifice.

'You see how much we value the dead over the living,' observed Christine's mother with a little laugh. She seemed surprised, as if she had noticed the oddness of this for the first time.

We crossed valley after valley. Standing *vatolahy* stones, like menhirs, deflected evil spirits from important sites or acted as memorials.

'There's a rice field here of my ancestors,' Christine's mother explained, 'but the ancestors said that everything that's grown in it has to be kept in the field itself. Nothing can be taken away.'

'You mean you have to sit in the field to winnow the rice and pound it and eat it?'

'Yes, it's *fady* to take the rice away. So we just leave it fallow.'

'That seems rather a waste.'

'Yes, but what can we do?'

She pointed out the field. 'It's that one, to the east of the little house.' Directions were never left or right, but always according to the compass points, a more precise system than ours but one I never got used to. Often the sun was behind cloud so it was difficult to know where east was.

By the time we reached the fields drizzle had set in. A bent old lady joined us and shook hands formally with Christine and her mother. This was Christine's grandmother. Once again I was struck by the respect – almost veneration – for the older generation. We lined up alongside a manured and flooded field, and the grandmother scattered some rice seed. The most respected having thrown the first vital handful, we followed suit.

'When we eat it, we'll have a souvenir of your visit,' said Christine's mother with her vivacious smile. 'I'm sure it will grow especially well.'

Christine and Brunoh escorted us back to Fandriana where we hoped to pick up a taxi-brousse, but we paused at Christine's uncle's raffia factory, and the pause turned into more than that. After it had been closed for years, Paul Rafamantanatsoa had recently re-opened his family's factory to weave hats and strips of cloth. In his thirties, he was dapper in neat jeans tucked into ankle boots and with a well-trimmed beard. He had the same gleaming smile as Christine's mother, the same bright eyes. He was delighted to have the chance to speak English.

'I *love* London,' he exclaimed. 'I've been there, let me see, twice. Tower of London yes, and ah the pubs! I spent so much time in pubs! And punks!' He turned to Christine and Brunoh with a shining face. 'It's a wonderful place. Bayswater, Soho . . .'

Sitting on a bench in the manager's office in a raffia factory in the heart of Madagascar, we began to share his enthusiasm.

'Hyde Park!' cried Richard.

'Albert Hall!' Paul crowed.

'Brixton market!'

'Feesh an sheeps! *Coleslaw!*'

Christine said wistfully: 'It's my dream to go there, to travel, but we'd never have the money.' It was true. Right now they did not even have the money to pay for a taxi-brousse back home to Ambositra. They could not tell Christine's parents because of Brunoh's pride. A husband must support his wife. Clearly Brunoh was not strong – his glass eye gave him trouble – but at times I felt irritated by their hopelessness.

'What are you going to do with your English degree when you get it?' I asked Christine sometimes.

'I just want to help Brunoh with his rice and his haricot beans.'

She showed touching devotion to her husband, but they would never be able to live off that. Because inheritances were divided amongst the children, Brunoh's farm extended to four small fields and thirty pine trees. And for all their longing to travel, Christine and Brunoh were utterly incurious about our lives in England. They never asked us what we did or how we lived. Perhaps they knew they would never come and see it. Or perhaps their hermetic lives and their poverty excluded everything but their own problems and their Malagasy *fomba*.

Paul, however, was refreshingly active and optimistic. 'Make yourselves at your ease,' he said, pouring beer. It was a relief to be with someone who had ventured out of this isolation; Paul had spent four years studying rural economy in Belgium.

'How did you like that?'

'Mmm, actually, not much. I found the Belgians very . . . mmm . . . narrow-minded. But I loved Amsterdam, and London. I love British music. The Beatles, all the music from the Golden Sixties. You remember the Golden Sixties?'

'Well, they were a bit before our time. Were the sixties golden here too?' I asked.

'The sixties? Of *course*! Just after Independence, lots of money and good things.'

Brunoh described the long gone days when he could buy baguettes of paté and salad as long as his arm, and the parties in Ambositra. 'I remember going fifteen days without sleep, just party party every night.'

'Surely the good days will come back?' I asked hopefully, but Christine shook her head.

'No, it can only get worse, this crisis. The good days are over.'

But Paul's vitality was undimmed. He had re-employed five out of fifty weavers, and was transporting raffia from the east coast.

'Why don't they weave it there?' Richard asked.

'They don't do anything there. It's only in the highlands where anything gets done.'

Brunoh added: 'We, the Betsileo, consider the *côtiers* just to be descendants of slaves. We think of them as lazy good-for-nothings. You see, here there's not just racism between black and white but between highlanders and *côtiers*. Stupid, isn't it?'

Raffia was being dyed in hot green vats and spread on grass to dry. It would have been a factory just like this one that wove our striped raffia *lamba* a hundred and fifty years ago, though now the colours were brighter, less subtle. Old women stirred the vat with stained green hands. Upstairs a solitary man was stitching ugly 'European' hats; Paul was hoping in a few years to break into the export market.

'You can wash it and iron it!' he enthused. One or two of the old looms were strung with the shiny fibres, though the warp was nylon. 'You'll stay for lunch, won't you?' Eyes bright. 'You like kidneys and heart?'

'No, not really . . .'

'Wonderful, wonderful.' He hurried out.

'He's telling someone to prepare it,' Christine explained.

His house was traditional, with the sitting room up on the first floor.

'Excuse me, it's very poor.'

'No, no.' Remains of faded patterned wallpaper could be seen below the ceiling.

'This really is the country, you understand. All my music, my wife and kid, they're all in Tana.'

His mother-in-law had come to stay en route to a *famadihana*. She was shy and spoke little French, but she was beautiful with sharp features, shiny hair and freckles. Her brother, who lived in a solid-looking house opposite, had been Ambassador to Britain in the early seventies, yet here she was, squatting over a charcoal stove in an unlit back room.

The table was set with yet more domes of the best red rice reserved for special occasions, and white wine from Fianarant-soa. Typical of the French, I thought, they had made life as pleasant as possible for themselves, and imported vines.

'It's delicious.'

'Wait!' said Paul looking round at us eagerly. 'Let me see . . . I remember: It's just your cup of tea!' Christine and Brunoh were bemused. 'Will you have some more rice?'

'No thank you, I couldn't.'

'Wait! I'm stuffed!' He slapped the table with delight.

Inexorably the conversation turned to death. 'In the Betsileo region,' Christine was saying, 'If you are invited to a *famadihana* you must go, or when it's your turn to hold a *famadihana* no one will come, and the zebu you have killed will be wasted. Just thrown away.'

Brunoh confirmed this to be true. 'There was that man here who recently died. They hired taxi-brousses and cars to take people to the tomb, but only about three people turned up because he had never gone to anyone else's.'

Paul added: 'Here, you *have* to participate. You have to conform.'

'When there's a big crowd at the *famadihana* how do they know if you've attended or not?'

'Because when you give your donation, your name's written in a book.' Christine nodded as Brunoh spoke.

'That's why there's so much hardship this year. It's not just the people who are organizing the *famadihana*, it's all the guests who have to spend money too. You *must* do it.'

Brunoh added: 'You don't just pay money at a *famadihana*. That means nothing unless you eat something as well. You must.'

'But don't you want to eat something?'

They all looked at each other. 'Not always. Sometimes there's a *gris-gris*. You can feel it. You just have to push your rice to one side.'

'Are you serious?'

'This is no laughing matter.' Paul, a teacher-turned-entrepreneur, educated in Belgium, slipped without hesitating from talk of pubs and coleslaw to sorcerers and ancestral spirits.

'It's true,' they all insisted. 'One shouldn't joke about these things.'

'What are these *gris-gris* then?'

'They're like a spell, cast by a sorcerer. Or a poison. It could be if your crops never grew while all those in the fields around were healthy. Someone would have put a *gris-gris* on your land. Someone you had spited in some way, perhaps without realizing it.'

'Oh yes? And who are the sorcerers?'

No one smiled. Paul said, 'Usually young women wandering the footpaths at night. It can be very dangerous for you if you cross their path. Very ominous. Sometimes they hold hands together, and block your way.'

'And do you know they are completely nude?' Brunoh added.

'You've seen that yourself?'

'Yes yes, it's possible. Many people have seen it. One has to keep an open mind. Their sorceries, they always work.'

'In what way? What sort of sorceries?'

'If for example a woman wants a husband, or you want to

harm your enemy, you get a *gris-gris* from a sorcerer. It's very dangerous. But don't worry, they don't affect *vazaha*.'

Brunoh added, earnestly, 'My grandfather could always tell. A waiter could give him a glass of water with a *gris-gris*, a poison, and instead of drinking the water, the glass would crack in his hand. Just like that. He would see that the waiter was trembling, and know that it was he who had put in the *gris-gris*, because he wanted to harm him in some way, but my grand-father was stronger than the power of *gris-gris*. He could defeat them.'

'Who are they?'

'It's the ancestors. Hereditary. Usually women who pass the charms down one to the next. They know all the secrets of the forest, of the plants and poisons. If you see them before they see you, you'll be all right. But if not, they sweep you off on a horse and ride through the night and then just dump you some-where.'

It was late afternoon when we left in search of our taxi-brousse. Red brick houses lined the road, wooden balconies sup-ported on flimsy brick pillars. It could have been a Victorian railway town, Tiverton, say, but for the stepped paddy fields around, and the chickens in the doorways. Another of Christine's uncles passed by, out for a stroll with his eleven grown-up children.

'Only eleven,' Christine joked. Her uncle fluffed up proudly. His army officer sons towered over him. He knew he would be well cared for after death. We shook hands with each of them when we met and again when we parted.

We sat on the roadside in the last of the sun, but none of the vehicles was going our way. When it got dark we jigged around to keep warm. Brunoh, a one-time basketball ace, performed press-ups across a ditch. For three and a half hours we talked of Madagascar, of religious sects and of the lack of family planning and of Brunoh's unmarried cousin who had recently got pregnant.

'It's a shame for us,' Christine kept saying, 'a shame.' Not daring to tell her parents, she had had a back-street abortion, and died. Her father had still not been told the cause of her death for the shame he would feel had been brought on the family. This was very different from what we had been told by the few English men we knew living in Tana. The girls, they said, you almost have to fight them off. They'll do anything to get a *vazaha* boy-friend. And they hate you using contraception, illegitimate babies are fine, especially in a society of extended families. I recalled the orgies outside the Rova for Radama's wedding, and David Jones, one of the first missionaries, fending off the licentious women. By being with Richard, perhaps I was spoiling his fun, but AIDS was said to be spreading, and there was no immorality in the highlands for well-brought-up 'nobles' like Christine and Brunoh, so mindful both of tradition and of Christian morals. The Norwegian Lutherans had managed to add fear of God to all the other fears. Anxiety lay behind everything.

By 7 pm it was too dark for Christine and Brunoh to walk the six miles home. Hoping their children would not be worried – and of course there was no telephone – we abandoned the roadside and returned to Paul's. He was finishing supper and pressed us into consuming yet another mound of rice. Even Richard was beginning to look pale.

We unrolled our sleeping bags on a mat downstairs. Christine waved a candle around. 'Aren't you afraid being down here? The sorcerers?'

We laughed, and she creaked back upstairs. The town was utterly silent now, no dogs, no cars, no radios. Then out of the stillness came the eerie thread of a young girl's voice, singing.

Six months later I heard that Paul's factory was closed, and all hopes of expanding the factory were abandoned. He had returned to Tana.

Soon after dawn the Grand Hotel in Ambositra seemed more of a haven than ever. The head of the diminutive Franco-Milanese *patron*, Monsieur Du Mesignil d'Engente, rose above his bar.

'Taxi-brousse?'

'Yes.'

He nodded. He knew. '*Chambre et petit déjeuner*,' he pronounced.

'And hot water, is that possible?'

'Yes, perhaps.'

The 'Volcano' boiler had erupted once too often; now water was heated in a bucket on a charcoal stove.

Last week we had barely had time to enjoy this place. When not searching for our friends we had stayed in bed, exhausted, and read romantic novels supplied by the *patron*. It smelt of cats and chickens but had a special charm. The heavy fireplace and metre-thick walls were those of a French hunting lodge, and there was a courtyard of potted plants and one-eyed dogs and jam jars full of lilies. The rooms opened off this courtyard. They had polished wood floors and iron-framed bedsteads with sagging mattresses and bolster pillows, and bidets on folding legs behind modest screens. Joseph was sole waiter, cook and doorman. He hurried about looking anxious while women in aprons pressed sheets with irons full of hot coals.

The centre of life was the bar. Behind it Monsieur Du Mesignil d'Engente listened to his wireless and held court, as he had done for thirty years. This was the throne from which he ruled his kingdom. Never, in all our days there, did we see more of him than his head and shoulders. These were always cosseted in one of four embroidered silk dressing gowns. Today's was pink. It was blotchily reflected in a mirror behind him, and framed by shelves on which were arrayed bottles of rum, and others hand-labelled '*Punch*' or '*Miel*'; there were tins of pâté, sardines, *jus de grenadille*. In a cabinet jostled Gauloises and Disque Bleu, toothpaste and embroideries.

There were hardwood carvings made by the Zafimaniry tribe who lived in the forest nearby, but they were unattractive and had not been moved for years.

'He must know every bottle, every spider, every gecko,' said Richard.

'Yes, every speck of dust.'

From here our *patron* bought vegetables and meat (passed over the bar in baskets by hopeful salesmen) and here he collected information about the town.

'Do you by any chance know anything about this *famadihana*?' we asked, perched on bar stools and peering over.

He was down near the floor trying to tune the radio which he pressed to one ear. Yes, he knew about this *famadihana*, even had an invitation himself. 'But in thirty years I've never discovered what all the ancestor stuff's about,' he confessed. He was in an unusually garrulous mood this morning. 'A few years ago they didn't like *vazaha* being there, but now they seem to encourage it, especially writers.' His stout tweed-suited Breton wife (who dared not trespass behind his bar) had lived here her whole life, and she sighed.

The invitations were expensively printed on shiny card. The

front was decorated with linear patterns while the back showed a photograph of the royal tomb on its hilltop way above the town. The *patron* peered at the card; in thirty years he had not learnt Malagasy.

'I think it says that the whole thing starts tomorrow.' So we were on time. All would be well, as long as the family gave us permission to attend. 'I'm sure they won't mind. Not if you've got an invitation. The host can't get here from Tana until the day after. That's the big day. He'll be staying here, along with all the government ministers and whatnot.'

Inside was inscribed:

Tompoko, sir, You are invited to help celebrate the exhumation of King I Mpanalina Faharoa, King of Ambositra, and his Prime Minister, Raramonja.

Normally royalty were not given *famadihana*. They did not need it. The polluting decomposition of a body that in most cases required the cleansing process of *famadihana* was not necessary for an ancestor who had already in life attained the ritual status almost of a god. This, however, was a special case. The Betsileo King had died with his Prime Minister in battle, and their bodies had been bundled together. Never unravelled, it was impossible to decide which parts were royal and which were not and as a result they had never been buried in the royal tomb. For four hundred years they had been shifted from grave to grave, until their mortal remains were simply placed on a rock on top of the royal tomb. Not a satisfactory resting place for a royal ancestor. But now, at last, a compromise had been reached. They were to be buried on the royal site not in the royal tomb, but in a new tomb of their own.

The *patron* said it would be obvious where the action was – we should simply follow the crowd. But there was no crowd. The town was deserted. We walked for miles, back and forth past the market and the big red Jesuit monastery. Richard got hitched up with a German doctor and his Malagasy 'guide' who led us to the wrong places and kept asking me for shampoo. I found myself striding along ahead in a worse and worse mood. By the time we found whatever it was we were looking for, it would all be over.

Eventually a taxi driver understood. As I was closing the door of his 2CV a young man whose face streamed with sweat tried to squeeze in too. I thought he was a friend of the taxi driver, and did not mind him sharing the lift, but the driver shouted at him and pushed him away.

We drove to a patch of ground fenced in at the bottom of a bowl of hills. Some two thousand people – dark skinned and muscular – craned over each others' heads, a field of straw hats. A tunnel of eucalyptus branches led down to the ring. Spreading excitement, two bulls inflamed with rum were herded down the tunnel and into the ring. The crowd closed in, pushing, and leaned as far as they dared over the fence to bait the bulls and prod them with staves. They threw in their hats and challenged each other to run the gauntlet of the bulls to get them back. Then the village president announced where the bulls came from and prayed that no one would be wounded. The crowd rustled and ten rough-looking matadors jogged into the ring. Another wave of murmurs, of jostling. Warily, they circled the now enraged bulls and then leapt at their humps to wrestle them to the ground. The bulls bounced and snorted, kicking up dust; a man lurched into the air and scraped the ground. Another was tossed on horns and lost his trousers: there was a two thousand-strong intake of breath.

Richard struggled down to the ringside. For a while I strained to watch, my view blocked by a teacher in a red waistcoat who told me his name was Mr He Who Does Not Cultivate The Fields At Night (clearly this was his family's *fady*). They'd had three bullfights already this year, he said. For all the best Betsileo circumcisions and *famadihana* there is always a bullfight. Oh no! They never kill the bulls, simply release them back into the field. The men? Last year a man was gouged in the belly and lost his intestines, and one had his skull trampled and was killed. Suddenly I was overwhelmed – the possible deaths, the heat and the press of bodies – and I found myself hyper-ventilating under a tree. A man with a hair-lip loomed into vision. He spat a lot and smelt of rum. He wanted to start a 'correspondence'.

'Perhaps,' I said, looking doubtful. I wanted him to go.

'Oh, I know my face is nothing. Nothing. But I love all the world.'

From my horizontal position amongst the tree roots I became aware that something was happening. A man had been gored, people said. Blood on his inside leg. Another wave of excitement and the crowd surged backwards. The fence had collapsed and maddened bulls were trying to escape; people were slipping down the slope towards their horns. Passers-by called down, 'Where's your boyfriend?'

'Husband. Down there.'

'Ah!' They squared their fingers round their eyes. 'Camera man!'

I recovered with a bottle of orange soda and made my way towards him. I found him in a melée of over-excited men who held him propped high on the fence. He was finishing a roll of film.

'Come on up,' he shouted. He was elated. He had taken close-ups of man and beast, of black bulls' flanks and men sprawled under shafts of light. It was he who had slid into the ring when the fence broke; someone had grabbed his collar and dragged him out. Men were now fighting around us, the bulls still snorting, boys under our feet.

'Join us,' urged the matadors. But exhausted and parched, we hitched back to town.

As we neared the hotel we became aware that someone was following us. It was the sweating man who had tried to get into our taxi. Tattered flares pinned together down his leg flapped round his ankles; he wore an idiotic but benign grin. He was the town *fou*. He did not beg, just strode a few inches away from us, mimicking our walks. People smiled from their doorways and called him to leave us alone; others tried to shoo him off.

'Go away,' shouted Richard. But he took no notice. Just kept on smiling.

'*Fou, fou!*' boys taunted him, skipping beside him and plucking at his jersey. He never spoke.

A tap on my shoulder. It was Christine, smiling. Somehow they had found the money to get back. She took me back to their home, bare and uncomfortable. Ambositra was Brunoh's town, to which in the Malagasy tradition she followed him. Even after his death she would have to stay here. And women must follow their husbands in death as in life, so she would be buried with him in his family tomb. Christine explained this without complaint. This was her fate, and she accepted it without question. 'For us, the men are considered very strong. We must follow them and do as they say.'

Though Brunoh was physically weak, unable to support his family, and though Christine seemed to be the more intelligent, she must obey and respect him. But away from her own ancestral valley Christine seemed deflated. Women, I thought, never really belong anywhere. They belong in their father's place and then in their husband's. (The Comoros are one of the rare places in the world where the opposite is true.) Through marriage women's names change and they side-step off the family tree. It is the lines joining males together that are inked in, while women are uprooted. In Madagascar at least women are not expected to take their husbands' names, but nevertheless they are buried in the husbands' tombs, and that for them is what matters.

Here in Ambositra Christine seemed more anxious than ever, worn down by poverty. And all the time the *fou* was at my heels.

'Don't worry,' she said, 'he won't hurt you. He just wants to be near you.'

A short man dapper in pin stripes: it had to be him. We met on the stairs.

'Excuse me,' I began, 'are you by any chance the host of the *famadihana*?'

He smiled. 'Not exactly. My father is the host.'

'Oh, I see. I am English –'

'I know.'

'You know about us?' It was a relief. The girl who had given us the invitation had, on our behalf, paid our *safon-drazana*, the guest's donation to the host.

'Let's walk downstairs together,' he said in English with a faint American accent. 'You're interested in our customs?'

'Yes.'

'Well, you're more than welcome to join us. I think you know today's programme. It includes a cocktail party to which you're invited. You'll meet my wife.'

She and Richard joined us. She was *soignée* in a knee-length silk dress and pearls, honey skin and soft hair. She was nervous. It was a big day for their family and, as she confided later, she was not from this area; she was not even from this tribe. She was Merina. She did not belong. They had met outside the system in America, where he was training as a surgeon and she was at university. 'I don't believe in all this tribal business,' she admitted.

'Why don't you come along now?' suggested Dr Razafinarivo. 'Things are starting more or less straight away.'

*

It was 8 am and the family house was in turmoil, trays of cocktail sausages being dashed back and forth. 'That's not the traditional food,' muttered Christine, who had joined us. 'All that's western. Normally we only eat beef. Pork is considered dirty.' In her way, Christine was conventional and proud of her traditions. Richard vanished with his camera. 'Let's get somewhere quiet,' said Dr Razafinarivo, ushering Christine and me into the best front room. We sat on a row of uncomfortable chairs and he gave me a small Malagasy history of the family.

'Most of it's hearsay,' he admitted. 'As you know, until the missionaries came nothing was written down. But it's thought that this king died sometime in the sixteenth century.'

'Why are you doing this now, after all these years?'

'Well, my father is eighty-two and feels he has done well in life. He's a pharmacist. So he wants to do this for the family and the people of Ambositra. He knows I'll never do it. My father's very proud of his family and its history, so I guess he wants to celebrate that. I don't really believe in all this, and he knows it.'

Music started outside, footsteps and shouting.

'Don't let me keep you,' I said and, looking distracted, the Doctor left. He had spent five years planning this event.

Below, in the shade of the sacred north-east corner of the courtyard, stood the two *tranovorona*, the biers. The bodies (or as we and not many others knew, the handful of teeth) lay rolled in mats beneath tents of pink silk. Literally *tranovorona* means 'bird house' or 'nest'; odd (and yet not odd, here) that the ancestors' resting place should be associated not with death but with birth.

They had lain here all night, the flautists summoning the spirits to return to their corpses and enjoy the party. Milling around the nests were the family elders dressed in pink silk *lamba*, and the brimless straw hats unique to the Betsileo. 'No brim means that the knowledge does not escape from the head,' whispered Christine. 'Many Betsileo love their hats so much that they sleep in them.' I was glad to have her with me.

Crowds pressed against the fence. 'The people are happy because they feel close to the ancestors, and have been with them all night,' said Christine. As the sun warmed up one band of musicians flung off their early morning blankets to reveal matching blue shirts and red neck ties. I realized we had seen the same band at the Tana *famadihana*. Christine explained that these troubadours spend their lives roaming the highlands from ceremony to ceremony – *famadihana*, circumcision, wedding. They were joined by the oom-pah-pah of a military brass band.

From nowhere, the *fou* materialized beside me. He was chased away with a knife but soon bounced back, like a rubber ball. Eventually he wandered off and I watched him notice Richard below us and follow him.

'He's curious,' said Christine reassuringly. 'He wants to see what he has in his bag.'

Again people tried to shoo him away but he was impervious, always smiling slightly, always puzzled, scratching his head, trousers flapping, feet rubbery and bare.

Two huge and unsmiling *vazaha* appeared, swinging cameras. They had driven from Tana.

'Perhaps the *fou* will adopt them instead,' Christine suggested. But he didn't go near them. Perhaps he was afraid. They were Russian journalists from *Tass*.

Soldiers escorted ministers from Tana, flutes whistled faster and faster, drums rolled and, pushing the *fou* out of the way, the elders hoisted the nests on to their shoulders and processed up to the main square. A thirty-foot granite stele, inscribed with the names of the descendants but otherwise bearing a confusing resemblance to the lamp post beside it, was to be unveiled. It was smeared with blood, and on its plinth, grinning lopsidedly, tongue lolling, was the head of a sacrificed zebu.

'The zebu's very important,' Christine whispered. 'It must have as white a forehead as possible, so as to light the path of the ancestors down towards us.'

The nests were placed beside it, and the elders perodically checked that all was well beneath their canopies.

Fanfares, hats off, the National Anthem, microphones tested. Monsieur Alphonse Andrianasolo, a renowned Betsileo speaker, was draped in a striped *lamba*, a pink hat placed on his head, and the *kabary* began. For an hour he discoursed fluently on the history of Ambositra, on the moral example set by the king, and on the worth of his descendants. Without notes he played with the intricacies of the language and dotted his speech with the proverbs of which the Malagasy are so proud, to the occasional polite titter. Unselfconscious, the *fou* sat alone between the speaker and his audience. A soldier hauled him away, but he soon thrust himself forward again. And again, until they gave up.

A select few followed the hosts to the cocktail party in the village hall. Arrayed under paper decorations were bottles of Coca Cola and J&B Rare. Most, I noticed, went for the whisky. Suit lapels were striped with medals, ladies' shoulders wrapped in silk *lamba*; we felt out of place – too tall and too scruffy. The Doctor and his wife also stood apart, outsiders from the city who did not believe; they seemed to feel more at ease with us than with their country cousins. They loved speaking English, they said kindly, and their son was an American citizen. 'But I like being here,' the Doctor added. 'It's my country, and it needs us.'

Unlike most people who studied abroad where they could earn far more than here, he had returned home to become one of Madagascar's leading surgeons. But his children would probably never come back.

'Why should they? They lead better lives over there.' His eyes wandered anxiously over my shoulder. At the other end of the room the toasts were beginning. Someone proposed a vote of thanks to the hosts (tossing down more J&B) and the professional orator, Monsieur Andrianasolo, replied (at length) on their behalf.

We filed out between an aisle of village drunks who shook our hands and touched the men in suits for 100 fmg.

We were not sure if we were invited to lunch, so we returned to the hotel, thankful for the rest. Not for long: to our delight we were joined by our English friend Simon, who had just arrived from Tana. It was a joy to be with someone with whom we had so much in common – mutual friends, mutual interests. But that would have to wait: the meal was in full swing, he said, and they were wondering where we were. We returned together to the family house. A woman took us each by the hand and led us into a stone-flagged room. By now trestles covered with lace tablecloths were strewn with detritus. A cheer broke out, and I noticed the Doctor in a corner trying to join in. His tie was askew.

'Where have you been?' he called, sounding jovial.

'Speech, speech.' Palms banged the table.

'You've got to introduce yourselves,' Simon whispered. 'Go on, I've already done it. Just say who you are.'

Typically, he had already made friends with everybody. I stood up and said how happy we were to be there, thanked them for their hospitality. They banged spoons on the table and clattered glasses in drunken approval. Then food was brought. A woman with cropped hair and glasses approached with a jug.

'I speek Eenglish leetle. You drink the coffee Malgache?'

'Yes, thank you.'

'Nothing,' she squeaked, and poured a thick dark stream. Simon's easy friendliness and English good looks seemed to make people relax around us.

'You Simon,' growled a drunken army colonel, 'and me Garfunkel. Tonight we dance.'

And dance we did. That evening 'the masses' as Christine called them (or occasionally 'the peesants') returned to the village hall and gathered in a circle beneath the paperchains. At one end, in state, lay the ancestors, and in front of them, some immediate members of the family, humourless as judges at a *thé dansant*. No sign of the Doctor. The music started. People were shy at first, but then an old man in shorts and bare feet – the oldest person present – was chosen to lead. Arms in the air, body swaying, he stamped the ancient tribal rhythm. This is what has filtered down to our western discos. A drunk youth joined him; at first people were amused and threw him coins but he could barely pick them up and at the end of the song he was hauled off. Things deteriorated when who should push his way on to the floor but the *fou*. A roar of hilarity almost drowned the music, amusement from one quarter and outrage from the organizers.

'He lowers the tone,' one shouted.

'We must respect the ancestors!'

The *fou* was dragged out, only to bounce back minutes later. The angry people yelled at him, but others shouted back, 'Let him stay! This is a festival for everybody!' But out he was pushed.

To get the party going again, Monsieur Andrianasolo took to the floor and made a quick speech.

The crowd thickened, straw hats banking higher and higher. Beside us a man with a face like a giraffe periodically cackled with laughter at nothing in particular. Everyone was enjoying themselves except the stony-faced descendants. We climbed onto a table at the back, hoping we could see but not be seen, but I heard the dreaded *vazaha vazaha* and knew our time would come.

'*Vous dansez?*' whispered a girl in a woolly hat, her arms wrapped around me.

'Only if you do,' I replied.

Eyes turned more and more frequently towards us. Each time the master of ceremonies paused I waited for what I knew was inevitable, only for his finger to point towards a group of teenage girls or a shy couple. Some shuffled self-consciously, others were showered with coins. I dreaded the staring but when the finger did at last come our way Richard said, 'Come on, we've got to do this now.'

Simon agreed so I followed them off the table, down between the crowds and on to the dance floor. The crowd erupted, the one word *VAZAHA* reverberating over the musicians and up amongst the paperchains into the roof. All around us they cheered and clapped and hooted but I saw nothing, everything blocked out except the music. I was aware of being grabbed by the toothless old man and swung round, then a young boy in checked trousers and a pork-pie hat took over. We danced on and on, and the space around us cleared until we were alone. I saw no staring crowds, no Richard, no Simon, only this boy's panting face and shining skin. The flutes stopped and left only the drum, pounding faster and faster. The clapping and the rhythm; the drum was never going to stop. Then the dancers closed in again and I was grasped by another man and then another.

When we left, exhilarated, and pressed our way out into the night, the flutes started up again in our wake. The dancing went on until dawn.

We set off before breakfast for the royal tomb. These early winter mornings were chill until the sun burned through. It was a steep climb but lovely, up between stepped fields of newly-planted rice (we could have been in Sri Lanka) and hedges of wild roses, honeysuckle, and passion vine loaded with fruit. Red-walled Ambositra dwindled below.

At the top of a rocky crag the royal family were buried in what, over the centuries, had become more a mound of grass than a recognizable tomb. Beside it stood the new tomb, a rough-edged bunker built of marble slabs and topped with concrete. How could they have desecrated this place with such ugliness, we wondered secretly, but if *famadihana* was to remain part of people's lives today, not simply a repetition of the past, I suppose it was right to use contemporary materials, even if they were so unattractive. Again, that hybrid mix of cultures.

A few men had gathered. Five zebu had just been sacrificed in front of the tomb and, flesh still twitching, they were being skinned and cut up, stomachs opened and emptied of half-digested grass. Throughout the day a man squatted on his haunches to squeeze clean miles of intestines. Another slipped nuts of fat into his pocket. He used it on his hands, he said, when he dug the fields. Birds of prey wheeled overhead. Tables were carried up from the town and stalls began to be erected at the base of the tomb. Doughnuts were fried, carrots grated. People flowed up in a steady stream. By mid morning the Russians had joined us, the drumming had started, and a truck hooted up the hill with the nests on the back.

Five hours of speeches began. Again Monsieur Andrianasolo was called upon. Through a megaphone he summoned each guest by name; in return for a small gift of money each guest received a portion of sacred meat.

The sun was merciless and we escaped to watch the *Mpira Gasy*. They were traditional Malagasy singers dressed in missionary garb of boaters, sashed shirts and long dresses. Back to back in concentric rings, they chanted in harmony of the ancestors, of the way things were, are and always should be. They admonished the audience to follow the ancestors' moral example, not to drink or be profligate with money. The crowd was thick, immobile but for one man who sat in the front imitating the *Mpira Gasy*, mouthing the words and remonstrating back, so wholeheartedly did he agree.

I was led aside by a man describing himself as an 'unofficial' historian. He was from Antananarivo University, and in an undertone in the far corner of the royal site, overlooking the valleys and hills, he repeated the now familiar charges of Presidential corruption. Ratsiraka must change the constitution, liberalize his policies, encourage foreign investment, exploit the country's natural resources. A man in a beret sat close by muttering. 'It's true, it's true.' Although I said I was unqualified for such a mission, they insisted that I should be a carrier of this Truth back to the west.

Suddenly we heard through the megaphone: '*Venez les touristes!*' The two fat Russians had gone home so Richard, Simon and I climbed back up the rocks and before the crowd we, too, were presented with handfuls of sacred meat. 'It is our mark of respect,' announced Monsieur Andrianasolo, 'and of our welcome to our foreign visitors.' The Doctor, who appeared for the first time, tie askew, shirt less than crisp, watched us ruefully and produced a plastic bag. A fat man in dark glasses trained his video camera on us. He was the host's nephew.

'Ah, I see you've met our bigshot,' smiled the Doctor. 'Our VIP. You know he's a good friend of the President?'

'I wouldn't say good friend,' the fat man replied modestly. 'Economic adviser, that's all.'

'Good adviser then.'

'Well, I don't know about that.'

With an MBA from an American college, he was making his fortune importing Tata trucks from India. So successful was this capitalist venture that he had been employed by the Christian-Marxist government. Predictably, he lived in a new villa in Ivandry, drove a BMW, and took holidays abroad. An economy '*a deux vitesses*'.

The band started up again, and the nests were prepared for their final move. The eight elders squabbled over who was to take which corner. The crowd surged back and forth. 'Have you seen my wife?' called the Doctor. 'No?' The wave of bodies beached him beside us. 'Oh well, I give up. Come and look inside the new tomb.' This was a great honour. Normally only the most respected members of the family were allowed in. Christine was shocked when we told her later. 'It's *fady*. I have never *never* been inside a tomb.' She wondered – covertly – what it was like. Other guests clustered at the entrance to watch us defy *fady* and descend the steps into an airy chamber. They did not dare to follow. Cool and quiet after the turmoil of the day: I almost heard the Doctor sigh. The tomb had cost millions of francs. It was smooth with concrete and whitewash, and in the centre stood a carved wooden boat that still smelled of beeswax. Its craftsmen stood shyly behind it. They seemed overwhelmed by the events of the day and by the magnitude of their now completed task. The Doctor congratulated them.

'This is where my ancestors will lie,' he said.

After laying the bodies on their boat, setting them free on the great ocean of the dead, the door would be sealed forever, or at least until some other wealthy descendant decided to build them another tomb and give them another *famadihana*.

Simon had researched into the history of Malagasy textiles and photographed the silk *lamba* in the Rova after Laura finished her work. Weaving as sophisticated as this had died out, so he set up a UN-funded project to revive the tradition while also creating work in rural areas. One silk *lamba* was being woven in a village not far from Ambositra, and when we told Simon about the *lambamena* in Uncle Ralph's attic, he was keen to show us what he was doing. These weavers were related to Christine, not surprisingly here where most people seemed to be connected somehow. Simon would take us all there the following day.

Meanwhile Richard and I exchanged the fleas at the Grand Hotel for a Benedictine nunnery at the other end of town. High red brick walls shielded a hushed and clean security from the hurly-burly outside; Belgian, French and Malagasy nuns flitted soundlessly across the cobbles in fawn habits. It was a world apart. Someone in the 1930s with austere but perfect taste had commissioned Arts and Crafts furniture in honey-coloured wood with creatures crawling up the legs; chair seats were exquisitely woven from sisal and raffia; rope mats covered smooth stone floors; niches were filled with books and carvings; colours were unbleached and natural. Every door handle and light switch had been lovingly crafted. A garden of magnolias, camellias and lilies was lovingly tended. After the crowds, the noise, the rush to reach Ambositra, this was a retreat for the senses as well as the spirit.

We sat in silence in our room (two chaste beds with hand-woven covers, a polished basin, smooth wood floors) wondering what time we were expected for supper, and where. The stillness amplified every sound, and we started at a bell resonating through the stone hall. We found a few other guests heading for the dining room set aside for visitors. (The nuns dined alone in their closed community.) The table was laid with starched napkins and bowls of soup, and eight other people stood to say grace. They were nuns from other orders, and a Polish priest, all here to learn Malagasy. We ate restrained portions of shepherd's pie and yoghurt, and this ordered life where bells segmented the day came as a relief. Briefly, we abnegated all responsibilities; sometimes I can see the charm of living in an institution.

I was sitting beside Sister Rosemary, a Canadian who was eager to speak English for the first time in nine months. She had spent twenty-five years in an order in North London, but in middle age had suddenly been 'called' to Madagascar.

'I'll spend the rest of my life here,' she said cheerfully.

She was short and pasty-skinned as if she had been too long out of the light. From this sepulchral haven she would sally forth into the depths of society. 'You've never seen anything like the prisons here,' she said. 'I've seen some things in my time, but after that I had terrible nightmares.' She described one room ringed with a shelf raised four feet off the ground where prisoners slept. Others lay on the floor amongst the rats and the excrement. Unless the prisoners have a family living nearby they get no food, just the odd manioc root. 'I saw a guard strip off his studded belt and beat a prisoner,' Sister Rosemary said, eyes wide. 'One nun took a photograph and the next day the police raided her house and demanded the film. She refused to give it to them and in the end they left it on the condition that she would send it to France and never let it back into the country. Amnesty International filed a report years ago, and as a result they were banned forever.'

Richard went to bed and Sister Rosemary invited me into her room.

'Forgive the chaos,' she said, though there was none. It was simple but not spartan. She wanted to tell me about *fihavanana*, and leafed through the notes she had taken during lectures on Malagasy culture. 'Ah, here we are. *Fihavanana*. This was a lecture by a Malagasy priest, a marvellous man who is also head of the Press Association. *Fihavanana* is at the heart of Malagasy daily life, and it means family unity. The family must be seen to be bonded, to be close.'

'I've seen that at *famadihana*,' I said. 'I envy that.'

'Ah, but you see the emphasis is on *must be seen*. The families must appear to be united even if they are not. You must always be seen to be smiling. And the basis of that is fear. Fear of what people will do to you if you are not smiling, not nice to them. Fear of revenge. Fear of spells and *gris-gris*. It's the same with the ancestors. You must be nice to them for fear of their revenge.'

'So you mean that at *famadihana* the joy is not genuine?'

'No. It's all fear.'

'I've noticed something of that, but happiness too. People have been very friendly to us.'

'They just want something from you. They must be seen to be happy and smiling, hoping you'll give them some money.' We were sitting on hard chairs and the nunnery grew quiet, muffled in sleep. I was beginning to feel depressed. I thought of all the smiles greeting us on taxi-brousses, and of Christine and her family. Were they just trying to get things from us? And were they afraid of what we might do in return if they were not nice to us? Suddenly I wasn't sure, but I was beginning to dislike Sister Rosemary. After all, what did she know? She had only been here nine months, and all her knowledge was from cloistered lectures and the underbelly of life, not from living amongst ordinary people.

She went on: 'This fear and all the ancestor worshipping is so strong that it makes our lives very difficult. They believe in God, in Andriamanitra, but it's all so tied up with ancestor worship that they have to un-learn everything before learning about Jesus. The family ties are so strong – the *fihavanana* – that before a Malagasy nun joins our order she must sign an agreement to renounce her place in the family tomb. That's very difficult for them.'

'But why do you want to convert people?' I asked. 'Why not just leave them alone?'

Sister Rosemary looked a bit taken aback. What was I doing in this nunnery, she was wondering. I felt a bit like a spy.

'Because they need us,' she asserted. Of this she had no doubt. 'The Jesuit father-journalist begged us to teach his people. Without you, he said, they'd be nothing. They can't sustain any work they do, they don't repair their roads or their houses. They work for a couple of days and then just stop. The country's in a dreadful state. Do you know that the Jesuit father doesn't know one person who will be capable of taking on his weekly column in La Croix newspaper when he retires?'

'Why not?'

'Because no one else will be able to sustain it for that long. All they care about is having a good time. And getting something out of you.'

When Simon suggested visiting the weavers' village, wading across a wide and fairly deep river was not exactly what I'd had in mind. But there was no alternative: the village was on the other side. Simon did this once a month to check how the work was progressing. The bridge had been swept away one monsoon and no one had the money or motivation to rebuild it. Christine and Brunoh guided us through the shallower waters. Christine's maternal grandmother lived here with two of her daughters and was teaching them the art of weaving, which she herself had learnt from Norwegian Lutheran missionaries. As we walked up to the village Simon explained that the silk had been grown, spun and dyed in Madagascar as part of his project.

'The great thing is that this is an entirely Malagasy art,' he enthused, while also being well aware of the irony that a *vazaha* should be trying to stop the art from disappearing.

It was a hamlet more than a village, paddy fields falling away below. The floors were smooth with beaten mud, and upstairs Christine's aunt sat at her loom.

'*Manahoana Tompoko.*' The weaver greeted Simon warmly.

We climbed the old stairs and entered a scene from Grimm's fairytales. In a light beam shifting with dust sat a young woman with two long black plaits. Behind was her spinning wheel, in front a loom on which was strung silk of the most brilliant colours and the most complex patterns. It was a copy of a *lambamena* in the palace in Tana. At once I recognized the patterns from the silk *lambamena* in Devon. Ours could almost have been woven here. Simon said these looms had not changed for over a hundred years. But he was disappointed by the lack of progress.

'It's nice what she's done, that's great. Now we can see the pattern forming, and the shine. But the problem is it takes so long! This is two months' work and she's hardly begun. And this is only half the *lamba*. Her sister is supposed to be weaving the other half and apparently she hasn't started at all.'

Christine looked on anxiously: her grandmother and aunts now depended on Simon for a living and they feared his anger.

'She's starting today,' said the weaver encouragingly.

'Today?' Simon laughed. 'It's always when I'm here that she starts. Isn't it?'

'We've had many problems.'

Simon turned to us, embarrassed by the scene. 'It's always the same. Quite honestly I'm getting a bit fed up. It could have been done in two weeks in India, but of course that isn't the point. The point is to give these people work. But all I ever get is demands for more money.'

I sympathized with his frustration, particularly as I knew how much he cared for Madagascar. He loved this place, yet he was growing disillusioned and thinking of leaving.

'They must think I'm a pain in the neck, coming in here. I feel like I'm a perfectionist. I want everything done just right. I guess

Europeans or whatever just do have a very different way of looking at things, and I'll never be able to adjust, not really.'

I could not stop Sister Rosemary coming to mind, and it made me feel uneasy.

We left Simon to sort things out, and I went for a walk with Christine. She too was embarrassed by the situation. 'Simon gets so angry that the weavers lose courage for their work,' she said.

'But he wasn't angry. He was very nice.'

'But he speaks so aggressively! We feel afraid. We are not lazy people, really we are not. It's just our way.'

I found myself repeating what Simon had already said. 'And he has paid them, very well too,' I added.

'But it's not enough for us. We need more just to live.'

Richard and I went north to Antsirabe to have a bath. A thick mist breathed up and down valleys as we climbed in a taxi-brousse through the highlands. The grey-green land grew rocky, and rivers shrivelled to streams beneath eroding crags. It could have been the Spanish Pyrenees, or even north-west Scotland without the heather, deforested with equal enthusiasm. We emerged on to a plain dotted with tall blank houses, windowless on our side in accordance with the dictates of the ancestors. Houses as inward-looking as the people. They stood not in clusters of villages but isolated in paddy fields which had been divided by inheritance into tiny patches. Some were flooded, others newly planted with rice unhealthily green, others being chopped with spoon-sized long-handled spades. Even their tools are delicate (if impractical). It was Sunday, and church-goers spilled onto the street in pin-stripe suits and high heels.

I recall little of Antsirabe itself. It was full of Norwegian-Lutheran churches and aggressive *pousse-pousse* drivers desperate for fares. All day they hung about beneath our hotel window, grinning and gesticulating whenever we showed our faces.

The baths overlooked what had once been a thermal spring and was now a foetid pond choked with water hyacinth. From a distance the turrets and pines trees lent the building a healthy Scandinavian air but it was deceptive. The heyday of these baths, when Queen Ranavalona II came to take the waters, and when Prime Minister Rainilaiarivony's son came to recover from the rheumatism he had picked up during a visit to England, was over. Windows were broken, the roof rusted, and the ground was encrusted with salts and smeared with rivulets of sulphur. It was closed for the evening but we peered round the back: a post-nuclear wasteland, silent and dead, just the dripping of old sulphurous pipes. A washing line was hung with corrective-looking pants and an old bathtub spilled clods of black mud. We were startled by a man sitting in a window picking stones out of rice. He came hurrying out.

'It's volcanic mud – you can spread it on your face.'

'Lovely.'

'Yes, you boil it here.' A brick fire beside the bath was clearly where this happened. 'Bring a plastic bag tomorrow and I'll give you some.' This doctor was keen on the mud. 'With massage, bath and medical consultation that will be 10,000 fmg.'

We returned the next morning.

'Ten thousand fmg?' The masseuse was incredulous. She had blackheads on her nose and she hated him. Perhaps they had been lovers. 'He was trained in Marseille, you know,' as if that explained everything. In the hallway the *curistes* sat in dismal groups in dressing gowns awaiting their turn. 'Didn't he tell you to bring soap? Typical. He's a drug addict. He's mad.'

Richard was led away to the male compartment, and I was ordered to undress and ushered into a dank sulphur-stained cell. A starched-white woman barked at me to get behind a mesh screen. She picked up a hose.

'Is it hot?' I asked hopefully.

'No.'

I stood there naked dreading the icy blast. I was her victim. But it was warm, naturally so.

'*Le dos,*' she droned. '*A gauche. A droite, levez le bras.*' Water powered through the nozzle.

Next door for the massage. Through the steam I saw a shapeless woman with long brown nipples climbing off a plastic-coated bed which stood like an operating table in the centre of the room. She clutched a towel, giggling in the corner.

'Lie down.'

I raised myself onto the slab. Three women closed in, with three hoses. I was soaped and kneaded until a hot sprinkler was cranked into action along the length of my body.

'That's it then.'

I was led back through the changing rooms, past a massage

cubicle in which a body lay splayed, like a hunk of cooked beef being tucked into by hungry women. My wet *lamba*, a thin piece of cotton masquerading as a towel, clung coldly as I entered the hall. The air had turned icy. I joined the glum convalescents (a few downtrodden *vazaha* amongst them) to await my bath. It was rusted like a Victorian hospital bath but was hot and deep, deep enough to wallow. A woman jetted me with more hoses. Whatever you do, don't swallow it, she warned.

'What about your mud!' called the doctor as we left. His voice echoed mournfully over the lake and up to the hotel. 'Where's your plastic bag? Don't you want your mud?'

We pretended not to hear.

For days we stank of sulphur but it was our only bath in four months.

CHAPTER NINE

THE NORTH-WEST

We planned to tour the north and paused in Tana to borrow a stack of novels from an English acquaintance before travelling by taxi-brousse 490 miles to Mahajanga. The tight hills of the southern highlands opened out to a rugged emptiness which made me think of Dartmoor. Cloud shadows manoeuvred over bald hills, tors and standing stones, all pulsing red in the evening sun. A few lonely huts dotted an otherwise marvellously unpeopled land. By nightfall the only signs of life were the caterpillars of flame that wriggled over dry grasses.

Where trees had been razed and bush fires burned, now the only living things pushing up through the ground were the termites whose red mounds pimpled the eroding prairie. Each year during the dry season over 200,000 hectares are burnt. Grasses send up new shoots for cattle grazing but in a few years the earth is barren. *Midi Madagasikara* had carried articles raging against this annual madness, but Tana's intellectuals could have little effect on tribesmen in these wildernesses whose herds of zebu might starve.

We broke down for several hours under the Milky Way and a moon too dazzling to look at. In the taxi-brousse the press of bodies stank of feet and sweat, but at least we all kept one another warm. A fat woman wedged me in.

'She's your hot woman bottle,' said Richard.

Amongst the passengers sat a bearded crone. She wore laddered black lisle stockings, a black dress and brown cardigan, her long grey hair wrapped in a scarf. She spoke fluent Malagasy, yet she was what she appeared to be: a peasant woman from the fields of France. With her was a middle-aged man, dark-skinned but with European features, feet padded like Malagasy feet from years walking barefoot. She had married a Malagasy man, produced this son, and at Independence found she was too poor to go home. In any case, her home was here. She had become a Malagasy peasant. Her toothless smile was kindly but we were all too tired to talk much.

As night wore on the temperature rose. We were coming down off the plateau into the dry north-west. At 3 am we were dropped at the roadside.

The driver hooted into the night, waking the dogs and a man who emerged from the forest and sleepily led us up a path.

'You can sleep there if you like.'

He pointed to a shed. The ceiling had collapsed and I feared rats, so instead we spread our sleeping bags under the stars and the glittering full moon on the sandy ground. Plate-sized teak leaves crackled underfoot and smelled hot and dry. We covered our heads in shawls against mosquitoes, the rattle of cicadas and the light. Every snapped twig sent my heart racing – I was still afraid after Mananjary – but it was only dogs and chickens. A grunting toad turned out to be Richard snoring. Before dawn I heard a pump or generator starting up, or was it zebu carts passing on the road? In the morning I discovered it was white Sifaka lemurs who sat above our heads in the leafless winter trees, and whose cries resonated through the forest.

We were in Ampijeroa, a 'forest station'. Gradually people emerged from a length of bamboo rooms. No one seemed surprised to see us lying on the ground. Soon smoke was rising. I walked through a scruffy village – we had left the land of bricks and returned to thatched palm-stem huts – and fetched water from a lake near the road. It was surrounded by deciduous forest – quite different from the east coast – and a few paddy fields. Other women fetching water led me through the mud into the shallows and promised it was clean despite the colour. We brewed tea on our stove and then with Rabe, the warden, explored the forest. As we climbed higher, the tall trees, each with their attendant liana, shrunk to saplings. We tracked brown lemurs, coua birds, drongo and small nocturnal lemurs that hide in holes with big scared eyes. Rabe was quiet and knowledgeable. Last year much of the forest was destroyed by a *feu de brousse* that got out of control; Rabe and the villagers worked night and day for a week clearing paths in order to stop the fire's spread. Thousands of animals and birds were killed, he said. He expressed no bitterness; the *feu de brousse* was just a fact of life.

Lake Ravelobe was sacred, Rabe said. He swore there were crocodiles here.

'But what about those people swimming?' we asked. (I thought of my own tentative steps to fetch water.)

'They never harm anyone. That's because it's sacred. People come here to ask for things from them. That's the meaning of Ampijeroa. Crocodiles are thought to be the embodiment of the ancestors.' I thought of Richard's hat – Ranavalona's hat. Was it perhaps a sacred hat? The *fady* surrounding crocodiles were numerous but changed from place to place. Nobody crossing a river should wear clothes of red material as this would challenge the crocodile; those crossing a crocodile river must keep their mouths closed, an open mouth suggesting the jaws of a crocodile. If the *fady* are observed, the crocodile will undertake not to hurt the people, and if the *fady* are broken, the witch-doctor must make a sacrifice and ask the animal for forgiveness. Killing the crocodile is the greatest *fady* of all the crocodile *fady*. We walked on the soft mud.

'Do you think it's really true?' I whispered to Richard. 'That there are crocodiles here?' At that moment Rabe pointed out a log on the shore that had begun to move. A young crocodile was sunning itself with its jaws apart. It slid off into the water at our approach.

Grey parrots shrieked, jumping fish slapped on the water, and in the evening high high above the empty lake wheeled a rare fish eagle.

'We're going to turn this into a proper reserve,' Rabe said, 'with a hotel here by the lake, and restaurants.'

'Oh.' It seemed a pity. Rabe himself came from far away to the east, from the shores of another sacred lake.

'Before, everything was sacred,' he muttered, almost to himself. 'Now nothing is.'

Richard made a fire and cooked rice. It was a convenient foodstuff, so cheap, never going off or getting squashed, and swelling to three times its bulk. We were getting addicted to it, almost sharing the Malagasys' misery if we did not eat it at least once a day. We even ate it for breakfast, with honey. Under a mango tree we put up the tent for the first time since Mananjary. It was disturbing to touch its slashed sides, so violent, and unpleasant to sleep in. The ground was hard, and again we both lay alert for footsteps.

Then we hitch-hiked to Mahajanga.

At last we were back on Newman territory. It felt almost like home ground. Here Robert Newman Hunt landed in 1837 and innocently tried to persuade the Queen to allow him to open his 'house of business' in Tana.

I wish to inform your Majesty that in the sea ports there are so few people that no trade can be done, and our ships are obliged to go away with the goods they bring from England, so that in future they will be able to run very seldom, unless the government should grant us permission to send our goods up the country.

He goes on in an almost pleading tone:

Mssrs. Newman Hunt & Christopher are only merchants, they have no wish to meddle with the government or the religion of the people.

The Queen was not moved by his appeal. She had other things on her mind, and in any case, three months earlier Jean Laborde had signed a contract with the government to create an industrial city outside Tana. Before long there were soap factories, blast furnaces, cannon foundries, reservoirs, all operated by some 20,000 forced labourers, none of whom (conveniently) needed to be paid. Silk was spun and bricks baked, paper milled, animals husbanded, orchards planted: Laborde was a universal man. What need did Ranavalona have of a patronizing trader like Robert Newman Hunt? She ignored him.

But clearly some trade was done in the port. In October 1840 Henry Angelo notes that $20 is owed to Robert Newman Hunt, and $8974.24½ – a huge amount – to 'Majunga employ'. $1,478 was owed by the Sakalava king. They must have had quite an establishment.

Of course Mahajanga has grown in 150 years, but it retains a desolate feel. We stayed with a Creole family in a shanty town of corrugated iron, relieved only by the occasional wind-torn banana tree. The town was the hottest in Madagascar and had been bombarded by cyclones. Near the port, shops were shuttered behind metal grilles; we could almost hear clocks tick and voices whisper. Arcaded streets were dusty and bleached by day – I half expected a cowboy to swing from saloon doors, gun in hand, to blast away the silence. By night beneath the moon they were as empty and shadowed as a de Chirico.

In Indian cafés desultory fans turned. Flies buzzed, and a gang of ragged boys flicked bottle tops in the sand and begged when they caught our eyes. We waited for something, though for what we did not know. Perhaps for some presence of the past.

We found a hint of it at the port itself. A few old warehouses and carved doors, and dhows marooned by the low tide, hinted of our return to ancient trade routes. The swollen baobab, fourteen metres in girth, was planted by Arab slavers a thousand years ago. Mahajanga was a short hop from the Comoros and had long been favoured as an outlet for Malagasy slaves, as well as hides and timber which were shipped to Zanzibar and beyond.

These warehouses might have been used by Newman Hunt & Christopher.

Robert Newman Hunt had profit in mind, but enveloped in higher ideals. He was an emissary from Britain, the greatest nation on earth.

England is famous for the goods which are made there, many of them would be useful for your Majesty's subjects, and they would be brought here cheaper than from any other country. England has few of the natural advantages which Madagascar has, and whatever grows there is only got by hard work.

Two-masted sailing ships that might have been the *Herrick*, or the *Rio Packet*, were being loaded in the harbour. Sadly, they were all heading south; we were on our way north.

We jolted in *pousse-pousses*, preoccupied by travel arrangements – visas to be extended, permission to travel by ship to be granted by the port authority. I also had a hideous haircut and sat under the drier reading French 'photo-love' stories.

What I remember most often is the intensity of life lived in one darkened house. A certain *salon du thé* had been recommended but the metal shutters were down. Richard rattled them, and out tumbled a family of Indians.

'I'm sorry, we're closed,' a surprised woman apologized. Then she smiled. 'But please come back later and drink lassi with us. You promise? Don't forget now.'

Nila was vastly fat. With her hair clipped back and a mole above her lip she was no beauty, but she was an enveloping cushion of warmth and goodness. So unlike the reserved Malagasy, she opened her large heart and took us in. She sat us at the end of their living room and from her cavernous kitchen, piled with dishes and electrical gadgets and of which she was ashamed (it's so untidy!), she plied us with sweet Indian *chai*, lassi and curries. Although she and her husband were fasting, however much we ate it was never enough for Nila.

As in East Africa and Zanzibar, most of Madagascar's Indians were relatively recent immigrants from Gujerat. The majority were Muslims and lived here, in Tulear on the south-west coast and in Diego Suarez. Mosques dominated this town. But Nila and her husband were Hindus, and they kept themselves to themselves. This long dark room with its shuttered windows was the centre of their world. After three or four generations here they were still outsiders. Their roots grew elsewhere, but though they kept their own traditions alive they had not yet been drawn back home.

'I'd like to go sometime,' said Nila wistfully, but I had the feeling that Mauritius was the closest they would get. Their ancestors had come over as traders. 'Newman,' pondered Nila. 'I may be imagining things but that name says something to me. I found some of my grandfather's papers. Maybe I read it there. Maybe our ancestors traded together. I wonder. It's certainly a familiar name.'

Rasmi, her husband, was distinguished-looking with grey-streaked hair and a hooked nose. (He decided Richard was a private detective. 'You know,' he said, 'Sherlock Holmes.' Richard was not particularly flattered.)

Though Rasmi had left school early owing to the death of his father, he now ran a successful furniture-making business, exported tables and chairs to Moroni and around Madagascar, drove a car, and could afford holidays in Mauritius. It was a relief to be with people able to get on and take care of themselves after the doom-laden passivity of Christine and Brunoh.

'Are there problems between the Moslems and Hindus?' I asked Rasmi, thinking of India.

'No, none at all.'

'And between the Indians and the Malagasy?'

'It's fine at the moment,' said Rasmi, a little discomfited by my question.

Malagasy resentment of the Indians had erupted a few years previously in race riots. People had died. I wondered if that explained the metal shutters. Nila kept hers closed and locked always. The Indians don't mix, was a common complaint. They don't inter-marry. In the past Malagasy culture was so strong that Arab traders who had settled over the centuries, as they did in East Africa and Zanzibar, here found themselves gradually absorbed. They did leave a few traces: the lunar calender, *vintana, ombiasy*, the earliest script. These were Arab infiltrations. Even today there are tribes in the south-east – the Antambahoaka and Antaimoro – who clearly betray their Arab origins. The earliest known writings, the *sorabe*, were written by Antaimoro scribes using Arabic script in the sixteenth century. But although they contributed to Malagasy culture, they merged with it. These newcomers held themselves apart. There were stories of hated Indian middlemen keeping back rice stocks during shortages and so doubling prices, but it was their separateness that the Malagasy most resented. *Tanindrazana* is the land of the ancestors, but not of Indian ancestors. We had noticed at the port that all the boat owners, stepping out of French and Japanese cars to inspect the loading of their ships, were Indian. Overfed Indian boys in shiny trousers ate ice-cream and buzzed around on mopeds, spilling over the sides.

'The point is that they're jealous,' Nila interjected. 'They're jealous of our success. They can't get it together themselves.' The Indians: the Jews of the Indian Ocean.

Rasmi shrugged. 'There are good and bad Malagasy just as there are with every nationality.'

Nila's ancestors' sea-faring trade had dwindled to a grocery shop *en brousse*. Until he died her father had run it. Now her mother was alone and eighteen-year-old Kirti, Nila's brother whom she had brought up, was dreading having to leave school in order to do his filial duty and manage the shop. He was learning English and wanted to go to university. He wanted to get on in the world, perhaps be an interpreter, not run a grocery shop. He showed us his records – British and American pop, mostly Michael Jackson.

The family insisted on us being with them for every meal, even breakfast. Each one was more lavish than the last.

'You need love when you're travelling,' Nila would say. 'You're far from home, without home comforts. So many people are unfriendly and try to cheat you. You need to be cared for.'

Along with the dogs and cats she had rescued from starvation, and the snakes saved from Malagasy cruelty, Nila was mother to all the world.

'I have spent my life trying to make happiness, not money,' she said, and we believed her.

She had opened her salon to take her mind off her troubles. After eleven years of marriage she had had fourteen miscarriages and three stillbirths. She tried everything. For eleven years she persevered, determined one day to have a focus for all her love, and to give Rasmi a descendant. Then the doctor suggested she worked to occupy herself. Not long after she began, her cat had kittens on her knee, and her masseuse predicted that she would have a child. Three months later she conceived. After nine months in bed she was flown to Réunion where she produced an adored and adorable son, Christophe. Triumphantly she closed the salon. She had better things to do.

Now Christophe played on a floor strewn with plastic animals and bright-coloured toys that we had seen nowhere else. 'I get all his things from abroad,' Nila said proudly. 'His clothes and his toys, from France or Switzerland or Réunion. Nothing comes from here. The colours fade.'

His every action was doted on, not only by Nila but also by Kirti and Bhavna, her sister. They showed no trace of boredom at hearing Nila's outpourings yet again – the day Christophe cut his chin, his first words – or of jealousy. Rasmi was equally devoted.

'Now I know I could have another child if I lost some weight.'

'But one's enough,' interrupted Rasmi, bouncing his beloved two-year-old in the air.

He was certainly a special child, with a high forehead, pale skin, and large grave eyes. Richard thought he looked like Krishna. Was his skin faintly grey-blue? Perhaps it was his clothes, but looking back now I see Christophe always in a blue haze. By coincidence (or was it some Malagasy sorcerer's whim?) the day we met was the eve of Krishna's birthday. It's like your Christmas, Nila explained. The six hundred-strong Hindu community would gather in their temple in the back of a shop for a midnight *puja*.

They wanted to take us to the temple but it was closed for preparations, so instead we visited a shrine in a friend's house. The livingroom walls were decorated with kitsch pictures of Hindu gods in wreaths of pink cloud; Hindu culture, the culture of their ancestors, transported intact across the ocean. A woman in a sari with a red tikka between her eyes led us in a respectful procession to a locked door at the back of the house. We slipped off our shoes, and stood before the bright-lit shrine. Miniature statues of Siva and Vishnu, Ganesh the elephant and Hanuman the monkey god were smothered in offerings from grateful suppliants whose wishes had been granted. A lanky pock-marked son grinned with pride. Indian movie stars shone on the wall. Nila placed a note on the altar.

'Don't you have some coins?' she whispered.

We made our wishes. Nila took my arm as we left.

'You know what I wished? It will definitely come true. That the next time we meet you will have a son.' Dear Nila: she wanted me to share her good fortune.

The woman was able, in a trance-like state, to allow the gods to speak through her. Nila's father had died, suddenly, of severe stomach problems. He had never been ill before and Nila suspected a *gris-gris*. She guessed that he had been poisoned by a friend to whom he had lent money and who could not repay it. Without knowing any of the circumstances, the woman had confirmed this during a trance.

'One must believe these things,' Rasmi said.

'Now I can't see that man without wanting to do something to him. I know he poisoned my father, and yet I could never prove it.'

This fear, and the eating of rice, were almost the only things Nila and Rasmi held in common with Christine and Brunoh.

We searched for a cargo boat to take us north, and found the *Hadji*, North Sea trawler-sized and carrying cement. Predictably, its owner was Indian.

'I don't advise it,' he warned. His ears, I noticed, sprouted hairs and the lobes dangled below his jaw. His mouth was free of the encumbrance of teeth, and he had not shaved.

'Why not?'

'The wind. Sometimes the crew have to shelter for several days somewhere while waiting for the wind to drop.'

Time was getting short; we didn't have several days to waste. 'But the wind doesn't look too bad.'

'It may not look too bad in the estuary here, but we're sheltered. You haven't seen it out there.'

He meant well but Richard was determined to get on this boat.

'We're prepared to risk it,' said Richard.

I was beginning to have misgivings.

'You're used to the sea, are you?'

'Yes,' said Richard.

I kept quiet about the sea-sickness.

'All right then. The *Hadji* leaves in two days.'

Sitting in her front room Nila abruptly said to me: 'You look tired.'

I was touched by her concern. 'I must admit I didn't sleep well last night. It was probably all that caffeine in your wonderful *chai*.' In fact I never seemed to sleep any more. I tossed about in bed, over-excited by the journey, worrying about how to reach the next place, where to stay, where to eat, and was then exhausted all day.

'No, I mean like someone really deeply tired.'

Richard looked at me oddly. Suddenly I was on the verge of tears.

It was hard to tear ourselves away. Around midnight Rasmi drove us to the dock. The modern port was, thanks to the UN, being rebuilt. But the gates were locked. We shouted and tooted the horn, but no one came. Eventually we climbed in and waved goodbye through the bars.

The *Hadji* was dark. Were we not expected? We lowered ourselves from the quay, footsteps banging on the metal deck, and down into the cabin. Seven berths, like so many shelves for the dead in a Merina tomb, held seven dozing bodies. There was an eighth berth free; even if it was barely wide enough for one, at least it had a mattress. We unrolled our sleeping bags, and within minutes were asleep. Not for long. The berth was for the crew: we were to sleep on deck beside the funnel on sacks of haricot beans beneath a makeshift canvas shelter. Embarrassingly, there was a row: the captain had no room for passengers but had paid for berths. This is a cargo boat, he insisted. He had not been warned of any extras. It was the hairy-eared owner who was to blame, but to wake him now and complain would only delay us.

For three days and three nights I lay as horizontal as possible on the haricot beans, which vibrated with the engine. Life belts were the walls and a ladder supported the canvas ceiling. We slid out to sea with much of the country's topsoil, sucked into the Betsiboka estuary by its octopus-like tentacles. A flat sandy coast grew, almost at walking pace, into red cliffs, even redder than the red cliffs of Devon, and I thought of Robert Newman Hunt narrowing his eyes against the sun and wind, on guard for hostile natives. When we landed at a fishing village hordes of people ran to the shore waving and shouting with excitement, and piled into canoes to row out to us. It could have been 150 years ago, but for the cotton dresses and shorts.

Uncle Ralph describes an incident which took place somewhere on that coast in 1837.

We have accounts of the Captains of the Firm's Brigs burying their goods in the sand for fear of the natives, and expeditions into the forests in search of gums etc etc. At about this date our Captains appear to have had a little engagement on their own account. Indeed it must have been exciting doing business in Madagascar in those days, as we read that two tribes in Madagascar were fighting each other, the Sackalavas and Ambolambos. The Ambolambos gained Moorsaanga, a Fort and village in which 'Our Ebony' was awaiting shipment, which they would not give up. They therefore sided with the Sackalavas, who it was arranged would attack the Fort by land, the Firm sending three ships full of Sackalavas and 100 canoes, they forced the Ambolambos to retreat to the fort, and silenced their fire. However, owing to the shallowness of the water they were obliged to run the ships up at high tide in order to load the Firm's Ebony; owing to the confusion the ships were badly shored up and fell over, consequently they had to throw ballast overboard in order to get the ships off on the next tide, and make a hasty retreat minus their eighty tons of ebony. 'It was a miracle the Ambolambos did not descend on them and wipe every man out.'

The three ships were square-rigged ketches armed with six twelve-pounders, twenty muskets, twenty pikes, forty pistols, six blunderbusses and twenty men with cutlasses. I never found any reference to this incident amongst the letters in the Pool or at the Public Record Office, and I never found the old log books from which Ralph quotes. Again Mervyn Brown came to the rescue: Moorsaanga was another name for Anorotsangana where fighting did take place in 1837 between the Sakalava and the Merina, ending with the Merina establishing themselves there and building a fort. 'Ambolambos' was probably a Sakalava name for the Merina tribe, derived from one of their early kings named Ralambo. I found Anorotsangana on our map, a village and fort on the southern bulge of the Ampasindava peninsular, just south of Nosy Be. We were passing so close by, though not close enough to see it.

The *Hadji*'s owner's warnings of rough seas were unnecessary, except when we crossed vast river mouths where fresh water collided with salt. Then we had to grip the life belts and hang on to our bags to stop ourselves from being flung about the deck. I swallowed Kwells, which did not always work. Did Robert Newman Hunt experience these lurches of nausea? After two years on his aquatic excursion he was probably used to it.

He would have dined in restrained elegance, with his surgeon and the captain as companions, perhaps the first mate too. A small glass of wine was advised for reasons of health, and a postprandial port, shipped of course by the Firm. Robert would have pondered over his glass what he saw as the deviousness of the Malagasy. Generals Ramiaramona and Rahaingio had been friendliness itself, but if they had sent up his letter to the Queen, as they promised, surely he would have received an affirmative reply by now. He sauntered moodily to the windows and stared at his collection of ferns, periwinkles and orchids that he had gathered from around the coast. Would they survive until his return to his beloved South Devon, he wondered abstractedly. Just as long as he survived this voyage! He was not feeling strong.

For us, cooking was slow. We were running out of fuel and the wind kept scattering the flame. Richard constructed a wall of bags around our stove but even that was not enough. We abandoned it and took to doing as the others did, handing a 'kapok' – a condensed milk tin's worth – of rice to one of the crew who added it to the great cauldron at the stern. An hour later plastic plates mounded with steaming rice were thrust back through the flaps of our canopy.

The kitchen was as usual a cut-away oil drum. Sea swilled round its base and the crew streamed fishing lines off the stern. There were shrieks of excitement when three tuna were hauled on deck. They lay panting pathetically until they were gutted and salted and hung out to dry. We did not participate much. Though the crew were friendly enough, after our row we lay low. I in any case was too weary to move. Even the sunsets which lit up the distant mountains and silhouetted islands, and which so moved Richard, were not enough to drag me to my feet. He reported back crabs swimming along on the surface, jellyfish and the suspicion of an albatross. He still had the strength for one more sniff of the night air, for one more look at the stars, but these days I just wanted to wallow in the monotony for ever.

Like Robert Newman Hunt we were heading for Nosy Be

(pronounced 'Noossy Bay'), the largest of Madagascar's off-shore islands. Even then the French were moving in, despite protests from Sultan Seyyid Said who claimed the island was his. By 1842 Henry Angelo writes to Newman Hunt and Christopher that: 'The French are completely established on Nos Beh and are drilling the natives for soldiers.'

At midnight the engines changed down, and we slipped into the capital, Hellville.

At once there was a change of mood. A French mood, a mood of wealth. The harbour was full of yachts and cargo boats, lights, and smells of mud and incense. Was it the rhythm of the *Hadji* that kept us swaying long after we trod on land, or the heady scents of frangipani and ylang-ylang, the petals of which form the base of French perfumes?

A boulevard between decaying colonial villas led to a small hotel. We wanted a drink and found a disco. It was exactly like a European disco, only better mannered and without any white faces save our own, but we were too exhausted to dance. It replaced the *Hadji*'s engine, throbbing through the night.

Dawn broke on a bay of unbelievable beauty. Mountains on the mainland formed a protective ring which receded in filmic layers of mauve, and one square white sail, framed by green banana leaves, moved soundlessly to the opposite shore. However, the cruel light revealed Hellville not as a haven of flower-hung villas but as another scruffy little port past its best.

We left for the nearest beach, a tropical heaven of suede sand almost deserted despite it still being high season on Mada-gascar's premier resort. With the relaxing of economic restric-tions hotels were being built, but they were mostly European-owned and though the Malagasy need the foreign exchange they seemed to participate reluctantly. A few women sold coconut oil and offered half-heartedly to plait my hair. The hotels provided jobs but, as in so many places, the extraordinary wealth of the tourists they waited on or whose beds they made was beginning to cause resentment amongst the locals. The Malagasy have always been ambivalent about *vazaha*, and here we felt ambivalent about being *vazaha*, so we avoided the tourist places. We stayed in a tin shack that had no windows and was parti-tioned into rooms. The rats and the snoring kept us awake.

A Sunday party of Comorians, perhaps descended from slaves

brought over by the Sakalava tribe, stranded here for one reason or another, collected on the beach beneath a mango tree. Cassettes played and vats of rice simmered on fires; quivering buttocks were swathed in bright Comorian cotton, hair was bunched like bears' ears, solid legs stomped in the sand. They circled a rice mortar for a rice pounding dance, tossing the pestle from hand to hand, chanting and clapping. Naked children with even smaller children hooked on one hip joined in. It was spontaneous and good-humoured.

Beer and more beer. Fully clothed ladies flung themselves on the waves, and glamorous young women in tight rubber shorts flirted with men who were muscular and dark. One woman was beautiful. She had patterned her face in the Comorian way with yellow dots of sandalwood paste and her smile was white. Her man was handsome and moustachioed, but I wouldn't have trusted him if I was her, especially as she was already running to fat. A more beautiful woman, long-legged and slim, disentangled herself from her French boyfriend to come and talk to him; there was an intimacy about the way they spoke, standing close together but apart from the other Comorians, that made me think they had been lovers. She shifted from foot to foot in the sand and looked up at him, then returned to the Frenchman who had been patiently staring out to sea. She held her shoes by their laces and tossed them over her shoulder as they strode away.

We peered into rock pools of electric-coloured sea urchins, white eels with yellow spots, undulating fronds of starfish, and fed them limpets. Sakalava children cavorted in the sand; Richard tossed them about in the waves, their skins glistening black. These Sakalava are more African-looking than the Merina; the Merina are hypocrites, they said. Eight-year-old Maurice brought us shells we did not want and unripe mangoes, but in the end he asked for money. Opaque crabs scuttled into holes. We found a secret bay, accessible beyond black volcanic rocks only at low tide and edged with forest, and spent the day there, reading and making a fire on which to cook our lunch. A scrawny and too brown French woman strode past carrying snorkelling gear.

'*C'est de la solitude, hein?*'

The French were in Nosy Be *en masse* until independence; they were resented, considered to have taken from the country and given nothing in return. But now all (or nearly all) was forgiven, and they were drifting back. Sugar cane plantations were run on sophisticated European lines with sprinklers and regimented rows of feathery spears the like of which we had seen nowhere else. One night we watched a French woman in her comfortable holiday villa screaming at her Malagasy maid. The maid collapsed to the floor and clung to her mistress's knees, begging for forgiveness.

Nosy Be was free of sharks, they said. But one morning Richard watched a six-foot-long hammer-head being unloaded from a fishing canoe. He bought two steaks and we chewed through them in tomato sauce.

We both admitted to a growing exhaustion, deeper than that of a few sleepless nights. The early days of this journey stretched back into infinity; I could barely remember Mombasa or Dar. The constant movement, the perpetual receiving of new people, new facts, new places: I was worn out. I was also suffering from a bad back and ankles that seemed to have twisted without my noticing. Then one morning I was woken by a pain in my shoulder that did not go away. I thought it was dislocated, but it turned out later to be a type of nerve palsy. I was not as strong as I had thought, and the prospect of going on was daunting. In the early days I seemed to drag Richard along but now our roles reversed and but for him I would have given up then. All I wanted was a room somewhere with white walls and a clean white bed, and to lie with my head buried under a white pillow and hear nothing more of Madagascar or of ancestors. We decided to splash out, and leave our squalid shack for this white room, rented in someone's house further up the beach. Richard explored Nosy Be with its volcanic lakes – a Comoro Island that got away – while I retreated into a spotless void.

Though my shoulder did not improve, a week of rest was enough to give me my second wind.

'Thank God,' said Richard, bored by beaches.

Madagascar was an early object of British pioneering dreams. Two employees of the East India company who had called at the island in 1630 wrote pamplets extolling its beauties, its abundant riches and favourable climate. A colony should be established on 'the chiefest paradise this day on earth', urged one. An expedition to Madagascar was planned, and King Charles I nominated his nephew, dashing Prince Rupert, to lead it and to govern the

colony. But when they failed to raise the funds the scheme collapsed. In 1644 City merchants financed an expedition which
established a settlement on St Augustine's Bay in the south-west.
The aridness of the region and the hostility of the inhabitants led
to its abandonment in 1646, when only sixty of the original 140
colonists were left alive. But this did not deter another attempt
three years later. Prestigious benefactors (led – ironically – by the
Parliamentarian General Lord Fairfax) gave it their blessing and
a party set sail in the *Assada Merchant* for Assada, or Nosy Be. In a
pamplet published after their departure the expedition's leader
wrote: 'I do believe, by God's blessing, that not any part of the
World is more advantageous for a Plantation, being every way as
well for pleasure as well as profit, in my estimation.' The author
had not yet been to Madagascar, but had read the glowing
reports. His name was Colonel Robert Hunt, and he was an
ancestor of our own hero, Robert Newman Hunt.

The pamplet began as a letter to his 'Deare Friends' who may
have wondered why he should leave his comfortable home and
his dear wife for such an adventure. Why would anyone do such
a thing? His nineteenth-century descendant had no dear wife to
leave, and his twentieth-century descendant was lucky enough to
have her dear husband with her. But Robert Hunt had a mission
beyond those of mere trade and adventure. He wanted to be
useful to his native country, to increase trade and navigation, but
above all his aim was to glorify God. He intended to settle a just
and honest government on the island, and place two or three men
as agents to the Sakalava court of northern Madagascar, where
the king was friendly and spoke English, in order to spread the
gospel. Blithely Robert Hunt asserted that this king had 'invited
our men to come againe and promised all his country should be
at their command'. Hunt would build a fort and town at the
harbour where there was already Arab trade, plant sugar cane,
rice, tobacco and cattle, trade in 'ambergreese, iron, tortle shels,
sandall wood, ibony wood, druggs etc' and create a Barbados in
the Indian Ocean. Any man prepared to spend four years as a
servant to him or his fellow adventurers would be fed and
clothed, and after four years would be given as much land as he
required, six months' provisions, and three negro servants.

The *Assada Merchant* set sail full of optimism and, in retrospect,
foolish bravery.

Unknown to Robert Hunt, soon after his departure from England one of the few survivors of the previous Madagascar expedition published a pamphlet of his own. 'I could not but endeavour to dissuade others from undergoing the miseries that will follow the persons of such as adventure themselves for Madagascar.' Had he read it, perhaps Hunt might never have left his home and his wife – who knows? It came too late.

After some three months at sea, Hunt and his adventurers landed on Nosy Be. These days it cannot be very different from his dream; it *is* a sort of Barbados.

For Robert Hunt this was not to be. In his pamphlet he mentioned diverse small islands which might be useful to the expedition. Perhaps he went exploring. All we know is that he decided not to settle on Nosy Be but on a neighbouring island which he called Goat's Island. But natives were hostile and fever rampant: within weeks the utopia was over and, tragically, Hunt was dead. Reinforcements arrived from England but just too late: the rest of the expedition had sailed on to the mainland where some were enticed ashore with promises of ambergris, but there they were murdered. After another false start the whole project was ignominiously abandoned.

Various historians of Madagascar are agreed that Goat's Island is probably Nosy Komba. From Hellville its wooded slopes looked just a few hundred yards away, but the journey took us two hours. Our vessel was a single outrigger canoe, twenty feet long and as wide as a narrow-hipped woman, and it was carrying beer crates to the island. Balancing our packs across the hull we teetered aboard. At first the captain and his young mate paddled, and unfurled the sail only when the wind got up at midday, as it does at this time, dutifully, every day. Two pointed logs balanced the craft and the sail was stretched open by two poles which slotted into notches in the hull. They could be moved backwards and forwards with changes of wind, but could not go about. Other sails looked, as they had done for centuries, like sheets pegged up to dry against crinkled blue hills.

The natives were still hostile, but through over-exposure to *vazaha* rather than fear. They were sick of bikini-clad day-trippers from Nosy Be who tottered off ferryboats on high heels to snatch photographs but ignore the pottery animals spread out for sale beside the sea.

The President of the village lived in a tin hut slightly larger than the rest. He was old and sat in his doorway grating carrots.

'Excuse me, I'm looking for a *vazaha* grave,' I began, standing over him.

He looked up, unsurprised. 'Yes? *Vazaha* grave?' A lone tooth glimmered like a moon in the black universe of his mouth.

I explained the story. 'He died somewhere on "Goat Island" which I am told is here. Have you ever heard Nosy Komba called that?'

He shook his head. 'There were never goats here. Lemurs, yes.'

'Well, names change. It was a long time ago of course, so I don't expect there to be anything, but I just thought you might know.'

He nodded gravely. 'There are *vazaha* graves on the island.'

'There are? Do you know where?'

He indicated with his head the mountain that swelled behind him. It looked rocky and inhospitable. 'Yes,' he said.

'Do you have any idea how old they might be?'

'Very very old.' He had led a group of *vazaha* archaeologists up there once, he knew the graves were special.

'Could you take us there?'

'Yes.' He asked for toothpaste (of little use to him) and European soap as payment.

We climbed steadily up a well-used path, the President barefoot and armed with a scythe. An Alsatian mission had long-since been abandoned yet we heard a piano playing, eerily, inside. The President thought nothing of this. Through bamboo fronds we caught glimpses of luminous sea and of Nosy Be and then, as we got higher, of other pimply islands with their rims of white coral expanding below. A boa constrictor slid aside, and black lemurs chattered from the trees, or what remained of them. Rice fields had been carved from the forest, manioc and bananas planted, the remaining vegetation burnt, yet through the devastation still hooted the bubbles of sound we had heard on the east coast, and cicadas rattled: magical noises of the tropics. Plump women squatted in the doors of their palm huts and the President called out our story again and again. Stubby bananas were pressed on us. The President pointed out the villages of the past too, a *vazaha* settlement high on the hill, now turned to fields which he had inherited from his grandmother. Here had been the hospital, the President said, here the school. Could this be anything to do with the *Assada* expedition? The President said it was old, even older than him, and he was born in 1913. They died of hunger, he said.

After two hours we reached the top; not only the pimply islands but now the mainland too hovered in blue way below. Perhaps the haze on the horizon was the Comoros, but we weren't sure. The graves were themselves buried in a clump of bamboo. Richard battled through it while the President scythed the hollow trunks. They tore at our hands.

'I've found something,' called Richard. 'Some crosses.'

'Any names? Dates?' I called back.

'This one's Muslim. So's this. And here's a French one.'

The President was scrabbling at the earth. There was something he wanted me to see, a tomb perhaps. We scraped it clear, and found a metal plate marked with a plan of the graves.

'Metal. That's too late for me. They wouldn't have had metal like this.'

'No, this was put here later,' he insisted. 'During the French times. But the graves were already here.'

In each rectangle was carved a name. Berthaud. Berhin. Gernay. All French. Nothing looked even remotely like Hunt. Richard was making his way back.

'The crosses,' he said. 'They're all concrete.'

I sat back on my heels. The President was watching me hopefully. 'It's no good,' I said. 'They're *vazaha* graves all right, but not the right one. I'm sorry. But thanks for bringing us up here anyway.'

We stumbled back down the hill.

It had been too easy. After 350 years it was unlikely that any grave remained. There was probably never any grave at all. Concerned with their own survival, the remaining settlers would have fled the island leaving him to rot. And if he had a grave its marker would surely have been merely a token, some hasty wooden cross smothered at once in jungle.

'I hear you're looking for Goat's Island,' said the German proprietor of the little hotel on the beach.

'Yes?'

'I heard it wasn't here. I heard it was Nosy Mitsio.'

— CHAPTER TEN —

THE NORTH

If we were to explore the north, we had no time for Nosy Mitsio; and what did this German know anyway? We abandoned Colonel Robert Hunt – he had probably nourished some tree centuries ago and was best left alone. Instead we sailed in a *pirogue* to the mainland. Before the wind rose the only sounds for four hours were the chop of paddles in flat water as Nosy Komba crept past, secret villages nestling between boulders, mango trees and the sea. Dolphins arched by, huffing like cattle. Robert Hunt may have died of hunger, but at least he could have feasted his eyes.

We walked and hitch-hiked in a gravel lorry to Ambanja, a long dusty town set in cocoa and coffee groves. What little we saw of it was through the back of a taxi-brousse, the Peugeot pick-up type with bench seats down the side and a roof too low to sit upright. For over an hour we cruised the town gathering passengers, until even the patient Malagasy began to object. Each stop was greeted with cries of disbelief as yet another body was pressed on board, some on the roof, others hanging off behind. A woman on the floor was squeezed between a man's legs, causing ribald mirth. Nobody really minded, except a Merina family who held themselves apart. They were well-dressed, on holiday from Tana, and almost as foreign as us.

A four-hour drive took us to Ambilobe, another flat hot town, where we spent the night. It was little more than a stop-off place on the way north to Diego Suarez; most people were passing through. We joined the Tana family on wobbling benches in a typically filthy mud-floored hotely for mounds of rice and chicken bone soup. In these parts the meal was accompanied by a bowl of tepid water in which green vegetables – *brèdes* – had been boiled. Sometimes one leaf floated on top. We soon came to like it. The proprietor wore an embroidered cap; he was from

Aden. He had come here in search of work forty years earlier, had married, settled down.

'Richard was born in Aden,' I said, stretching the truth a little. I didn't know the word for 'conceived'. The proprietor grasped Richard's hand. 'You're an Arab! My brother!'

The next morning a lorry dropped us at the roadside. Fifty miles to the west rose the Ankarana Massif, a castle of limestone pinnacles where caves had collapsed into valleys with a private ecosystem of their own, and where crocodiles lurked eighteen feet long. Bleached blond grass rolled away to either side of a red dust track. There were no vehicles in sight, but something was sure to pass by. Until then we would need water. We approached a collection of roadside huts and four young boys clutched each other in alarm, and fled. I peered through a doorway. A family sat on the floor around a rice pot, spooning it in with morsels of banana, a meal of starch, and without a word they ladled water into our bottle.

Off on another adventure. The ritual greeting as amazed faces appeared in doorways went something like: 'What's new?'

'Nothing. What's new?'

'Nothing. Where are you going?'

'Matsaborimanga.'

'That's a long way. Your bags look heavy.'

'Yes.'

Although we paused at oases and bathed our feet in the shade of flowering mango trees, almost at once my weariness returned. My shoulder was also not improved by days of rough roads and pack-carrying. Our tent, meths stove, sleeping bag, books and medicaments all weighed about seventeen kilos for me and twenty-three kilos for Richard. He was tired too. He thought travelling with two was more tiring than being alone, I suppose because he had to cope with our relationship as well as the stresses of being foreign and being constantly on the move. We were not getting on. He was preoccupied with his future – how would he earn a living when we returned to England? We walked separately, wrapped in separate thoughts.

No vehicles passed, except a couple of thatched zebu wagons rattling on wooden wheels which we quickly overtook, and by midday the heat was pulsing, the earth baked. In the only village with shops we stocked up on beans, sweets and dried bananas

wrapped in banana leaves like Christmas crackers before stag-
gering on, the landscape changing from Andalusia to the Wild
West. Then, after six hours, the pinnacles towered abruptly out
of the undulating land, a sheer forest of grey spikes above a forest
of green. They were not earthly, more like a gigantic wall of
concertina metal zig-zagging into the distance. But at the top,
amongst the hostile shards and well out of man's reach, lay
pockets of green. Eagles turned.

We left the track and found a perfect campsite. I dropped my
rucksack and fell to the ground, flat on my back, blissfully thinking I might never move again. After six exhausting hours we had
made it. The wind was gusting here, but we had a view of the
spikes turning gold beyond the honey-coloured grasses. We
found ourselves making jokes again, liking each other. Richard
searched for fruits of the forest while I put up the tent. A peaceful
evening alone, watching the sunset, lay ahead.

He returned, and lit a fire. Sparks hit the grass and within
seconds an orange-fringed black stain was spreading outwards.
Stupidly, I picked up a rock and threw it at it, and then yelled at
Richard for being such an idiot.

'Shut up and just get the things out of the way!'

This was serious. We hauled our packs outside the ring but it
was spreading so fast that Richard ripped up the tent and flung
the whole lot on to the sand path. The flames were still small and
we both kept expecting them to burn themselves out as they
neared trees, but instead they spread around the edges of the
trees and swelling with each wind gust gripped the longer grasses
and roared into action. After all our condemnation of the *feux de
brousse* we had our own bush fire on our hands. Richard tore at a
branch and began to beat the flames, and I followed. We
smacked at them and managed to extinguish some, only for a
gust of wind to flare them up again. We beat with all our
returned strength, racing for new branches when ours were burnt
and useless.

'It's hopeless,' I sobbed into the wind. 'It's impossible. It's
going to get the village.'

I envisaged torches of huts and people, court cases, prison.
Egrets flocked around, squawking and bouncing with each surge
of flame.

After what seemed like hours we heard a shout, and some boys
ran towards us over the hill. A man was with them. He hoisted

his *lamba* up between his legs and did not waste time on recriminations.

'Have you got a knife?' he shouted.

'Knife! Rich, get him the knife!'

Richard ran to the packs and we slashed at branches to make more flame beaters. Now the heat pushed us back; when the wind dropped we could get in close, then back we were pushed again, flames rearing overhead as they hit a clump of man-high grasses. I followed the man, hitting at the small flames he had missed and which would soon take off again while Richard disappeared round the other side. Another man arrived, and this time the two managed to exchange greetings, even to laugh. I wanted to scream at them, 'Shut up and just get on with it!'

I was desperate by now, streaming with sweat, my bare feet and arms scratched, and blistered by the heat. A piece of grass flicked my eye and my vision blurred: it had flicked out my contact lens. From then on I was stumbling into rocks, stubbing my toes, crunching on to scorched ash. The older man was obviously a professional, grinding out the fire with tiny sandalled feet, but I was barely aware of him; I could think only of beating and beating.

An hour later we put it out. It was the paths that cut it off.

We lay slumped on the grass, faces soot-blackened, feet shredded, toenails gone. The men – there were four by the end – helped us search for charred remains of our tent that had stayed in the ground when Richard tore it up, and they asked for a *cadeau*. I would willingly have given them everything but in the end they had money and shirts. They led Richard to an irrigation channel to wash, but it was half a mile away and I could not walk that far.

It was a long night. We had been reunited against the fire, but now it was over we lay side by side on the hard ground not speaking or even looking at each other, just blaming each other. At dawn the pinnacles were a black wall of crenellations silhouetted against the eastern sky, forbidding and jagged. We packed up and strode across the bleached scrub as sun shafted into the valley. The scrub edged a forest of cathedral-high trees and the pinnacles vanished. Brown lemurs scattered, unused to humans. We bickered about the path – should we stick to it, though it appeared to be going in the wrong direction, or break away and penetrate directly through the undergrowth to where we knew the pinnacles were? I followed Richard through the trees, grumbling all the way. Lianas snagged at my rucksack and tangling my legs caught me up short, their webs suffocating and impenetrable. Frustration, resentment, criticism: as the pinnacles reappeared through the foliage our hostilities exploded into a full-scale row. I can see us now, Richard beating a tree trunk with the banana cracker, his voice rebounding off the pinnacles and around the valley. Absurdly, I hear myself saying, 'Ssh, people will listen.' As if there were any people.

I suddenly realized that the pinnacles were our mood – spiked, brittle, aggressive – and that the lianas were our relationship.

We forgave each other and recovered quickly; though we trod carefully for some time it had cleared the air. We decided to struggle on towards the rocks that now reared overhead, grey and formidable as Gormenghast which we had both just read. It was strangled with creepers, trees like Clarice and Cora's growing on flat places high above our heads. I could imagine Lord Sepulchrave pacing behind these turrets, gloomily enacting the rituals of tradition, evil Steerpike lurking in the shadows. Madagascar would have suited the family of Groan.

We had hoped to climb to one of those flat fertile places and make ourselves a nest, but it was impossible without ropes and crampons. We retreated. At once the forest closed in. I have no sense of direction, and no direction seemed right. As a child I had got lost in woods above the river Dart; every turn seemed wrong and I had run, sobbing and claustrophobic, down to the water's edge. That gave little relief: there was a boat house, but it was no ordinary boat house, it was Agatha Christie's boat house, full of murdered corpses; I fled back into the woods.

It returned to me now, the horror. If we ate only rice we had food for three days, but no water. I swallowed fear, and avoided Richard's eyes in case he was panicking too. If he was frightened, then it was certain we had had it. But he knew where we were going, and we soon reached the path.

After another attempt we abandoned the pinnacles of Ankarana for the light and air of the open grasses. We were now barely able to walk in the heat and exhaustion, physical and emotional. We hobbled back to the irrigation channel to bathe our feet and drink and drink, and found another campsite in a grove of spiky trees. Cautiously, we lit a fire. This time it worked and we ate sardines with haricot beans – surely no meal has ever tasted better. In the sunset the crags turned to a Fascist memorial with rows of iron-grey regiments clutching green banners; then it softened to a red curtain hanging in folds. Our tent went up; it was now singed around the base and torn where Richard had ripped it from the ground. It was an ill-fated piece of gear. We lay looking at branch shadows cast on the flysheet by the moon, shifting in the breeze like a living Chinese scroll. We slept surprisingly well despite the stony earth and an odd snuffling in the night, dancing feet, flapping wings. Richard thought they were wild boar and an owl.

We never got to Matsaborimanga but we could not regret it. Perhaps we would return one day and try again, though as journey leads to journey I doubted it. Instead we turned back along the red road to Diego Suarez, leaving before dawn. Parrots, eagles, kingfishers, palm huts, rice pounding, chickens pecking at bare ground. The going was hard but time – the sun – was against us and we couldn't afford to rest. Luckily there was a breeze and some cloud, but this thickened until it collapsed in a downpour just as we reached a village. The men in a bar eyed our boots.

'How much do they cost?'

I made up some likely-sounding sum, not so cheap they would insist on buying them, and not so expensive that they would think we were rich enough to rob. They were ordinary trainers, but they cost more than these people could earn in two months. They tried on our packs and were impressed by the weight; they liked the packs too. It was another eight miles to the main road, they said.

Now the wind was against us, and rain slashing – it was one extreme or the other here. Andalusia and the Wild West turned to Dartmoor, swathed in purple cloud. Wet topsoil clung to our soles like platform shoes. Car tracks – of cars we had never seen or heard – now creased the ground. Again we flopped, this time in grasses, other walkers discreetly looking away from our indecorous abandon. We began to talk of puddings. Chocolate pudding. Summer pudding. Yes, that was it. We disputed over just blackberries, or blackberries and redcurrants, or redcurrants and raspberries, but were united on juice-sodden white bread and cream.

I could hardly go on when a man beckoned us to follow. His possessions hung from a shoulder pole and his white shoes from one hand (he was barefoot), and he led two women with sacks on their heads. He knew a short cut. At a steady trot we scrabbled up narrow dirt paths behind villages, down into steep wooded valleys, forded streams, skirted rice fields, waded through rivers, the man in front, the two women behind. No one spoke, just kept moving for the last three miles to the road-side sprawl of Anivorano. Miraculously, a taxi-brousse – this time of the estate car variety, into which squeezed thirteen adults and three children – was waiting to speed us north.

Diego Suarez was reputed to be a major port with the largest harbour in the Indian Ocean, as dramatically sited as Rio. This, however, is visible only from the air. From the ground Diego is a dusty empty left-over place: straight roads lined with shuttered *épiceries* lead nowhere. The only activity was in the Bohra mosques (we were back with the Bombay Bohras, their women clothed in hideous shiny nun-like habits) and in the house of ill-repute where we stayed. As this was a metal construction every movement resounded, even opening and closing the door. The slatted window revealed in horizontal strips a passage without light, but at least we had a shower; red dust and soot poured off us.

The *patronne* of a well-known restaurant bemoaned the collapse of her country. Her four children were far away in Paris and her husband drank. We caught the eye of the only other client, a stocky Frenchman in his sixties who strode about in shorts and sucked his lobster with tremendously French gusto.

'It's hopeless here,' he assured us cheerfully from a neighbouring table. 'She can't get bread because there's no flour. She can't get good meat any more. Things are getting worse and worse. And you know why? No French. Well, it's their choice, but that's how it is. No French, no British, no money.' He lived on Réunion but despite the impoverishing absence of the French here came over whenever he could. 'It's much better here,' he added, confusingly.

'Why?'

'Ach, the people in Réunion.' He banged his forehead with his palm. 'They're in a bad mood.'

'Is Réunion still a French colony?'

'No, it never was a colony. It's a province of France. The people are French. They vote in the French elections.'

'If it makes them so bad-tempered, perhaps they'd be better off without the French,' I hazarded.

He shrugged.

He spoke good English and turned out to have lived in London during the war. 'I was seventeen. Ah, those were the days. Balham! Let me see, the Northern Line, yes? I've never been back but I remember it so well. Clapham South, Clapham Common.'

'What were you doing there?'

'I was in the Navy. The British Navy, fighting the Germans. Clapham North, Stockwell. Yes, I had a good time. I trained in the south-west, in Dartmouth.'

Richard and I laughed. It seemed too much of a coincidence. 'Dartmouth! My family comes from there,' I said, but he ignored me. His mind was on that long black line. 'Oval! Wait, wait, Morden! Oh yes, I remember Morden.' His eyes softened.

'But Dartmouth,' I persisted. 'Did you like that?'

'Oh yes, very much,' he replied casually. Then he smiled. 'Blackfriars!'

'No, that's on the Circle Line.'

'I lived in Kingswear you know.'

'Kingswear!'

'Yes, opposite Dartmouth. And I had a girlfriend.' This was a wicked confession. 'She lived ... let me see ... it's forty-seven years ago now.' He chuckled. 'It was near Newton Abbot.'

'Newton Abbot? But that's where we got married!' He took no notice. 'And Richard's family come from there too.'

He would not grasp the significance. 'Oh yes? Elephant and Castle! Remember that? Elephant and Castle. Aah. Northern, Circle, Central, District.' He sighed.

'And Dartmouth?

'It was OK. I was in the submarines you know, torpedoing the enemy boats with the Free French. Very dangerous.'

Diego was always more important to the rest of the world than to Madagascar. The rugged hinterland of trackless mountains prohibited any useful link between it and the capital for transporting goods. But from this northern tip of Madagascar the entire western Indian Ocean, from the Mozambique channel up the coasts of Tanzania, Kenya and Somalia, could be controlled.

After the closure of the Suez Canal in 1941, Madagascar rode the sea route from the Cape up to the Middle East and India.

In June 1940 the colonial bureaucrats of France decided to opt not with Britain and the Allies but with Vichy. It was a bad decision. A year later the Japanese were winning battles in the Indian Ocean and were, the Allies suspected, on their way to the westernmost outpost of Asian culture, Madagascar. So the British decided to invade first, but without informing General de Gaulle. Previous Anglo-French attacks had not been a success (not least the combined effort on Tamatave just less than a hundred years earlier) and perhaps Churchill wanted to avoid the spectacle of the French fighting each other. So in May 1942, 30,000 British, East African and South African troops were landed at Diego. The fight spread to Mahajanga, and then closed in from all around the coast until the Vichy surrendered and the island was handed back to the Free French.

Our man from the Northern Line had been among the first Free French to land after the invasion, and had been demobilized here after the war. He joined the Civil Service, and at Independence left for Réunion. He would never go back to Europe. He stood up abruptly, 'Good night,' and stomped off. A few minutes later he passed us again. 'By the way, the *patron*, he's a good fellow really, but he likes too much the rum.'

The next morning we saw him in the street. He did not greet us but frowned and said: 'You know there is a cemetery here with about three hundred British dead? Sad huh?' Then he walked on.

We had come to Diego to meet the Bishop. We knew only his name, but two helpful nuns led us to his house. He was thin and grey and hurrying along in a purple shirt with a briefcase under his arm. Without asking who we were or what we wanted he invited us in.

'What language should we speak?' he asked hesitantly in French. 'French? English? Malagasy?'

'English,' we said.

'Aha. I see. Well, will you sit down?' His accent was strange; for a moment I feared the nuns were mistaken and that this was the Bishop's French assistant. We were expecting a burlier man, with a beard perhaps and muscular legs. Only when an old lady emerged from the kitchen to great him with great humility were we convinced of his identity.

'You must excuse me,' he said. 'I haven't spoken English for – let me see – the British Ambassador was up here last November so it must have been then. That's almost a year. And hardly any French.' Sometimes he searched for words – inflatable became 'pumpable'. 'You never forget your native tongue,' he said, 'but you do lose words.' Gradually, as he regained confidence, his Scottish accent returned.

Bishop Keith Benzies was born outside Glasgow some fifty years ago and studied French and Czech at Hull University in the hope of one day joining the diplomatic service. 'I thought that if I studied an obscure enough language they might take me on,' he said in a typical remark against himself. After graduating he became a teacher and then joined the Anglican church. One day twenty-three years ago he answered an advertisement for people to work in Francophone countries and found himself in Madagascar. On his second day he was abandoned in the highlands. No one spoke a word of French. 'So you see I came here under false pretences really,' he observed, smiling. He remained *en brousse* for thirteen years. Now he is tri-lingual in English, Antakarana, the local Diego dialect, and Malagasy. 'I know that I'm fluent when I can take an evening service in Malagasy and think of something else at the same time. I find it quite an advantage not being French,' he added. 'I never speak it unless I have to. The older people still resent it. It still has difficult associations for them. And the younger ones don't speak it much anyway.'

He was a modest, slightly-built man, dedicated to his job. When he kicked off his sandals I noticed that his feet were swollen and padded with use, like Malagasy feet.

'Your reputation is that you eschew all forms of modern transport and visit your flock on foot,' I said.

His diocese, covering the northern third of Madagascar, is about the size of England.

'You have to!' he cried. 'There's no other way. There are no roads.'

Sometimes he walked three days to reach a tiny church, or to take Bibles to an Anglican village. He passed through 'heathen' villages on the way, and heterodox Muslim villages, and was sometimes forced to stay the night there, but they welcomed him in. 'That can be really tiring because there when people say, "What's the news?" you don't just say "Nothing", you tell them. They really want to know. They're so isolated! They have no newspapers of course and not even any radios because they can't afford the batteries.' His Scottish voice was gentle, now that he had got back in the swing.

'How many hours do you walk a day?' I asked, thinking of the agony of our six-hour Ankarana walk.

'Oh, about thirteen and a half hours or so. Sometimes we'll stop for an hour to make lunch, and sometimes we won't bother, we'll just keep on going until the evening. Miles? About fifty. But listen, this is pure boasting. It depends on the terrain of course. In the mountains a little bit less.'

'Barefoot?'

He laughed. 'No, in these sandals. And now that I've reached the exalted heights of being a Bishop I even sometimes have the privilege of someone else carrying my luggage. The Bibles, our food and so on.' We spread maps over the floor and he traced some of his routes: he must have seen more of this region than most Europeans, or even Malagasy.

'What do you think about on your walks?' I asked, assuming he would say God. I remembered our own summer pudding fantasy.

'What do I think about? I think about trifle.'

'Trifle?'

'Yes. I imagine every layer, from the bottom layer up.'

I liked him already.

His fridge was empty but for one small bottle of orange soda which we shared between the three of us. His was a spartan existence. The house was painted flat hard colours and was spare, like him. There were few ornaments – a crucifix on the wall, a plastic vine, and a hanging saying in Malagasy: 'A Happy Home is an Earthly Paradise'.

The devout lady in the kitchen was his one extravagance, and she was paid by the church. His salary was a Malagasy salary: £24 a month. Yet he seemed content. Though unmarried (and marriage would never have fitted his rigorous schedule) he had 'adopted' four Malagasy sons. They all came from broken homes, or had been abandoned. Bema, who at twenty-seven years old had despaired of ever passing his baccalauréat, had just opened a small grocery shop in the front of the house; Boniface and Desiré were at university; and Bébé was away visiting his grandparents. Bébé had lost the use of his legs through polio. Bishop Benzies had rescued him from destitution in his remote mountain village, where he had chanced upon him one day.

The Bishop was a busy man; it was time to leave.

'But it's been so good to speak English again,' he said. 'Are you free this evening? Why don't you come back and have dinner? Good. But I'll have to apologize in advance, it will be very simple.'

'We're used to things being simple,' said Richard. 'But can we bring a bottle of wine?'

Bishop Benzies hesitated. 'All right, go on then, a bottle of wine would be lovely.'

(In fact it was not lovely and he drank none of it.)

When we returned, Bema was chatting on the verandah to a friend, who vanished over the wall at our approach. Bema was a brawny young man with huge arms swelling out of a blue T-shirt. He dwarfed his adoptive father like a cuckoo in the nest, making Keith Benzies seem even more frail than he was. Judging by the distances he walked he must have been fit, yet he often referred obliquely to the possibility of death, to continuing with his job 'God willing'. He did have chronic bilharzia, but preferred to live with the disease than to go through the horrific cure (as he had done once) only for the disease to recur. One effect was that the evening before a day's walk he could not eat or drink.

Bema spoke a little English but was shy, so the Bishop courteously translated for him when necessary. Bema was big-hearted, a gentle giant, and he responded to the Bishop with equal courtesy. The lady in the kitchen genuflected and announced that dinner was ready. The Bishop said grace, tentatively, in English, and we sat down to *crudités*, rice, liver and papaya – simple, yes, but good.

We spoke of many things, of Britain and Madagascar and of the ancestors. 'I hope you won't be like that American who paid someone a thousand dollars to trace his past, and then another thousand to cover it up again.'

'I'm afraid it might be a bit like that. There's a possibility that there might have been some slaving going on.'

'Very likely, that early. You know there are still some freed slaves alive here? It is possible. All slaves were freed by the French when they arrived in 1896. One woman was only three years old then, but she was a slave, and she's still going strong, or

at least she was when I last heard. She was proud of it – well, you
would be. It's something special to be the last.'

We talked about *famadihana*.

'Do the church and the ancestors clash?' asked Richard, recal-
ling an Evangelical missionary from Nottingham we had met in
Tana airport and who had been vociferously opposed to the
practice.

'Not really,' he replied. 'I see *famadihana* as being something
like a memorial service really. Of course it's very easy for the
Catholics who in any case are prepared to worship relics, but
for us Anglicans it's a little more tricky. But you've got to be
tolerant, haven't you? I'm often asked to *famadihana* myself.
I've even had to invent a suitable liturgy for it. But the
Catholics do go one stage too far I think when they are prepared to
invoke Jesus and the ancestors in one breath. That is pushing it a
bit.'

I liked his answer. He was no missionary fanatic (and with
predictable discretion, guessing that we were not church-goers, he
never once mentioned God) but was a genuinely good and self-
effacing man, here to help the underprivileged as well as to spread
the gospel. No wonder he was so well respected that he had been
elected Bishop despite being a *vazaha*.

But I felt a great sadness, the sadness of exile, albeit self-
imposed. He was white, he was an outsider, his roots grew near
Glasgow, but it was as if he had been cast off. In twenty-three
years his family had never once been to visit him. They had never
met his sons, or seen his house, or witnessed him at work. And
though as a Bishop he would return to Britain every ten years for
the Lambeth Conference (his flight paid by Canadian Anglicans)
and though he still kept in touch with his friends, he had made his
life here. It seemed a lonely life – the only other British in the city
were a couple of Indians who had British passports but had never
been to Britain – but this was now his home. He wanted to stay
here until he died, and to be buried here. I felt in him a yearning to
belong. He was (justifiably) proud of being trilingual and he
identified with the Malagasy – he spoke of 'We', not 'They', and
always called cities by their Malagasy names, so Diego Suarez
was Antseranana, Tamatave was Taomasina. But he never would
belong, however hard he tried. Perhaps his sons could root him
here, who knows, but they were not his real sons.

Richard said, 'He seems perfectly happy. He leads a fascinat-

ing and fulfilling life. You're just imposing on him feelings of
your own,' and he was probably right.

The Bishop appeared the next morning at our hotel; he sat on
a metal chair and ignored our dirty clothes and half-packed bags.
'This could damage your reputation, being here in the house of
ill-repute,' I warned him.

He laughed. 'I've always wondered what this hotel was like. It
doesn't seem too bad. I dare say at this time of day I might get
away with it.'

We planned to cross the bows of Madagascar to Vohemar, a
small port on the north-east coast. Our map marked the road as
only 'seasonal', and no buses could get through. Bema had
kindly scouted the truck stops but the Bishop reported that
nothing was going to Vohemar today.

'There'll be a taxi-brousse back to Ambilobe and you'll find a
lorry there. I will accompany you to the taxi-brousse station if I
may?'

'Of course you may! We'd be honoured.'

'I must take you on the way to meet the British consul. He's
French really, has a car repair business, but he'll be furious with
me if he finds out you've been here and he hasn't met you.'

Unfortunately the consul's garage was closed, so we continued
on to the Bishop's 'cathedral'. Even he spoke of it in inverted
commas.

'It's not much, I warn you.' It was a corrugated-iron barn, and
the door was locked. 'It's sad to have to lock it, but recently
someone broke in, some lunatic, and ripped up all the vestments
and chucked them and the Bibles and prayer books in the sewer.
That'll teach us to be high church.' (This he had inherited from
his Malagasy predecessor.) Without hesitating the Bishop
unhooked a shutter and climbed in on Richard's shoulders.
'They'd arrest me if they saw me,' he said, laughing. Green walls,
strip lights, a few sad lilies, stations of the cross. 'Not quite up to
some standards . . .' But he was not complaining. It had recently
been enlarged: half the congregation had been praying on the
steps.

With a few hours to kill we had a drink, avoiding what he
called a rum den. Rum is the greatest destroyer of families, he
said, along with all the other hooches made from mangoes,
papayas, sugar cane and so on. 'I think the Malagasy would
make alcohol from carrots if it was possible.' It probably is.

A youngish man thrust a piece of paper at the Bishop. He had been arrested in Vohemar for stealing clothes, and after six months in prison in Diego had been freed yesterday. Now he had no money to get home.

'He knows I have a fund for this,' the Bishop explained. 'Money gets sent from parish churches in Britain. If we didn't provide for him, how would he get back? He'd be forced to steal something else. And that paper says he stole clothes but the police and *gendarmes* use such methods to obtain a confession that these people will confess to anything.' Both Richard and I had been struck by the Bishop's innocence, yet he knew what went on down in the depths of society, more than we could ever imagine.

'What methods?'

'The usual beatings, cutting the flesh and putting chillies inside, electric shocks, anything.'

'Good God. I had the feeling that here the police were better than in many countries. In Kenya or Tanzania. They seem so friendly.'

'Oh no, they're awful. Terrible. I wanted to set up a human rights organization because there's nothing here and there's a great need for it, but I got a very sniffy letter back from Geneva dismissing the proposal. Of course there are a lot of political prisoners too.'

The Bishop was full of stories. 'I always say that if I was to write my memoirs no one would believe me.' As we sat in the forecourt of a garage waiting for the taxi-brousse to load up, he told us of how British parish churches had helped him to rescue a young illiterate named Eugène. The Bishop had found Eugène in his village suffering from facial gangrene. The whole of the left side of his face had gone, the eye, nose, mouth. All that remained were his tongue and bottom lip. Most people were so horrified they screamed and fled. He was a monster. But Bishop Benzies launched an appeal and brought him to England. Eugène wore a mask on the plane and the Heathrow customs officers were suspicious. Despite his return ticket, letters of recommendation from bishops, clergymen and hospitals, they nevertheless questioned him for fifty minutes. It was very hot and Eugène was suffering.

Eventually, driven to desperation, Bishop Benzies said, 'Clearly you don't believe that the man in the passport is the man behind the mask. Eugène, will you take off your mask please?'

There was a gasp, and he was through at once. He was taken

to a hospital in the New Forest and throughout the eight months of painful plastic surgery Bishop Benzies lay on a camp bed at his side. 'It was wonderful,' he said. 'All the plastic surgeons were top people who had never seen a case as bad as this, and they all gave their services for free. Then there was a tiny piece in the church news in the *Daily Telegraph*, and a flood of contributions started coming in.' Now Eugène was back in his village, married and expecting his first child. His face was restored. But not completely. When he removed his glasses each night, off came his nose too.

We left the bishop and back-tracked to Ambilobe, down off the hills into the stifling plain. A lorry was leaving for Vohemar tonight but it was carrying fish and had no canopy, was open to sun and dust; we decided to wait for the morning and travel with beer crates instead. For the first time we managed to get seats in the driver's cab. The journey would take eight hours, they said.

We were joined, inevitably, by the driver's floozie. Every driver has one, jolly girls with plastic bangles who make a little money and get a free ride. The Malagasy call them 'Bakoly', a girl's name, like a 'Sheila'. The Mpira Gasy at *famadihana* sing of Bakoly, warning her against handsome and rich chauffeurs. Ours was Florence, a flowerprint-clad mound of brown flesh. She was a primary school teacher in her thirties, recently divorced with three children.

'Is that your mister?' She indicated Richard with her head.

'Yes, that's my mister. Is the driver yours?'

She nodded and grinned gold and swung her plaits. They had met two weeks ago, she confided, when he came through from Diego in his lorry. 'This is our honeymoon,' she said.

He was anxious about the journey. It was his first time on this route, and his articulated lorry was unwieldy. His assistant stood outside on a bar behind the cab, his face clenched against sun and wind, shouting directions. Often he jumped off to guide us through the worst troughs in the pitted red earth and over rivers. This route would be impassable when the rains came; then Vohemar was accessible only by air or ship. Frequently we were all asked to get out so that the driver could go it alone, his face fixed in concentration while his lorry bucked and reared over crevices and rocks.

After eight hours we had got a third of the way. Then we stuck, central wheels suspended, over a dried-up river bed. We squatted in disconsolate groups in the shade; I scratched patterns in the earth with a stick; Richard read; Florence hunkered down beside me and picked her feet.

'I've got pus,' she said, informatively.

Eventually, after much negotiating ('They're not Christian,' muttered Florence, frowning), another lorry pulled us out.

For fourteen hours we climbed into the mountains. As a true floozie Florence should have been flirting with her man and squealing with giggles but she had toothache and swallowed handfuls of our painkillers. She lay down on the gearbox with a towel on her head. But when she woke she chattered; she lolled on the engine and bared a shaved armpit; then she leant over to whisper in my ear theatrically, clamping her sweating pit to my arm. I smiled weakly and prised her off. At heart she was a good sort but her mister had other things on his mind. He looked tired.

As darkness fell we tried to sleep, but there was nowhere to rest our heads and the ruts were too violent. At last we stopped in a mountain village named Deraina. Thirty weary passengers climbed down, disoriented, and made their way into a candle-lit hotely whose gregarious *patron* welcomed us all and showed us to clean tables with clean cloths. Even napkins were produced, an unprecedented event. We sat numb and silent as rice and chicken (why are Malagasy chickens all neck?) were served for the second time that day. Florence whispered, giggling, that they had been promised a room to themselves, and we should ask for one too. 'Don't be shy,' she urged. We were shown to a tin hut lit by a petrol lamp made (predictably) from a condensed-milk tin. In one corner a small bed covered with a quilt and a scented pillow proffered a few hours of bliss. Soon all the women and children joined us on mats on the floor. They rolled in blankets and settled down in rows like mummies; the room quickly filled with snores and farts. I blew out the light.

We left before dawn, Florence beautifully coiffeured and in a new shiny dress, but the lorry continuing its lurching. It was not long before we got out to walk for several miles. Someone knew of a short cut, and we crossed fields and tiny villages, the lorry revving in the distance. Sometimes Florence lunged for the trees, and disentangled herself triumphantly clutching exotic fruits, mostly still unripe. Custard apples she called 'Bulls' hearts', a horribly accurate description of their looks though fortunately not of their taste. There were bee-eaters too and birds of prey. Midmorning saw our descent towards the east coast, the river widening, and we paused to wash. Clothes were rinsed and hung about the cab to dry, teeth cleaned. And there was the fish lorry that had left twelve hours before us. Thank God we didn't take that, we said to each other. Two hours later we met it again, this time wedged immovably and almost on its side in the mire. Its passengers were strewn around disconsolately while a few tried to dig it out. We were on a bleak plateau where the only signs of life were a zebu cart, and wind and marshes. We lay amongst them for an hour while our driver tried to tow the fish lorry out. He gave up and we left them; they began to unload the cargo and, I presume, wait for some other passer-by to help. For all I know they are there still.

Sixty hours after leaving the Bishop we rolled into Vohemar. 'Don't forget your sister Florence,' she called. They were going on to Sambava and later we glimpsed them there, high up in their cab like gods.

Was it worth it? Vohemar was a scruffy little port, flat and windswept, and like all these coastal towns frequently battered by cyclones. But its bay was one of the most beautiful we had seen, bright blue sea rimmed on three sides by bare golden hills – it could have been the Scottish highlands – and on the fourth by jagged waves breaking over a reef, with islands beyond. A wreck and talk of sharks added an edge of danger. We walked into the wind along the endless stretch of white sand, and then back down a grass track, snakes whipping away from under our feet.

We found a yellow chameleon over a foot long. More than half the world's species of chameleon live here and only here, miniature dragons that puff out their necks in rage, eyes swivelling, scaly skin changing colour not only with surroundings but also with emotions. Is yellow the colour of cowardice for a chameleon? Or is it simply the colour of dried grasses? It grasped a branch with gloved hands and moved with unwatchable slowness. We placed a grasshopper a foot away from it, and watched as a snot-like tongue oozed from its mouth, then shot out the length of its own body. The insect was gone.

Arabs were here first in the twelfth century, spreading south from settlements like Mtwapa. They built up a civilization called Iharana that lasted well into the seventeenth century, and left behind luxurious tombs filled with Chinese porcelain and silver jewellery. But these were now swallowed by forest, much as the Iharanians were gradually absorbed by the local population. Their descendants had built two pretty mosques. (These and the bank were the only buildings of interest.)

In their wake came the pirates. Ever since Mary Newman's husband gave the Indian Ocean its first view of a British swash-buckler on the deck of the *Golden Hind*, holds bulging with treasure, the Indian Ocean was seen as a source of riches, booty and adventure. Drake was a privateer with royal backing, but his successors in the Indian Ocean found that a lack of any clear enemy – like the Spanish in the Caribbean – meant that privateering licences hardly applied. They turned to piracy instead, became freebooters, outlaws of the sea, liable to arrest and perhaps to execution by anyone able to overpower them. However, there was no strong naval power and during the late seventeenth and early eighteenth centuries piracy flourished. The crews included French, Dutch and Danish, but most of the captains were British, many of them Devon men. Some were naval deserters, others from merchant ships, others captured by pirates and so perforce joining them, others rescued by them from worse horrors. They stole cargoes, tortured passengers, raped women, and their favourite places of refuge were the Comoros, the Mascarenes and above all Madagascar. Here were ample supplies, hidden bays, long beaches suitable for careening their stolen ships, and no colonial authorities to interfere, unlike in the West Indies. Madagascar became one of the world's great pirate havens.

If and when they survived their adventures and returned to England, some of these renegades got into conversation with a man calling himself Captain Charles Johnson. An odd fellow this, snooping round the docks asking questions, haunting inns frequented by the lowest types of seamen, and noting down evidence at pirate trials. Eventually he published his findings as *A General History of the Robberies and Murders of the Most Notorious Pyrates*. His real name was Daniel Defoe.

One of his heroes was Captain John Bowen, a British seaman captured in the 1690s by French pirates who were making for Madagascar. They were drunk and mad and they wrecked their ship, and Bowen managed to escape to St Augustine on the south-west coast where the local king was friendly, spoke

English, and looked after him for eighteen months. But the king insisted he left on the next ship that passed, which unfortunately happened to be a pirate ship. A pragmatic fellow, Bowen saw where his best interests lay and this time instead of fighting, joined them. When the captain died, Bowen took over. From then on he and his freebooting cronies ruled the waves, cruising from St Augustine to Zanzibar to India and Mauritius as if this was their criminal manor. The Indian Ocean was their pitch to plunder, and – if they took care – without much inconvenience; when Bowen ran aground at Mauritius, far from arresting him the then Dutch governor gave him provisions and helped him fit out a new sloop.

My great-grandmother, Uncle Ralph's mother, was a Miss Bowen. Was there some connection, again through the female line? I hoped so.

Because of the fierceness of the Sakalava kings and the danger from pirate-hunting warships on their way to India, the west coast of Madagascar was considered unsuitable for pirates. However, on the east coast there were perfect hideaways. Vohemar was not ideal but it was a useful stop-over north or south. Bowen would have called in here to re-provision, and later, during the eighteenth century, the Mulatto descendants of him and his cronies travelled in outrigger canoes past Vohemar, past Diego Suarez, past Nosy Be and then on to the Comoro Islands for their annual slaving raids.

Following John Bowen – uncomfortably close – came the firm into which his descendant (perhaps) married, Newman Hunt & Christopher. From pirate to merchant was not as big a step as it might seem, as Defoe's *History of the Most Notorious Pyrates* pointed out. Merchants and the governments that backed them robbed and cheated too. But if only the Newmans had been as successful as John Bowen! As usual they got embroiled with an unsuitable character, for their client in Vohemar, its Governor, General Ramaharo, did not pay his debts. By 1842 he owed $188 and from England, thousands of miles away, it was hard to persuade him to pay. The worthy Henry Angelo was summoned to recover the money, but I found no receipt amongst the letters in the Pool, and I wondered if he succeeded. I enjoyed the possibility that the President of Vohemar still owed me this sum (plus interest). The President was absent, and though his underlings were interested in my story I was unable to make them understand when it was.

Dates meant nothing. Fifty years, 150 years, it made no difference. The past is not a linear series of numbers, but just the Past, the time of the ancestors. And before the Europeans arrived no records were kept, no archives. No one had heard of General Ramaharo, let alone Robert Newman Hunt, and when I mentioned the debt their faces went flat.

I discovered more in the Annales of Raombana, a diary written by Queen Ranavalona's English-educated private secretary. According to Raombana, in 1834 Khamis bin Othman had arrived with other ambassadors from Zanzibar at the Merina court. They requested 2,000 soldiers for Sultan Seyyid Said to help subdue a rebellion. Ranavalona demurred, and sent five ambassadors back to Zanzibar. Amongst them was General Ramaharo, Governor of Vohemar. This must have been how the connection with Newman Hunt & Christopher was made. Trade followed, but Ramaharo was a terrible governor who impoverished the town for his own personal gain. He was clever, however, and played on the Queen's superstitions by convincing her that he had special powers over the winds and the waves. He could, he claimed, turn topsy-turvy any vessels that came to fight her (and the Firm was not here for that, merely for trade) but only if money and cattle and other supplies were given to him for the special 'conjurations' that took place on certain days each month. She believed him and ordered that he should be supplied with whatever he needed. But his avarice and foolishness brought Vohemar to the edge of ruin, and he was not missed when he died. His corpse was buried in Imerina, brought up to the highlands by his 'provincial wife' (not his Merina wife) who lived off his ill-gotten gains for a few years until by 1847 she was forced into prostitution.

Raombana speculates that Ramaharo died from fear, fear of the *tangena* test that had brought the life of his brother to a painful end. Under the circumstances it is unlikely that Henry Angelo managed to extract the $188. Not the type to do business with, I'd have thought.

CHAPTER ELEVEN

ON THE PIRATE TRAIL

My shoulder now sent twinges of pain down to my hand and ankle and up into my head. It kept me from sleeping, and when I looked in a mirror – the first mirror since Nosy Be – I looked old. Perhaps all this talk of death was making me morbid, but for the first time I could imagine being decrepit, being at the end of my life. It was unpleasant. Richard was bearing up better.

Lines of Robert Frost's repeated themselves in my head: 'But I have promises to keep, and miles to go before I sleep, and miles to go before I sleep.'

I longed to rest but our visas were running out and we had no time to waste. Two favourite pirate hideaways lay to the south: Maroantsetra in the crook of Antongil Bay, and the island of Ste Marie, both haunts of Bowen and trading posts of Newman Hunt and Christopher.

The following days have blurred. There were more lorries, more taxi-brousses, more cyclone-wrecked bridges reduced to piles of concrete stuck with reinforcing rods, more rivers to wade. There were spread-out vanilla-producing towns – Sambava and Antalaha – prosperous enough and calm, not desperate like the highlands or Mananjary, but with little of interest, just pleasant places to be. I remember staying in Sambava in a hut on stilts beneath coconut palms by the sea. Moonlight oiled the waves and cloud shadows hurtled down the beach, swallowing us then surging on leaving us unscathed. I remember too the flowers – hibiscus, wild gladioli, frangipani, orchids sprouting from trees – and gusts of scent invading the taxi-brousses; there were meadows of cattle-bitten grass like cricket greens with huts ranged around. Medieval England might have looked like this, though surely never so tidy. We were happy (then) to have crossed from the dry savannah of the west to this greenery.

But at Antalaha the road petered out.

*

Our map marked a track across the Masoala Peninsula to Maroantsetra and Antongil Bay, pirate bay, but no one had ever upgraded it into a road. It appeared to follow one river from sea to source then cross a watershed to descend with another river from source to sea. Rivers meant tributaries, and tributaries meant scrabbling down into gorges, wading across streams, then climbing up the other side, again and again. There were green lumps on our map: forested mountains. The route was just under a hundred miles long and Richard was excited.

'You must be mad,' said the French *patron* of our little hotel. Married to a Malagasy, he had stayed on after Independence, waiting for life to return to the way it was. While waiting he had grown coarse until this delicate bungalow on stilts trembled under his step. He shook his head dismissively.

'No no no. Walk to Maroantsetra? After three months of rain? OK in the dry season, but right now it's just not possible.'

'Leeches?' I asked.

'Everything.'

I looked meaningfully at Richard and back at him. 'Is there any other way of getting to Maroantsetra?'

'Mmm, probably not. Sometimes there are ships, but there aren't any in at the moment.'

The 'port' was a concrete jetty with a tumble-down warehouse, and the only boats were rusted wrecks abandoned on shore.

'Flights?'

'There are flights, but right now they're probably booked up. There aren't enough planes.'

'But there are always ways of getting a seat somehow.'

'I'm not so sure. And it's very expensive for *vazaha*.'

'I see. Do you get many tourists here?'

'Not any more.'

He stomped off into the back regions.

'So what do we do?' I asked Richard gloomily. 'We're going to be stuck here. We're going to have to go back the whole way to Vohemar, aren't we? And then to Ambilobe? To get to Maroantsetra we're going to have to go back to Tana.'

'No, we're going to walk.'

'But you heard what the guy said?'

'Yes, but that doesn't matter. What's a bit of mud? Anyway,

it's not raining now. Maybe the rain's stopped. We're coming up to the dry season.'

He was always optimistic.

'What about my shoulder? I can't carry my pack all that time, not with all our books and everything.' (We had now read them all, but had to return them to Tana.)

'We'll sort everything out. Maybe there are some things we can dump. Maybe I can take some more things. And we'll take only just enough food for one meal a day.' He was determined. We discussed him walking and me taking the plane if there was one, meeting him in Maroantsetra, but I knew that eventually he would win me round. We were joined on the verandah by the *patron*'s wife. 'I hear you want to go to Maroantsetra.'

'Yes. What do you think?'

'It's fine. My cook comes from there. He does it all the time.'

Richard looked meaningfully at me.

'What about the mud?' I asked, my last hope.

'Mud? That's no problem. But you will need a guide. There isn't one clear path. The cook knows some honest people.'

We were introduced to the grandly named Jean Chrysostome. He was stocky, nervous and a beautiful honey brown. His father, who worked for the electricity board, had been moved here with his family from Maroantsetra: Chrysostome knew the route well, he said. He often walked to visit relatives, and he spoke a little French and was strong.

'Could you carry Helena's pack?' Richard asked. 'It's about seventeen kilos. Yes? That solves it then.'

But Chrysostome wanted to bring his brother, a bigger, darker, more silent youth who sat moodily on the hotel steps.

'I'm sorry, we only need one porter.' Richard said. Chrysostome looked stubborn.

I touched Richard's arm.

'Let's go with them both. Then you won't have to carry your pack either.'

Richard was doubtful, his manly pride at stake.

'Then your hands will be free to take photos. And in any case, they'll be much happier together.'

It was a bad night. I lay awake listening to rain cascading off the tin roof into barrels. The walk would be hell. I almost wanted it to rain more so that Richard would agree it was impossible, but not at all, he was more enthusiastic than ever. 'You'll love it when it's over,' he said. At 6.30 am we set off, explaining to the boys how to adjust the rucksack straps to ease the loads, guilty that we carried nothing. However, Chrysostome had luggage of his own, a blue plastic suitcase full of books and ironed shirts and a bottle of coconut oil, so Richard heaved that on his back: it was not much of a deal as far as portering was concerned (his own pack was more comfortable) but it made him feel better.

A bit shy of each other, we took a taxi-brousse to the end of the road, rutted and muddy from the start.

'Are there roads like this in France?' asked Chrysostome.

'We live in England, but no, no roads like this.'

He jumped down to push when we were stuck, to lighten the load when we wobbled over log bridges, and to peer in the engine when we broke down. Though only eighteen he took control, in the nicest way.

All too soon the road ended.

'On the map it goes quite a lot further.'

'Rains. Last year,' said Chrysostome.

At first the track was wide and fairly flat, and it was possible to leap from dry mound to dry mound. The sun came out in patches and the landscape was beautiful: what had I been worrying about? To our right, moving in and out of bananas and coconuts, Jac trees swinging testicle-like fruit, oranges, pomelo trees, was the wide Ankavia river; waves of bright green hills broke against distant mountains and bamboos fired salvos of feathered fronds. It was lush and there were birds and villages. These people were Betsimisaraka and Christian. Bamboo churches were lifted out of the mud on stilts and only distinguished from the houses by being slightly larger. Before leaving these villages for the wilderness of the peninsula we stocked up in a tiny grocery shop on extra rice and candles, our last chance to do so.

'Hello, *vazaha!*' Children shrieked with amusement, as did their parents, running to tell each other the exciting news of our presence, peering out of doorways with toothless grins. '*Vazaha vazaha vazaha!*'

'Hello, *Gasy*,' we sometimes replied.

Nonplussed for a moment, they burst out laughing.

'They said, "Hello *Gasy*,"' they repeated to each other, the words pursuing us down the single street long after the inhabitants had vanished.

We passed walkers, singing and whistling and overtaking us.

'*Salama*,' they called. '*Mbola tsara*.' One man carrying puppets with angry expressions travelled from village to village giving shows; others, grim-faced in mud-spattered skirts and shorts, trotted past with luggage on their heads.

'They've come from Maroantsetra,' Chrysostome said admiringly. 'Only three days.'

'How long will it take us?'

'About five.'

One family were out ploughing, waist-deep in mud, shouting at their zebu, chasing them round the field to churn up the ground.

We paused at stalls selling banana and manioc jelly wrapped in banana leaves, and boiled sweet potatoes. Chrysostome commandeered a raw manioc root from a basket on a girl's head, hacked off its muddy skin with his *panga*, and shared it out. It was crunchy and white and tasted of chestnuts. He pointed out plants he knew, and cut twigs of cinnamon for us to sniff and chew. What smelt so deliciously of jasmine was, he said, coffee, in full white flower. He waved at acquaintances and sped on ahead, apparently untouched by the weight on his back, and then waited for us while Be Jean (*Be* meaning 'Big') lumbered silently behind.

On a bridge a chameleon, turned mottled blue-grey against the concrete, high-stepped gingerly above the deep and fast-flowing river. We paused to admire it. A trio of men followed, one of whom without a second thought raised his *panga* knife and flicked the chameleon into the river. It writhed against the current, tried to clasp a branch and nearly made it, but was swept on. They stood around watching, and sniggering.

'Why did you do that?' I shouted, overcome with rage. 'Why?'

The man shrugged, his face shrouded in stupidity.

'Why should he want to kill a harmless creature, so rare?' I demanded of Chrysostome.

He replied gently, 'He's a countryman. He doesn't know any better. He's afraid of the chameleon.'

'Why? Is it *fady*?'

Chrysostome looked faintly embarrassed. 'Yes.'

The chameleon was a magician, evil, powerful. There's a species, a man had assured me, that can whistle like a bird and so

attract small birds to its branch where it devours them, one by
one. (Nonsense, Richard said.) The chameleon is a dangerous
dragon. Snails were *fady* here too, but it was hard to find out
about other things – it seemed that talking about *fady* was the
greatest *fady* of all. But having been so intrigued, suddenly I
hated these people's stupid ignorant *fady* that caused so much
fear. I was close to tears.

'They're very good swimmers. It's bound to have survived,'
said Richard, kindly. (Nonsense, I said.)

Several hours passed before my dislike of the Malagasy
evaporated.

It was not long before our broad flattish path with its dry
mounds began to narrow, and to climb and drop. Soon it was
simply a red swill of glutinous slime. Trying to protect our boots
we teetered round the edge, either crumbling down towards the
river on the right, or skidding on the sheer mud bank to the left.
We reached for steadying branches which came loose in our
hands or were studded with prickles which we picked out of our
skin. What looked like mounds of firmer earth were now swell-
ings of soft mud that rose to our shins and squelched in our boots.
Already we had blisters. We replaced our boots with sandals but
they were sucked off at once. Richard tried bare feet but stones
and sharp ends of sticks lurked unseen.

'Jesus Christ. Shit.' He skidded and flailed in front. 'Jesus!' He
ski'd down the steeper slopes, arms rotating, performing an
elaborate mud ballet. I had to laugh.

Chrysostome and Be Jean waded unconcerned on flat feet like
leathery plates. Though only eighteen, Chrysostome's soles had
wrinkled with use and swollen until his mangled nails had
become mere details on his splayed toes; for years he had walked
barefoot into the forest to gather wood.

At last the day ended at the village of Antsahabe, which spread
above the river. The inevitable crowd of children vanished when
the village President arrived. '*Inona kabary?* What news?'

'*Tsy misy*. No news,' Chrysostome replied formally, and
explained who we were.

The President, in his thirties and young for the job, nodded
and led us to his house. We slumped on his wooden verandah
and peeled off our socks while his son swept the house. This was
relatively substantial, with a tin roof and a red plastic three-piece

suite on which we sat while the President continued his murmured inquisition. Where were we from? Where were we going?

Chrysostome answered for us, having absorbed all the relevant information as if by osmosis. He had asked no questions, but picked up and stored every morsel of information that we had let fall. He already knew the entire contents of my pack, where I kept what, down to the smallest safety-pin buried in the lower left pocket that I had not seen for months. He was not snooping, he was just intelligent, and had decided to take over our lives. We gave them up with little struggle.

Washing took place in the river at the bottom of a sheer mud slope. Ragged children followed us down, but Chrysostome thoughtfully shooed them away and we sank into the wide brown water in the last of the light. A youth, ignoring us, stripped naked and waded mid-stream. Richard gleamed white beside him. The return journey covered us in mud again.

Our supplies were unpacked, and Chrysostome measured out five *kapok* of rice, one each for us and one for the President, which his wife took away to cook. She had matted plaits and a scarred face and the narrow hips of a rice-pounder. She laid a mat on the floor, and plates of vegetables and beans on the mat; we sat on its edge while she ladled out domes of the sodden white rice. The form was to break up the lumps, then spoon in mouthfuls as large as possible with tiny bits of 'extras'. There was no greed, nor any ceremony; as soon as it was over and we were drinking our burnt rice water, the mat was whipped away and shaken out of the door, the floor swept again. The President's wife and children did not join us.

While we spoke the President lit petrol lamps and sat at his table measuring out bundles of vanilla and entwining the glossy black pods in raffia. Throughout the day we had seen the vanilla industry at work, the pods laid out in the sun to dry on tables, filling the air with their sickly scent, then being carried into town. Vanilla is one of Madagascar's main cash crops, and the island was the world's greatest exporter, mostly to America for the ice-cream industry; but a lack of quality controls in Madagascar means that vanilla from Réunion, where the *Vanilla planifolia* vines were first grown in the nineteenth century, is now better quality. Surprisingly, vanilla is an orchid. It was harvested first by the Aztecs in Mexico and brought to Réunion by a Frenchman.

Unfortunately the pollinating *melipoma* bee did not travel with it, but in 1841 (or so the story goes) a Malagasy slave developed the technique of pollination by hand, which is how every plant is grown to this day.

Vanilla is now hugely expensive; the loving way in which the President handled his pods was a testimony to their preciousness. It had been a bad year, he said, too much rain.

Chrysostome and Be Jean were given a separate hut, and we – despite our protests – were shown to the President's bed. He and his family slept on the floor beside us.

We were woken by the usual cacophony of farmyard noises, and the pounding of rice, Madagascar's heartbeat. There is no privacy here; every sound from every hut can be heard, the crying baby, its parents' intimacies. Odd in such an under-populated country that people should choose to huddle together, but then in this village they were probably all one elastic family.

During the night it had rained and clouds still hung low between the hills which, when the sun briefly shone, steamed. A rainbow arched from hill to hill against a dirty purple sky. After more rice we sat quietly while Chrysostome and the President held another formal exchange of courtesies, and then we set off. It was 7.30 am.

The President and his family waved, smiling and hopeful: how could they know? At the time I decided it was the worst day of my life, the worst journey in the world. We must never forget it, said Richard, because the rest of life will seem so good. The path was ever muddier and narrower, and we lurched with our eyes and all our concentration fixed to it, skidding, slipping, slithering, sloshing through the paludal morass – a thesaurus of mud words occupied my brain. I was dimly aware of the river's glitter and of the anticipated tributaries that we boulder-hopped, but nothing mattered except the mire, and staying out of it. Progress involved gauging the quality of mud before each step. The deepest-looking puddles were sometimes deceptively shallow, and what appeared to be rock was often a mound of sludge. Worst was the earth puckered like cellulite: that was the deepest and most treacherous. And we were trapped: going back now would be even worse than going on. We waded through marshes and flooded paddy fields, tempers roughening. Why don't they do something about it? Why don't they make rock trails and suspension bridges, like the Nepalese? Why are they so indolent?

They don't even have stepping stones in the villages. It's all their fault.

After many hours I insisted on a stop at a waterfall and lay on a mossy rock while Richard prised off my boots and squeezed my socks. Bearing up better than I, he kept me going with rhymes about mud. The only other pleasure was wild raspberries.

When we staggered into Andrakadila I knew I could go no further. It was a hamlet so small that it did not have its own President, but the members of the *Fokonolona* provided us with cooking utensils and wood, and with the hut of someone who was away. It was almost Stone Age in its simplicity, raised above the mud on stilts, its only feature the fireplace in one corner which consisted of rocks embedded in earth on which to balance saucepans. No chimney, no possessions except a mat on which we ate and slept.

Chrysostome rose to the occasion, buying green vegetables and a twist of salt in a banana leaf, and fetching a bucket of water from the river. Cold and exhausted, we managed only a token splash, to Chrysostome's covert dismay. He scrubbed himself in the river, washed his clothes and (unasked) my boots, prepared the rice, hung up our wet clothes, and cooked dinner while we and Be Jean could only watch. It was hard to believe they were brothers, one so bright, the other such a kindly dullard, and later we discovered that they were brothers in their sense but not in ours. *Mpiraya tampo* means brother or sister from the same source, and Chrysostome had twelve of these; Jean lived with Chrysostome's family but was in fact his *rahalahy*, meaning brother but also cousin.

Thanks to Chrysostome we revived enough to spend a convivial evening singing Malagasy pop songs, including 'our' song which had haunted us for so long and which for the rest of the journey none of us could forget. The villagers watched from a verandah opposite, but they were shy and we had no strength to make friends.

That night we squeezed together in a row on the floor, and I was asleep before Chrysostome had even finished sifting rice for tomorrow's breakfast. Not for long: the floor was so hard that none of us could get comfortable, and we knocked each other with elbows and knees as we shifted about. Poor Be Jean was longer than the hut so spent the night doubled up. Then it rained and the rain streamed through the thatch. Richard and

Chrysostome struggled in the dark to fix a mat against the roof, but the rain seeped round it.

It continued with more or less force all the next day, when we encountered our first major series of river crossings. Initially we unravelled our boots and pulled them off to wade across barefoot, then struggled with laces and blisters to put the sodden things on again. But the attempt to keep dry proved futile, and when we decided to keep them on life improved. The boots were abandoned to the mire; now instead of skidding round the edge of the path we strode through, mud often up to our thighs; but progress was faster.

It was that day too that we entered the rainforest. Topless trees were buttressed by plate-like roots; from every crevice dangled hair-like tendrils of birds-nest ferns; and everything was dripping, dripping. High up in the canopy we saw light and some bird life, but down at human level near the ground the jungle was muffled.

Only now did I understand the cause of the slime, for under the trees the path solidified, held together by roots. I caught up with Chrysostome.

'You know why the path is so bad?' I demanded. 'Because they cut down the forest.' I sounded hectoring.

'Yes,' he replied. 'The people need to plant rice.' It was that simple.

Swathes of burnt land and scattered match-stick trunks stretched before us, to be only briefly swallowed in the majestic creeper-hung gloom. Cut the trees, sell the timber, clear the undergrowth, expel all animals and birds, plant rice, then move on leaving a wasteland of wild ginger and seeping bogs. Since 1950 Madagascar's rainforest has been reduced by half. Even the government still sold tracts of land to timber companies.

We never stopped that day, never even paused, climbing over a mountain and the river's source, and then plunging down a red cascade, deeper and deeper into a valley below. Suddenly a new river, travelling in the opposite direction, was our companion. Tributaries were unbridged torrents, waist-deep. After seven hours we heard a cock crowing and came upon our first signs of habitation that day, a lone hut beside a coffee grove. Then other walkers, and at last a village.

That night we lined the roof with the tent's flysheet (the boys used the tent itself as a blanket) but nevertheless by morning all our possessions were wet. None of us could stretch: the hut measured five foot six by seven foot, even smaller than the last. The President, to Chrysostome's shame, demanded clothes and medicines as payment for the hut and 1,500 fmg for a stringy pullet. This so outraged the boys that the story was re-told at each village, people sucking in breaths of disapproval.

The journey continued with more of the same, but as the valley broadened so its beauty increased – small zebu-grazed fields, clove groves, flowering shrubs, a backdrop of forested hills – and the villages grew. Being Sunday people were out strolling and big-breasted girls plaited each other's hair. Civilization was returning, houses enclosed in neat picket fences and main streets lined with pollarded trees. There was even an *épicerie* or two, though when we tried to buy bananas no one had change for 500 fmg – about 20p. But this was incidental, since at midday Chrysostome and Be Jean changed into clean clothes and sandals and we hobbled into Mahalevona, their *'village natale'*. They were greeted as heroes, pausing every few seconds to shake hands and be clapped on the shoulder, Chrysostome in particular. Polite, good-humoured, energetic, everyone liked him, and Be Jean followed along behind.

Be Jean's mother lived in a compound of four huts, and she greeted us without surprise, though she cannot have expected us. She had Be Jean's big African nose but paler skin and an anxious look. Life was hard, and more so since her husband divorced her and went to Maroantsetra. We dropped our packs in a hut where a woman turned a sewing machine and hens roosted, and were led to an irrigation channel to wash. Paddy fields stretched in a green haze, dotted with straw hats and backsides: it must be the most beautiful valley in Madagascar. Richard was happy, but I was more concerned with my feet. They were almost completely raw.

The main hut was raised hip-high and smoke-blackened. We squatted on stools while Be Jean's mother cooked. He slumped in the doorway, suddenly a surly adolescent in her presence, while Chrysostome sparkled, chatting, laughing, peeling vegetables. After lunch he organized willing children to draw water from the well and wash more vegetables while he boiled green plantains which the neighbours came to sample.

There were two doors to this hut, and we were puzzled by the way in which each visitor did not enter through the door nearest them, but went out of their way around the house to the opposite door. It transpired they were travelling clockwise around the hut in the direction of *Rohontany*. *Rohontany* is a force of destiny which circulates a house, and to go against the force of destiny is *fady*. The visitors, who arrived from their houses to the east, had to enter through the door on the west. We did the same. Who knows what other *fady* and mystical forces were at work? The air over Madagascar buzzes with them, invisible to all but the villagers who have made them their own.

Though excited to be united with his family, Chrysostome was as assiduous as ever in his care for us, erecting a line for our damp clothes and lovingly washing my boots, tutting at the state they were in. He had his eye on those boots. When he noticed our tiredness, he led us to his uncle's hut which – joy of joys – contained a bed. A crowd of children watched our every move and took over the bed in order to study our map, but as soon as we lay down and firmly said goodbye, they vanished.

Chrysostome and Be Jean came back sporting our jackets and banana-leaf rain hats. They had brought supper – a chicken far better than the wicked President's, they promised – and more neighbours to welcome the *vazaha*.

Damp mists wavered over the dawn valley; rain dripped from darkened steaming eaves and girls in cotton dresses scrubbed saucepans in the water channels. We set off in a farewell party, Chrysostome at its centre distributing sticks of sugar cane, full of life. The end was almost in sight and today Chrysostome wore his town gear: a T-shirt defying the cold with cut-away arms and slashed sides. It declared: Alt – Police Line – OK. He had added 'Well Done', his personal motto.

Be Jean's mother was smart in a straw hat with a red flower in the band that would not have looked out of place at the Dartmouth regatta, her plastic sandals in her hand. People emerging from their Stone Age huts were often as elegant as her. She was going visiting and when she reached the next village she peeled off calling '*Bon Voyage*' without giving us a chance to thank her.

We almost flew, the path now an old colonial road, broad and firm. And at Navana we glimpsed the sea. Antongil Bay at last: we had crossed the Masoala Peninsula. This final stretch was the most lovely, not just because in four hours the journey would be over, but because the fern-filled canyons and the steep woods dropping to the water and the sounds of the waves reminded us again of the mouth of the Dart. These waterfalls and lush growths were surely the reality of every south coast gardener's dream, of Uncle Ralph's dream.

The track rounded a wild beach lined for several miles with Betsimisaraka graves. Crossed bamboo poles like pony jumps marked the recently buried. After a certain time the remains would be exhumed and packed into small cement coffins with domed lids that rested at all angles on the ground. In front lay enamel plates and bottles: at the time of second burial the ancestors had been fed. We came across a funeral but it seemed a private affair so we hurried past.

On the banks of the Andrianafotsy river we caught a ferry. It was the hollowed trunk of a gigantic tree – two people wide – and with two men paddling we sped downstream, low down and invisible in this watery land. (While we waited to leave someone shouted 'Look out!' and before I could turn the bows of a boat poled by two out of control floozies smashed into my ribs. This prompted the usual floozie giggles and added yet another ailment to my list.)

We collapsed in Maroantsetra.

While Richard ate, I spent the rest of the day and all the next in bed, limping on sores that had begun to fester. Our parting with 'the boys' was almost tearful. We had lunch together at the small hotel, and they changed into their smartest clothes: matching orange trousers and shirts with writing on, Be Jean glued as ever to his raspberry hat. After a day in town they would return to Be Jean's mother and help her with the rice fields. Then they would walk home at their own pace: instead of five days it would take eighteen hours.

Some shuffling of feet led to the request we dreaded: our boots. We still had far to go in these boots but they were desperate for them.

'Helena's will do for me,' Chrysostome had decided (they had clearly discussed this at length) 'and Richard's for Be Jean.'

But like the Ugly Sisters, however hard they pressed their splayed plates into the boots, they could not get them on.

It was not hard to imagine Antongil Bay in its heyday when,

three hundred years ago, the pirates made it their lair. What looked like earth and grass were often islands of floating vegetation and between these it would have been so easy to give a pirate-hunter the slip. Any number of pirate boats, roughened and patched with over-use, could have lurked up the delta to watch the approach of a threatening vessel. Friend or foe? The pirates could see before they were seen. And it was sheltered too.

Here the pirates repaired after successful raids to distribute their booty and to drink the barrels dry. When they had slaked their thirst for adventure and loot, many turned instead to the lovely women and allowed themselves like the Arabs before them to be sucked into the Malagasy apathy. England in the early eighteenth century with its cold winters and dock-side slums, its pirate trials and executions, must have seemed a long way away. Here they had families and lived a life of ease, fish swimming on to shore, fruits pressing themselves to their lips, and they murmured *mamy ny aina*, life is sweet.

By 1730 there were few pirates left. Malaria and dysentery took their toll, and so – predictably – did poison. Some were disposed of by their wronged or greedy wives, others killed in inter-tribe fighting. They did leave some trace, however: it was Ratsimilaho, the mulatto son of an English pirate who returned after a brief and unhappy sojourn at school in England to rise up and, like Andrianampoinimerina, unite the squabbling clans into one powerful tribe which he named the Betsimisaraka, 'The Many Inseparable'. Now they are the second largest ethnic group in Madagascar and extend as far south as Mananjary.

Apart from a flare of prosperity during the colonial vanilla era, Maroantsetra has changed little. Lethargy lay like a damp blanket over a town as empty as a garden suburb, but had not quite extinguished a few sparks of hostility. For the first time since the highlands we were warned of thieves and hustled by beggars. They were kept at bay by roaming packs of dogs that savaged each other in the dust at night. Our gaunt Creole *patronne* sat all day long on the verandah of her once pretty colonial bungalow, while her sulky daughters painted their nails and waited for something to happen. There was no flour, she complained, no clothes, no meat, no tea. She was desperate. Almost no produce was getting through: cyclones meant there were no roads either to or from the town. Not even the lorries were making it now. There were few boats, and planes were booked up two months in advance.

Having got here at last, we were going to find it almost impossible to leave.

There was said to be a cargo boat being repaired in the bay of
Nosy Mangabe, a forested off-shore island, and that it might be
going south to Isle Ste Marie. It was our only hope. For a huge
sum the *patronne* persuaded her brother-in-law to take us there in
his canoe. He was a shifty sharp-featured man with reddish hair,
surely a descendant of the mulattos. His outboard phut-phutted
out of the lagoon but soon expired; we bobbed uncertainly for a
while, thinking of sharks. Walking the plank must have been a
favourite sport. We rowed back to shore where Sharpy produced
a replacement engine, but soon that gave up too. *En panne, la vie
est dure*: Madagascar's motto. He cursed the damn thing, and we
paddled.

At Nosy Mangabe we paused at a beach where an inscription
carved into the rocks was said to be the work of pirates. On the
sand stood a tent made from banana leaves; I half-expected a
wild European castaway to emerge, naked and raving, but it was
deserted. As the waves sucked back from the cliff the writing was
revealed, looped and ancient, but we could not make it out, and
no one knows what it says. There was no sign of the name
Bowen.

The main bay of Nosy Mangabe was hidden and perfectly
calm. How many pirates, secure in their hideaway, must have
careened their ships here over the years, just as another pointy-
faced man was doing now. It was hopeless, he said; he would
have to go to Tana for a spare part and it would take him at least
two weeks. Having got here at last, we stayed; Sharpy would
collect us in the morning.

Sixty years ago the aye-aye, one of the rarest and most obscure
species of lemur in the world, was thought to be extinct. Thirty
years later a French zoologist 'rediscovered' it, and in 1966 it was
introduced to the uninhabited island of Mangabe. Isolated, protected by sea and by the Department of Water and Forests which
forbids anyone without a permit to land on the island, it was
hoped it would survive. Only here, in a few coconut plantations
down the east coast, and in zoos in Paris, North Carolina and
Tana, can this creature be seen. In 1960 David Attenborough
came to Madagascar with what now seems the repulsive inten-
tion of trapping animals to take them back to captivity

in London, but he never saw an aye-aye. Its nocturnal habits made it even more elusive.

In a tiny encampment by the beach we met an American ethnologist. She had lived here six months and had twelve more to go. Her concrete house was strewn with charts and half-unpacked bundles of belongings; each night she and a bespectacled scientist spread out their sleeping bags on the hard floor, and each morning they washed in a waterfall. I suspect they resented our intrusion: who wouldn't? So we put up our tent at a distance and left them alone. She couldn't say if we would see an aye-aye – sometimes she was lucky, sometimes not.

Nothing would be visible until after dark, but we explored the forest anyway. It rose steeply from the sea and grunted with angry brown lemurs with haloes of grey-white hair; we would normally have been excited by these, but today only the aye-aye was on our minds. Nevertheless we followed them off the narrow path and came upon a collection of tombs sheltering under the lip of a boulder in the dripping jungle. It was a secret place and sacred. The distant shine of the sea flickered as the wind shifted branches below. Later the American woman told us that the descendants of these ancestors had died out, and the tombs had been abandoned. Untended, the ancestors roamed, hungry, cold and full of vengeance.

Mysteriously another family in Maroantsetra had 'lost' their ancestors, so they adopted these instead. It was an excellent compromise. Now the dead would be cared for by the living, and vice versa; it didn't matter who the ancestors were or who they belonged to, they were simply powerful inhabitants of that great ocean of the dead.

We squatted by the grave, idling, but the forest was oppressive and monotonously green, and my pustulating feet could not take me far so we spent the rest of the day on the beach trying to cook a Malagasy meal – burnt rice included – on damp wood.

We arranged to accompany two Malagasy naturalists into the forest that night. We had little hope of success, but they did at least have a solar-powered spotlight. We waited in our tent while they finished supper. I was tired and secretly dreaded struggling through the dank forest for what if we were lucky would probably be a very brief sighting of the shy creature, and I felt worse when the naturalists appeared in rubber boots. Did they know something we didn't? I would not be able to keep up: I could only wear sandals.

Whispering, we followed them down the flat path behind the beach, brushing through ginger and bamboo and fireflies and wading through swamps, their torch shafting the canopy. Incredibly, there was no rain. Almost at once there was a shout and above us peered down one of the ugliest and most fascinating animals on earth. Its gargoyle head was oversized and topped with huge bat ears; the eyes bulged; the snout was pink and raw and the teeth rat-like and protruding. Its two-foot-long body was top-heavy and covered with scraggy grey fur, and dangled with a tail wiry as a pipe-cleaner. It was a devil from one of the Buddhist hells, a monster by Bosch. Most horrible was the middle finger of each hand which was skeletal and used to gouge insects out of trees and to scratch its fleas. No wonder the Malagasy fear it as a harbinger of death, pointing the crooked finger at its next victim. In some villages the *ombiasy* is thought to gain great powers if he defies death and bites off that middle finger; in other villages a trapped aye-aye must be anointed with oils used in human burials before being released.

Oblivious of the light and of us, it did not leap from branch to branch like other lemurs but climbed cautiously, steadily going about its business.

'Eating, eating!' whispered the naturalists, noting it down. 'Moving! Scratching! Good, good. We're very lucky.'

When it was first spotted by Europeans in 1788 it was classified as a squirrel. Then it was thought to be related to a midget primate in Borneo. They might have called it a woodpecker, which does not exist in Madagascar, since that is the ecological niche it occupies. It was not until 1863 that a British zoologist convinced the scientists of the world that it was a very special and primitive type of lemur, the sole member of its family.

Another shout: there was a second male. It stalked the first male through the canopy and lashed out with the hideous claw. 'Good! Good!'

Then there was a third, then a fourth, and then a fifth, the cause of their excitement: four lecherous males, pink erections shining, in pursuit of a squint-eyed female. She kept ahead, hugging the trunk like a koala, and paused to clasp her tail between her front paws and use her finger to pick off insects and eat them. The naturalists were overcome when she started to eat flowers.

'She did that last night! It's never been seen before. It's our discovery!'

After two and a half hours of neck-craning, we reluctantly left them to it.

Eventually we managed to leave Maroantsetra. Luck led us to the *Managnara*, a forty-foot cargo boat. At 4 am it would head south to Antanambe on the east coast. The young pale-skinned captain, dressed in an Arsenal T-shirt and flowery shorts, noted down our names (and, oddly, our ages) on the back of a cigarette packet and shook hands. He was puzzled by our effusive thanks. At 3.30 am we walked the deserted streets to the 'port'. Three boats huddled by the quay. A lamp glowed on the *Managnara* but no one moved. We sat on a pulley smelling of piss, and waited. Slowly other passengers gathered, and waited too. Three hours later, as pale yellow slit the sky and mountains hovered through the mist and the boat's reflection stretched into the still water, the cabin door opened and a toothless black-skinned bunch of rogues staggered out, stinking of rum.

Pirate boats caught a ride on our engine and raised their sails when they cast off at the lagoon's mouth.

We all huddled on deck, bags, baskets, a motorbike and tiers of straw hats piled in the bows, while Maroantsetra and Nosy Mangabe receded through a belch of black smoke. A woman swigged medicine from a bottle. 'Sea-sick,' she explained grimly. The white liquid smeared her lips. 'I take it in the Malagasy way – drink it down. We don't know the dosages.'

'The more the better I expect.' I was not feeling too good myself. Richard nudged me: there was something in the water not far away, perhaps a huge shoal of dolphins. Water glittered on black flanks rising and falling.

'I don't think it can be dolphins,' said Richard. 'They're too big.'

'But what else can they be? It's just that there's a lot of them.'

'No . . . it's not possible . . . it is!'

As we drew closer I saw a flick of a vast tail and realized that for the first time in my life I was seeing a shoal of whales. And we were on a collision course. No one else seemed interested (later we were told it is *fady* to point at whales) although the captain did veer slightly as the majestic beasts cruised effortlessly past our stern. With lithe grace three humpback whales arched and plunged, snorting, slapping their glistening tails on the sea's surface, spouting as whales should, their scooped-out heads dipping through the waves. They turned north and headed straight for Maroantsetra. Aye-aye one day, whales the next.

Their dark shadows moving over the sea were pursued by rain clouds. We hid under the partly unfurled sail, but when the sail went up there was nowhere to escape. I did retreat under the tin roof behind the cabin but it was so low I couldn't stand and so narrow I couldn't sit. I found a place on a plank at the stern, and braved a man's halitosis to chat about this and that. He was a Malagasy teacher and he asked unusually personal questions: why were we making such a grand tour of Madagascar? He had never seen so much, not even of the east coast. Was I Mrs or Miss? Was that my husband or my brother? Did we have children?

'Next year they'll come,' he reassured me.

'Do you have any?' I asked.

He laughed. 'Of course! I have six or seven – I forget now. Listen, it's different for us. In a capitalist country you have plenty of distractions. You can go to the cinema, watch TV, read books, anything. We have nothing, not even electricity, so we spend our time caressing . . .' He stroked his own thigh. His face was blotchy and fat, and when he turned to me and laughed, I reeled. 'We have sexual education in schools,' he was saying, 'but the theory is quite different from the practice.'

'Quite.' I was feeling bad.

A huge floozie in a pine-green jacket swung her plaits from the cabin window and handed me an apple-like fruit which oozed white milk. She had it for her morning sickness, she said, but it was good for sea-sickness too. I returned with it to the bows, away from the smells of the engine and the breath, and felt better.

Rain was superseded by burning sun; seven hours passed slowly as the crinkled coast chugged by. No one could keep the sail up and the engine spewed oil; bailing was continuous, and the pump was tied together with string. They were not natural sailors on the east coast – the sea had always been too rough. It was a relief when we stopped for the night at Mananara.

There was a broad bay and a half-mile walk to the town, a friendly tranquil nowhere place. Tin shacks butted on to boulders and furrowed dirt tracks, but the roofs clinging on with

tyres and rocks spoke of more turbulent times. The streets glittered and for an instant I thought it was smashed car wind-
screens, but of course there were no cars. It was rock-crystal. A
snow-field of it spread in front of a bungalow.

'It's to protect the road,' explained its clean-cut owner. 'Are
you interested in crystals?'

Richard replied that most certainly he was.

The man shook our hands with a grip exceptionally firm for a
Malagasy, and introduced himself as a Commandant from the
French army; on retirement he had taken up dealing in quartz.
He employed twenty-five people on inland mines, and he invited
us to see his collection. Every corner of his house was stacked
with shining rocks. They were piled in the dining room, leaning
against the wall in the sitting room and even – craggy and hard –
in the bedroom. There were sacks of smaller chips tagged for an
optical instrument company in Hamburg.

'One of my clients will only buy prisms. He's in San Francisco
and he walks about with a crystal in the palm of his hand giving
himself special powers.' The Commandant imitated the spacy
Californian. 'I don't believe all that,' he said stoutly. 'I live with
this lot all the time – I even sleep with them – and never feel a
thing. But you never know . . .'

We mentioned the name of our tall English friend who dealt in
crystals.

'No! Wait here!' said the Commandant and returned with a
folder of letters from this friend. 'I can't believe it. I do lots of my
business with him.' Richard had picked up a miniature iceberg,
most of it as clear as glass but parts shadowed with fissures. He
held it against the window, fracturing the light into rainbow
colours and I knew how much he longed to buy it.

'It's a present,' the Commandant said impulsively.

We protested.

'Yes, I insist. That one's for Madame. Monsieur, choose
another.'

It was Richard's dream. The Commandant pre-empted him
by picking out a piece at random and full of thanks we carried
away our precious trophies. Weeks later we were admiring them,
and Richard suddenly fitted them together. They were two
halves of one stone.

We were instructed to be at the quay by 3 am. Nothing and

nobody there. The *Managnara*, moored off shore, was dead. Richard threw pebbles at it but to no avail. We waited for three hours in the dark until 6 am but no one complained.

'Ah, they meant 3 am Malagasy time,' said the halitosis school-teacher, 'not English time.'

We still had not learnt. Malagasy time meant whenever the driver felt like going, something that infuriated the French during the colonial era. It was the British missionaries who introduced the notion of time; there are no words for 'what time is it?' in Malagasy, just '*quel'heure?*' and the reply is always in French.

Bishop Benzies had once been on a taxi-brousse when a woman turned to him.

'*Quel'heure?*' she asked.

As a tease, he replied in Malagasy. The woman frowned.

'*Quel'heure?*' she said again.

Again he replied in Malagasy. Her neighbour translated it into French. '*Quatre heures et demi.*'

'Tch,' she tutted, to the hilarity of the bus. 'The *Monsigneur* has been here all these years, and still hasn't learnt Malagasy.'

It was four hours south to Antanambe where we waded ashore and found a lorry ready to go further south still. We were doing well. I remember little of the journey except its discomfort. We sprawled on baskets of live lobsters, cloves, gas canisters, chickens with a floozie with a parrot wrapped in chicken wire. Again and again we had to crawl over this, jump down, wait while the lorry negotiated a perilous bridge or a ferry then haul ourselves in, crawl back over the lobsters, bump along for another hundred yards. My body was packing up. By the time we reached Manompana I could only totter to bed. I couldn't even wash. I saw nothing of the village, but then there was nothing to see.

Here we hoped to find a ferry to Isle Ste Marie. But there was no ferry. Instead a fisherman named Jean-Maurice agreed to take us there in his *pirogue*. 'We'll go at 3 am,' he said.

This time we knew better. 'You fetch us,' we said.

He tapped on the door at exactly 3 am and led us between coconut palms to the beach. Under a clear starlit sky lay his tiny two-masted canoe. It was one up from the dug-outs of Nosy Be, built of planks, but it had no seats. We sat in a row in the hull on a piece of sacking, each of us wedged between the other's legs, elbows resting on the gunwales. Jean-Maurice and his son poled us over the shallow bottom, no lights but the stars. The trees were even darker than the sky. We slid up beside another *pirogue*, and one boatman lit another's cigarette. The boy chattered with the excited sing-song voice we heard so often here, squeaks of emphasis and gesticulations. His laughter seemed unnaturally loud. The bay was almost completely enclosed so we had no idea what the wind would be like once we got out to sea, but we could hear the waves crashing on to the reef.

'Wind's good,' murmured Jean-Maurice.

As we approached the mouth the handkerchief sails went up, patched and mouldy. The sky clouded and it was much rougher out here, and our smallest movement rocked the boat dangerously. A week earlier two fisherman had disappeared, undoubtedly eaten by sharks, but we did not know this then.

Jean-Maurice asked Richard for a cigarette but we had only biscuits to offer. Then he lay down beneath the mast for a snooze, leaving his son in control. A cloud lifted its skirts on a glimmer of light and Jean-Maurice looked up groggily.

'There's Ste Marie,' he said.

Above the waves on the horizon rose the bumpy outline of the island.

'And there's the rain,' I said, pointing at the loaded sky.

'No no. No rain.' And he was right.

Bowen cruised these waters with impunity. After being re-equipped with a sloop by the Dutch governor of Mauritius he settled on the east coast south of Mananjary. His life of peace grew dull and when, in 1702, two Scottish ships moored off shore, Bowen and his men could not resist. The captains and crew were enticed ashore, their ships seized, and off Bowen sailed, laughing into the wind, leaving them stranded. Bowen sailed away to the Comoros where he joined up with another villainous English pirate and together they had success after success. By now his ship was the *Defiance*, armed with 164 fighting men and seventy Indians to do the drudgery on board. Isle Ste Marie was a favourite place of refuge.

We seemed barely to move along an endless spit of land, but after five hours we did at last round it, whereupon the wind suddenly changed and drove at us from the island. The sails came down at once, and Jean-Maurice and Richard rowed the rest of the way, beating against the wind. By nine o'clock, just as the sun illuminated a turquoise sea, coconut groves, rocks, and just as I thought I could sit still no longer, we reached our goal.

Once the forests and bays of Isle Ste Marie echoed with the raucous laughter of bearded freebooters, brawling in their drunkenness. They were so well established that even bona fide merchant ships called here to trade, selling mostly madeira and rum. Still today the main bay is called Pirates' Bay, though now it is dominated by the oldest church in Madagascar, built in 1837 (the year Robert Newman Hunt arrived).

Ste Marie became a French colony long before the rest of Madagascar. It was inherited from the pirate's mulatto son King Ratsimilaho by his favourite daughter, Princess Bety. She is said to have fallen for the charms of a Gascon corporal named La Bigorne, which means 'Anvil Horn', an obvious reference to his sexual prowess and, through love for him, gave the island to the French. It sounded like a typically French story to me – a beautiful woman, a sexy man, and at the end of it the French acquire another colony.

It was a silent, sleepy place, decaying gently under stunted coconut palms, wilder and wetter than Nosy Be.

We ate breakfast and then rented gear-less, brake-less bicycles and rode the nine miles into town, whizzing down hills, loving the speed, and then toiling up again on foot. Though many of the hills were deforested, it was beautiful, with clove groves and glints of blue sea beyond empty curving beaches, and from nowhere – everywhere – hooted the descending bubbles of sound, some mysterious bird. *Presque Paris.* Older people raised their hats as we passed, but younger ones were resentful, and children called out demands for money and sweets. It was a shock to see the effects of tourism after so long on the untouched Masoala Peninsula, and this before 'real' tourism had even started. There were still no proper hotels, though despite local opposition, plans were afoot to change that.

Abandoned on a promontory overlooking Pirates' Bay lay a cemetery which was said to contain a pirate's grave. Might it be the grave of John Bowen himself? We followed a path through mangrove swamps and over log bridges. *'Donnez-moi de l'argent,'* croaked a witch-like crone from the door of her hut. The sea thundered in the distance. Grave stones were cock-eyed, strewn like rubble, inscriptions obscured by moss. But we could make out that they were all Europeans, buried appropriately beneath the fanned leaves of the Travellers' Palm. It was a sad place of exile, of lonely deaths far from home. Perhaps some of them could not face the journey back – after all, like Robert Newman Hunt it would have taken them at least 111 days to get here – but how easily an island can change from a haven to a trap.

Robert Newman Hunt did get home, full of optimism after exchanging gifts with Queen Ranavalona I. The early success was never repeated, and, as if the wickedness of Norsworthy and Khamis bin Othman was not enough, the partnership of Newman, Hunt & Christopher then broke up acrimoniously. Most of the ships were sold, and Christopher went on to become 'Christopher's' the wine merchant. In 1845, the European traders in Tamatave, twelve of whom were British, appealed for protection from Queen Ranavalona. The result was a disastrous Anglo-French invasion which left sixteen French and four British dead. As the British and French commanders retreated, so the heads of the corpses were cut off and impaled on stakes along the beach, where they stayed, staring out to sea, for eight years. As a result, Ranavalona closed the ports to all Europeans – only the Firm's arch rivals, the Americans, were allowed to continue – and so ended Robert Newman Hunt's dreams of a trading empire in the Indian Ocean. He died soon after, having never returned to Madagascar.

Amongst the graves – better kept than most – was the one we had come to see. Carved deep into the stone was a grinning Jolly Roger. I thought at once of Dartmouth, of the pirate's grave in the church overlooking the harbour mouth. But perhaps it had been too much to hope for. '*Passants – Priez pour lui*' begged the inscriptions: this was the grave of a French pirate, not of John Bowen. I discovered later that he had retired to Mauritius, and died there of 'the dry belly-ache'. In 1879, more than one and a half centuries later, another Bowen, my great-great-grandfather, became Governor of Mauritius. Would he have behaved like his Dutch predecessor and fitted out his piratical ancestor with a new sloop when he was shipwrecked off the island? Who knows?

We stood in the graveyard and wondered if we should go on to Mauritius. But if Mauritius, why not also Hong Kong, Queensland, New Zealand and all the other places where Sir George Bowen had been governor? Why need this journey ever end? The answer had arisen during the journey. I had come to see our lives as being lived at the end of elastic, able to stretch across the world but pinned down by the base point of our home and our families. They waited to spring us back. When we returned we would miss the elastic tension, feel at a loose end, but I was beginning to fear that if we stretched too far and too long the elastic would snap and we would whirl away into oblivion, as rootless and hungry as an unloved Malagasy ancestor, as sad as these foreign exiles. We looked at each other; we looked at my left foot too, turned red and inflating – a new disease, infected insect bites – and we knew what we would do. What I like best about islands, I decided, is leaving them.

APPENDIX: NINETEENTH-CENTURY SULTANS OF ZANZIBAR AND RULERS OF MADAGASCAR

SULTANS OF ZANZIBAR

Ahmed bin Sultan, Imam of Oman	1741–1804
Seyyid Said bin Sultan, 1st Sultan of Zanzibar	1804–1856
Majid bin Said	1856–1870
Barghash bin Said	1870–1888
Khalifa bin Said	1888–1890
Ali bin Said	1890–1893
Hamed bin Thuwaini	1893–1896
Hamoud bin Majid	1896–1902

RULERS OF MADAGASCAR

Andrianampoinimerina	1787–1810
Radama I	1810–1828
Ranavalona I	1828–1861
Radama II	1862–1863
Rasoherina	1863–1868
Ranavalona II	1869–1883
Ranavalona III	1883–1897 (exiled; died 1917 in Algiers)

GLOSSARY

SWAHILI

(Spoken in Mombasa, Dar es Salaam and Zanzibar. Some of the words are also used in the Comoros.)

Asante	Thank you
Buibui	Long black veil worn by Moslem women
Dhow	Traditional Arab trading vessel
Habari?	How are you?
Kanzu	Full-length white garment worn by Moslem men
Karibu	Welcome
Koffia	Embroidered cap worn by Moslem men
Jambo	Hello
Matatu	Small Kenyan bus
Mazunga	Foreigner/white
Mzuri	Good
Nakhoda	Dhow captain

MALAGASY

(Spoken throughout Madagascar but with regional variations.)

Andriana	Nobles of Merina tribe
Andriamanitra	God
Antakarana	Literally 'People of the Rocks', tribe living around Diego Suarez
Betsimisaraka	Literally 'The Many Inseparables', the second largest tribe living on the east coast

Betsileo	Literally 'The Many Invincible', a tribe living in the southern highlands
Fady	Taboo
Famadihana	Exhumation ceremony practised in highlands
Feu de brousse	Bush fire
Fihavanana	Family unity
Fokonolona	Council of elders governing village
Fomba	Malagasy customs
Gris-gris	Spell/curse
Hotely	Restaurant, sometimes with room to rent
Hova	Middle class of Merina tribe. Also another word for Merina
Imerina	Plateau inhabited by Merina tribe
Inona vaovao	Literally 'What news?', used as greeting in north
Kabary	Speech
Lamba	Literally 'cloth', but also strip of cotton or silk worn wrapped around shoulders in highlands
Lambamena	Literally 'red cloth', used as a shroud
Manahoana	Hello
Mbola tsara	Literally 'More good', used as greeting in north
Merina	Literally 'People of the Highlands', the largest tribe
Mpira gasy	Singers of traditional songs
Ombiasy	Witch-doctor
Pousse-pousse	Rickshaw pulled by man
Rainilaiarivony	The Prime Minister who married Queens Rasoherina, Ranavalona II, and Ranavalona III
Ranovola	Literally 'money water', water boiled in pot lined with burnt rice
Razana	Ancestor
Safon-drazana	Payment to the ancestors
Sakalava	Literally 'People of the Long Valleys', a western tribe
Salama	Hello (in north and north-west)
Sampy	Ancestral idols
Tangena test	Trial by ordeal
Tanindrazana	Land of the ancestors

Taxi-brousse	Literally 'bush taxi', meaning minibus or estate car used outside towns
Toakagasy	Illegally distilled alcohol
Tompoko	Sir/Madam
Tranovorona	Literally 'nest', meaning bier
Vatolahy	Standing stone
Vazaha	Foreigner
Vintana	Destiny
Zafimaniry	Wood-carving tribe in southern highlands
Zanahary	God the Creator
Zebu	Hump-backed cattle
Zoma	Friday, and name of market in Antananarivo which is at its biggest on Fridays